Implementing the ISO/IEC 27001 Information Security Management System Standard

For a complete listing of recent titles
in the *Artech House Computer Security Series,*
turn to the back of this book.

Implementing the ISO/IEC 27001 Information Security Management System Standard

Edward Humphreys

ARTECH
HOUSE

BOSTON | LONDON
artechhouse.com

Library of Congress Cataloging-in-Publication Data
A catalog record for this book is available from the U.S. Library of Congress.

British Library Cataloguing in Publication Data
A catalogue record for this book is available from the British Library.

ISBN-13: 978-1-59693-172-5
ISBN-10: 1-59693-172-8

Edward Humphreys has asserted his right to be identified as the author of this work in
accordance with the Copyright, Designs and Patents Act, 1988 and similar international
instruments and conventions.

Cover design by Yekaterina Ratner

© 2007 ARTECH HOUSE, INC.
685 Canton Street
Norwood, MA 02062

10 9 8 7 6 5 4 3 2 1

This book is dedicated to my father, Thomas Edward Humphreys,
and my mother Alice Theresa (Stewart) Humphreys, Anji and my sons Alexander,
Thomas and James.

"To see a World in a Grain of Sand
And a Heaven in a Wild Flower,
Hold Infinity in the palm of your hand
And Eternity in an hour."
William Blake

Contents

Contents

Acknowledgements

I would like to thank all those reviewers for their suggestions and invaluable comments. I would also like to thank Dr. Angelika Plate for her astute and detailed review of the text, which as one of the ISO/IEC ISMS editors was especially appropriate and useful.

Chapter 1

Introduction

"All things appear and disappear because of the concurrence of causes and conditions. Nothing ever exists entirely alone; everything is in relation to everything else." Buddha

Information security management is a global issue affecting international trading, electronic commerce and communications. Also managing information security is critical to various systems and services that make up national and global infrastructures. For example, processing information is essential for those systems and services we rely on to provide transportation, telecommunications, healthcare, the supply of sources of energy (such as electricity, water and gas) and many other common things we accept as being there when we want them. The information systems that provide vital management support for these different aspects of this public infrastructure are vulnerable to a whole range of threats.

Our dependency, use and application of information is not only all pervasive but so are the risks to this information. Information could be lost due to a system failure, corrupted by user processing errors, modified as part of some computer fraud, or disclosed to unauthorized users. Understanding what the risks are and assessing how these risks affect and impact business are vital to being able to manage these risks effectively.

An organization needs to assess its risks in terms of the threats it faces and the vulnerabilities of its assets to these threats. It needs to adopt an approach to risk assessment that is suitable to its business environment and to invest in the management of risk.

Organizations depend on information assets for their business processes and efficiency and need to protect these assets, even more so as they take up new ways of doing business electronically. Assurance that the integrity, availability, and confidentiality of this information is preserved is important, whether the information is being processed and managed, or exchanged between business partners.

1

Implementing the ISO/IEC 27001
Information Security Management System Standard

This book covers the international standards on information security. These standards (the so-called ISO/IEC 27000 series) were developed over a number of years to meet the needs of the international business market to protect information, one of the important assets and a valuable currency and commodity for being able to survive and prosper in today's dynamic business world as referred to above.

This book covers what is contained in these standards as well as practical advice on their implementation. In particular it includes what is involved in establishing and designing, implementing and deploying, monitoring and reviewing and updating and improving an information security management system (ISMS). The use of a well-tried and tested process model and use of the standards not only enables a business to establish an effective information security regime but also to deploy a number of management controls to continually improve the ISMS, to ensure that they still have effective information security.

The processes deployed involve assessing the risks the business faces, how to treat these risks in the business environment, particularly the organization deploying the ISMS and the selection of appropriate controls to manage these risks.

A number of case studies are provided to illustrate the use of these standards in real business situations.

Also process of third party certification is covered which enables business to demonstrate through independent audits that they have in place an information security management system that effectively protects their information assets.

Chapter 2

Information Security

2.1 IMPORTANCE OF BEING INFORMED

"Do nothing secretly; for time sees and hears all things and discloses all."
Socrates

Historically information has always played an important role from Biblical times to the present day:

- From the military campaigns of Caesar and the Roman emperors as well as those of the ancient Greeks, Persians and Chinese, ancient trading routes in Europe and of the Phoenician, Greek, Persian and of Roman empires,
- As well as those of the silk and spice routes, involving countries in Europe and the Near, Middle and Far East and trade and navigation of the Renaissance merchants and seafarers,
- From the invention of the printing press and the telegraph system, to the German encoding machines such as Enigma and UK code-breaking machines such as Colossus which took down the power of the Enigma,
- To information warfare of the twentieth century, encyclopaedic CD/DVD ROMs, information highways and global villages in Cyberspace.

The list is endless as history provides us with many examples of an evolutionary path to a global *Information Society*, a phrase coined by the European Union.

Information then as now is threatened in many different ways. All along this evolutionary path to an informed society, man has been confronted with risks based on:

- Threats to his information (e.g., disclosure of his discoveries and inventions, modification of his plans and loss of his possessions and estate),
- Threats from information used by his opponents (e.g., a competitor knows more than he does, traders in the Renaissance times know a better trading route without getting lost or falling foul of rocks and uncharted waters[1]).

The very market innovations, products and services that have shaped this electronic world of which we are a part have also given us a world where the information we use and rely on is at threat and more difficult to protect.

2.2 GLOBALLY CONNECTED

"I'm not afraid of storms, for I'm learning to sail my ship." Aeschylus

Today's so-called *Information Society*, especially in its electronic form, is increasingly dominating the way we work, live and play. Organizations around the world are doing business across public and private networks. Every type of business, from the very small to the very big, is affected by the *Information Society*. Citizens in many countries of the world are connecting to the Internet doing on-line shopping and banking and hotel and airline reservations. Industry and governments alike are seeing the benefits of going down an electronic commerce route.

Today's technologies make it easier to have access to information, to store more of it, to process it faster and to communicate it globally in seconds. This capability gives us the means of being more informed and more capable of exploiting and taking advantage of business and private opportunities. But the same technology can be used to damage or destroy information.

The network technology and services available today make it easy to access the world, to be globally connected and to be on-line at any time, from almost anywhere. This makes information more vulnerable whether it is business, government, personal, or private information.

---

1 The Spanish and Portuguese explorers and seafarers used notion of risk in the sixteenth and seventeeth centuries to refer to sailing into uncharted waters. This use of risk is associated with a notion of uncertainty related to space. We then adopted a notion of risk related to time, as used in financial processing and investment. In this later case it is related to the probable consequences of investment decisions for borrowers and lenders. Today the notion of risk relates to a wide range of other space/time situations of uncertainty including risks to our organization's financial and non-financial assets.

2.3 MORE ADO ABOUT RISKS

"Every man has a right to risk his own life for the preservation of it." Jean
Jacques Rousseau

Our dependency, use and application of information are all pervasive but the
risks to this information are a serious issue. Understanding what the risks are and
assessing how these risks affect and impact business are vital to being able to
manage these risks effectively.

An organization needs to assess its risks in terms of the threats it faces and
the vulnerabilities of its assets to these threats. It needs to adopt an approach to
risk assessment that is suitable to its business environment and to invest in the
management of risk and to minimize any business impact.

Managing the risks involves taking action and implementing controls to
reduce or minimise these risks. It is important that an organization deals with
information security at all levels to ensure business continuity, to reduce
business risks and avoid any potential damage and impact to the business.

2.4 DECODING INFORMATION SECURITY MANAGEMENT

"Commonsense is the realised sense of proportion." Mohandas Gandhi

Organizations depend on and need to protect the information they use for their
business processes and efficiency, even more so as they take up new ways of
doing business electronically. Assurance that the integrity, availability and
confidentiality of this information are preserved is important, whether the
information is being processed and managed, or exchanged between business
partners.

Electronic commerce allows an organization to do business and transactions
on-line. This way of doing business has been growing by leaps and bounds and it
could become the future standard way of doing business. Standards such as
ISO/IEC 17799 (previously BS 7799 Part 1) provide many best practice
management controls to deal with the possible threats and vulnerabilities of on-
line business. Things that need to be considered include, for example,
authentication of customers and suppliers, integrity controls on transactions,
payment protocols, liabilities, procedures for disputes and legal measures.

*"Is my organization (are my trading partners) fit to do on-line business in a
secure way?"*

More and more organizations are advertising their business presence on publicly
available networks such as the Internet. Care should be taken to suitably protect
information about your organization that you might publish (e.g., like

information put on a publicly accessible Web server). This is another area of concern related to electronic commerce that ISO/IEC 17799 addresses. An organization needs to consider how to protect the integrity of information on publicly available systems and the laws with which it needs to comply.

Assurance associated with publicly available systems "Is my organization's publicly available information secure?"

There is a growing need to ensure the secure use of mobile computing devices and equipment such as laptops, mobile phones and notebooks. This is especially the case in public meeting places, conference centres, hotels rooms and other unprotected environments.

Assurance that the mobile environment is secure to work in.

There are various threats and vulnerabilities that need to be considered when using mobile computing devices: theft, unauthorised use of remote connections and insecure exchange of business information, eavesdropping by overhearing of communications, access to information by overlooking, lack of backups and a lot of other issues. ISO/IEC 17799 provides best practice on mobile computing.

Teleworking enables employees to work remotely from a fixed location, for example from an office at home, outside the organization's premises. This requires suitable protection of the teleworking site to be in place to guard against various threats and to ensure that procedures and arrangements are implemented for this way of working. ISO/IEC 17799 defines the issues that should be considered to control and manage teleworking activities.

Confidence in the teleworking arrangements "Are the location and working arrangements suitable and secure enough for business?"

Organizations are using a range of services from different service providers and external third party suppliers to support their business. This includes information processing that has been outsourced to an external third party. It is important that the security of an organization's information and information processing facilities accessed by third parties is appropriately managed and maintained. This includes all forms of third party access: by service providers and third party suppliers, on-site contractors, maintenance and support staff, outsourcing to other organizations, or through some joint business venture or trading partner arrangement. Access to an organization's information may involve the exchange of information across a network connection, direct physical access to information systems, or the sharing of databases.

An organization needs to consider the risks from third party access and outsourcing arrangements. Once the risks have been identified, then the organization must consider what action it should take to reduce and minimise the risks of such access. This can be done by implementing a suitable set of controls and procedures and by ensuring that a contract with the third party defines a set of security requirements governing these controls.

Confidence in third party arrangements "Are they fit to have access to my organization's information processing facilities and to share information with?" Confidence in outsourcing arrangements "Are they fit to look after my organization's information and information processing facilities?"

We depend on information processing facilities at the local level (i.e., our own working environment or private sphere) within a domain of interworking business partners, at an infrastructural and international level. Information is an all-pervasive commodity. The risks to this information are all pervasive and so should information security management be all pervasive to counter these risks and to protect information.

2.5 LEGISLATION, REGULATION AND GOVERNANCE

"Man is by nature a political (community) animal." Aristotle

Over the past decade or so, more and more legislation has been published that has some aspect related to information, for example, be it data protection and privacy, computer misuse and hacking, electronic commerce and the use of electronic signature, or corporate governance. This has an impact on businesses who need to comply with this legislation and also demonstrate their compliance.

The growth in on-line business has further increased the need for legal protection to protect businesses and their transactions. Of particular concern is the need to protect global business especially when transactions traverse national boundaries and hence interface with different jurisdictions.

Some examples of current legislation detailed in Section 5.6.6, include:

- SoX or Sarbox (Sarbanes Oxley) also known as the Public Company Accounting Reform and Investor Protection Act of 2002, deals with the Public Company Accounting Oversight Board, which has the responsibility with overseeing, regulating, inspecting and disciplining accounting firms in their roles as auditors of the public,

- GLBA (Gramm-Leach-Bliley Act), also known as the Gramm-Leach-Bliley Financial Services Modernization Act, deals with those providing financial services and how they govern the gathering and collection of consumers' nonpublic personal information; or personally identifiable information and the protection of this information from foreseeable threats in security and data integrity,

- Basel II (as called International Convergence of Capital Measurement and Capital Standards - A Revised Framework) deals with issues governing the separation of operational risk from that of credit risk and quantifying both, how banks and depository institutions (also called capital allocation) must handle their capital to ensure the allocation of capital is more risk sensitive and the alignment of economic and regulatory capital more closely to reduce the scope for regulatory arbitration,

- EU Directive on Data Protection (plus the Member States interpretation) covers the gathering, handling and exchange of personal data,

- EU Directive on Electronic Signatures (plus the Member States interpretation), which provides legal provisions regarding the legal admissibility of electronic signatures for example, those used for on-line transactions and other similar pieces of legislation, appear in other parts of the world such as in Hong Kong and Japan,

- UK Computer Misuse Act deals with criminal activities to criminalise unauthorised access to computer systems,

- US Computer Fraud and Abuse Act of 1986, intended to reduce "hacking" of computer systems,

- International Copyright and Licensing Laws, provide legal measures against piracy and theft of intellectual property.

2.6 EN ROUTE TO A CERTIFIED BUSINESS ENVIRONMENT

"We are what we repeatedly do. Excellence, then, is not an act, but a habit."
Aristotle

A number of countries around the world have taken up ISO/IEC 27001 (previously BS 7799 Part 2) to manage information security and have, in addition, introduced schemes for certifying organizations against ISO/IEC 27001. This provides a common benchmark for assessing an organization's information security management system. Certification reassures management, customers and suppliers and business partners that an organization is applying best information security practice. It opens up new avenues of business based on a protected business environment.

ISO/IEC 27001 and the process of certification (see ISO/IEC 27006) provides a tried and tested framework for determining whether your business is "fit for purpose" from an information security management perspective.

- Do you have an information security policy?

- Are your employees aware of and trained in security for the organization in general and their job in particular?

- Are you physically protected?

- Have you the controls and procedures in place to securely use, manage and monitor your networks and communications?

- Are you controlling access to your sensitive and critical commercial information?

- Do you protect the integrity and availability of your business information and processes?

- Do you have business continuity plans in place?

- Are you abiding and compliant with the law?

ISO/IEC 17799 provides the controls, procedures and elements of best practice for organizations to establish a certified business environment to demonstrate confidence to management and your business partners that your organization is "fit to do business with."

Chapter 3

ISO/IEC 27000 ISMS Family of Standards

3.1 OVERVIEW

3.1.1   The 27000 Family

This chapter presents details of the current series of information security management system (ISMS) standards called the ISO/IEC 27000 family:

- ISO/IEC 27000 ISMS Overview and vocabulary,

- ISO/IEC 27001 Information security management system requirements,

- ISO/IEC 27002 (previously ISO/IEC 17799 before July 2007) Code of Practice for information security management,

- ISO/IEC 27003 ISMS implementation guidelines,

- ISO/IEC 27004 Information security management measurements,

- ISO/IEC 27005 Information security risk management,

- ISO/IEC 27006 Accreditation requirements for certification bodies.

3.1.2   Structural Relationships

The relationship between ISO/IEC 27001 and the other standards in the 27000 series is summarized as follows:

- ISO/IEC 27000 provides an overview of the concepts and terms and definitions used across all of the ISO/IEC 27000 family of standards,

- The relationship with ISO/IEC 27002 is to obtain a common approach to select controls suitable for initiating, implementing, maintaining and improving information security management in an organization in accordance with the requirements given in ISO/IEC 27001,

- The relationship with ISO/IEC 27003 is to provide practical implementation guidelines common to allow the establishment, implementation, operation, monitoring, review and improvement of an information security management system in accordance with the requirements given in ISO/IEC 27001,

- The relationship with ISO/IEC 27004 is to provide guidance on measurements used to assess the effectiveness on the implementation and management of the ISMS in accordance with the requirements given in ISO/IEC 27001,

- The relationship with ISO/IEC 27005 provides a consistent approach to the application of information security risk management for the PDCA processes given in ISO/IEC 27001,

- The relationship with ISO/IEC 27006 is to ensure bodies involved in accreditation and certification process provide a consistent approach to support the auditing and certification of the ISMS.

In addition to this supporting layer of standards there is a more detailed layer of standards and specifications in specific areas of interest such as:

- Incident handling,

- IT network security,

- Disaster recovery services,

- TTP (trusted third party) services.

Figure 3.1 illustrates this structure.

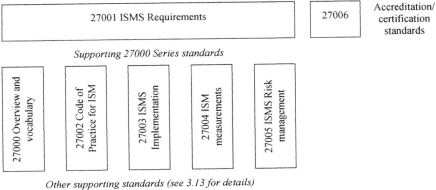

Figure 3.1 Structure

3.1.3   Status of Standardisation

The current status of these documents is that ISO/IEC 27001 and ISO/IEC 27002 were published in 2005 and ISO/IEC 27006 was published in 2007. ISO/IEC 27003 to 27005 and ISO/IEC 27000 are under development and are expected to be published in 2008-2009.

3.1.4   OECD

The principles provided in the OECD Guidelines for the Security of Information Systems and Networks (Towards a Culture of Security) are applicable throughout the ISO/IEC 27000 family of standards. These OECD principles cover:

- Awareness of the need for information security,

- Responsibility assignment of information security,

- Response to prevent and detect information security incidents,

- Ethics respecting legitimate interests,

- Democracy to ensure information security is compatible with society values,

- Risk Management providing levels of assurance towards acceptable risks,

- Security design and implementation incorporated as an essential element,

- Security management ensuring a comprehensive approach,

- Continuous improvement of information security.

3.2 STANDARDISATION PROCESS

3.2.1   Committees and Working Groups

The work in ISO (International Standards Organization) and IEC (International Electrical Committee) is carried out by Technical Committees (TCs) and Subcommittees (SC). These committees are responsible for the executive decision making and overall management of the standards programme. In addition Working Groups are established in the SCs to carry out the development of the standards. The Joint Technical Committee (JTC 1) is a joint ISO/IEC committee responsible for IT related standards.

3.2.2   ISO/IEC JTC 1/SC 27

3.2.2.1 SC27 Structure

ISO/IEC JTC1/SC27 is the Committee responsible for ISMS standards as well as other security standards. Figure 3.2 shows the current structure of SC27.

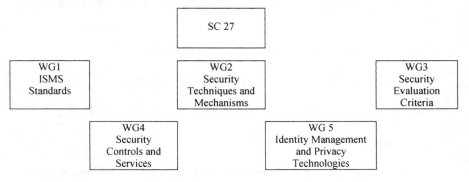

Figure 3.2 Structure of SC27

The current officers in SC27 are:

SC27 IT Security Techniques,
- Chair: Dr. Walter Fumy (Germany),
- Vice-Chair: Dr. Marijike de Seote (Belgium),
- Secretary: Krystna Passia (DIN),
- Secretariat: DIN,

WG1 ISMS Standards,
- Chair: Professor Edward (Ted) Humphreys (UK),
- Secretary: Dr. Angelika Plate (UK),

WG2 Security Techniques and Mechanisms,
- Chair: Professor Kenji Namura (Japan),

WG3 Security Evaluation Criteria,
- Chair: Mats Ohlin (Sweden),
- Secretary: Dr. Mike Nash (UK),

WG4 Security Controls and Services,
- Chair: Meng-Chow Kang (Singapore),

WG5 Identity Management and Privacy Technologies,
- Chair: Professor Kai Rannenberg (Germany),

3.2.2.2 SC27 Membership

The P members (those National Bodies that get involved in the development of standards and are registered to vote on ISO/IEC standards) are:

Austria	India	Russia
Australia	Italy	Singapore
Belgium	Japan	South Africa
Brazil	Kazakhstan	Spain
Canada	Kenya	Sri Lanka
China	Korea	Sweden
Cyprus	Luxembourg	Switzerland
Denmark	Malaysia	Ukraine
Estonia	Netherlands	United Kingdom
Finland	New Zealand	United States
France	Norway	
Germany	Poland	

The O members of SC27 (those National Bodies registered as observers only they have no voting rights but they can get involved in the development of standards) are:

Argentina	Indonesia	Romania
Belarus	Ireland	Serbia
Hong Kong (China)	Israel	Slovakia
Hungary	Lithuania	Turkey

3.2.2.3 SC27 Liaisons

ISO/IEC JTC 1/SC27 has contact with a number of liaison organizations in order to facilitate the sharing of information on the future needs for security standards and also to engage in collaborative working arrangements for the development of some of the security standards. This includes:

International Standards,

- ISO/IEC JTC 1/SC7 (Software Engineering),

- ISO/IEC JTC 1/SC17 (Identification cards and related devices),

- ISO/IEC JTC 1/SC25 (Interconnection of IT equipment),

- ISO/IEC JTC 1/SC36 (Information Technology for learning, education and training,

- ISO/IEC JTC 1/SC37 (Biometrics),

- ISO/CASCO Committee on Conformity Assessment,

- ISO/TMB (Technical Management Board),

- ISO TC 68 (Banking security),

- ISO TC 204 (Transportation systems),

- ISO TC 214 Health Informatics, WG4: Security,

- ITU-T (Telecoms security), Study Groups 13 and 17.

Regional Standards,

- CEN (Comite European Normalisation)/ETSI (European Telecommunications Standards Institute),

- NIST (National Institute of Standards and Technology, United States),

- RAISS (Asia-Pacific)

Industry Groups,

- CCDB (Common Criteria Development Board),

- ECBS (European Committee for Banking Standards)/EPC (European Payment Council (past European Committee for Banking Standards),

- ECRYPT,

- IETF (Internet Engineering Task Force),

- ISSA,

- ISSEA (International Systems Security Engineering Association) Open Group,

- Master Card Europe,

- Visa Europe,

- WLA (World Lottery Association).

3.2.3 Stages of a Project

The following paragraphs describe the various stages of a project from the initial Working Group internal study period, via a New Work Item Proposal (NP) initiated by the Committee Plenary, various stages of development to the eventual publication of an International Standard/Technical Report.

3.2.3.1 Study Period and New Work Item Proposal (NP)

To evaluate the necessity and the potential of a new work item, a Working Group may initiate a Working Group internal study period based on written contributions. To further the ideas, the Working Group may solicit contributions at the Working Group level or, upon consensus within the Working Group and with unanimous concurrence from its parent Committee Chairman and all Working Group Conveners, at the Committee level.

The Working Group study period shall not exceed one year. After this period of time the work shall either be abandoned by the Working Group or the Working Group shall propose to the Committee Plenary to initiate a Committee study period, a New Work Item Proposal (NP) or a subdivision of an existing project.

3.2.3.2 Working Draft (WD)

Once a project has been approved by JTC 1, a Working Draft (WD) is prepared by the Working Group based on contributions received from National Bodies (NBs), Liaison Officers/Organizations or Working Group experts. This WD is circulated to NBs for study and comment. Several rounds of review and comments might take place before the WD becomes a mature document.

3.2.3.3 Committee Draft/Final CD/Proposed Draft Technical Report

Once the WD is considered to be a mature document it can proceed to the next stage of standardization that is the Committee Draft (CD) or Proposed Draft Technical Report (PDTR). Authority for the initiation of each first CD/PDTR ballot is vested in the Working Group's parent Committee and may only be granted by the Committee Plenary. The Committee may delegate this authority to a Working Group for use at the next Working Group meeting. The authority, subject to review, for a second or further CD/PDTR ballots is delegated to the Working Groups. This authority may be exercised if sufficient support is received.

After every ballot an editing meeting is held, most commonly, in conjunction with a Working Group meeting. Participants to this meeting are, in particular, representatives of those NBs, who responded with comments to the ballot. Abstentions are interpreted as no expertise available. The experts representing the NBs shall have been authorised by their NBs to reverse or confirm the votes of their NBs in the light of changes to the documentand in particular to determine whether the conditions given with their NB votes have been satisfied.

3.2.3.4 Final Draft International Standard/Draft Technical Report (FDIS/DTR)

Authority for the initiation of an SC27 FDIS/DTR ballot is vested in SC27 and may only be granted during a Plenary session. When a draft is submitted for FDIS ballot all technical issues must have been resolved, since if the FDIS is approved, only minor corrections as judged by ITTF will be taken into consideration as modifications to the FDIS ballot text. Technical and editorial comments will not be considered.

3.3 EVOLUTION OF THE ISO/IEC 27000 FAMILY

3.3.1 Formative Years

Managing information security from a people, policyand procedural and business process point of view is the core objective behind the approach taken in the ISO/IEC 27000 family of ISMS standards. Although we are highly dependent on technology and the role it plays in today's business environment as part of the information systems and as our information-processing workhorse, it is just one aspect. People are one of the major problems in information security. People are the greatest of all vulnerabilities and the management of people presents the greatest of challenges regarding the management of information security. People are risk takers when it comes to a range of everyday tasks they are involved in as well as being risk adverse in other tasks they perform. Training, investingand motivating people, as well as giving them responsibilities for security and making them feel that they are part of a security culture are some of the key parts of establishing an effective awareness and management system that will help businesses to protect their information assets.

3.3.2 Baseline Controls

Best practice controls have been the essential element of information security management and the pre-history of the ISO/IEC 27000 of ISMS standards. Protection by applying best practice had been around for many years but in the 1980s best practice controls really came of age. More and more use of controls used commonly by business was brought together: controls that business could employ without the need to undertake any costly commitment. Businesses could set a level of protection across their organization using these "common use" best practice controls to establish a "baseline" level of security as a common security standard. In addition, of course, businesses had to build upon this baseline where security controls dealing with specific risks were necessary.

Catalogues of baseline controls were produced in many business sectors and user groups such as I4 (the International Information Integrity Institute). The I4 work adopted those controls in "common use" by industry as per the criterion "if the majority of organizations uses a specific security control then it is defined as control in common use and is thus a baseline control."

In the early 1990s the DTI (Department of Trade and Industry) in the UK set up an industry group to establish a "code of practice": a code developed by industry, for industry. This code was a catalogue of best practice security controls including some of the baseline controls discussed and adopted by industry in the 1980s. However this code went one step further, introducing the notion of risk assessment as a way of matching the controls to the business value of the information and information system of each organization. This code would thus allow organizations to customize their information security to the needs of their business: specific information systems they are using, their business processes and applications and their trading and operational environment. The DTI Code of practice for information security management also included advice and guidance on the implementation of the controls. This code was published in 1992 by the DTI.

The idea of applying a risk assessment was also introduced into the Code as management tool for establishing the security requirements of the business and for selecting a set of controls to match these requirements.

3.3.3 BS 7799 Part 1 and Part 2

In 1995 the DTI Code of practice was published as a British Standard BS 7799: 1995. In 1998 it was decided to carry out a review of the 1995 version to check whether there was a need to revise it or to leave it as is: this is normal practice with all standards. This led to a decision to revise the standard to improve and update it whilst retaining backward compatibility with the 1995 version. An editing team under the management of the BSI committee BDD3 set about reviewing and collecting comments from a range of interested parties.

From 1998 onwards a family of BS 7799 standards was then progressed:

*   BS 7799 Part 1 of this family was the DTI "Code of practice for information security management",

*   BS 7799 Part 2 is a specification for an information security management system (ISMS). This development arose after a public consultation on the need for a third party certification scheme for ISMS. The certification and audit process model used for BS 7799 Part 2 is the same as that used for ISO 9001 for quality and ISO 14000 for environmental management systems.

The emergence of the second part of the standard BS 7799 marked a second significant milestone in information security. The idea of applying a risk assessment, although mentioned in Part 1, is specifically introduced in Part 2 as a mandatory requirement as a means of establishing the security requirements of the business and for selecting a set of controls to match these requirements.

Organizations could establish and implement an information security management system (ISMS) based on Part 2 and subsequently went for third party certification of their ISMS to demonstrate that their information security was "fit for purpose". Such certification provides a means of measuring the effectiveness of the ISMS giving assurance to their customers, business investors and shareholdersand trading partners.

The family of BS 7799 provides best practice suitable for organizations, whether small, medium, large and in every market sector, including government commercial organizations. They give organizations best practice for use in various trading relationships including customer-supplier chains, collaborative ventures, third party services, outsourcing arrangements and virtual private networks of organizations distributed around the worldand emergence of global B2B electronic commerce as well as G2B, G2C and B2C relationships.

3.3.4 Internationalization

Up until 2000 these standards were being used world-wide by many different industries and businesses and so they became de facto international standards from an industry perspective. The next stage in the development of these standards was to formalize them as international standards. This led in 2000 to the proposed introduction of BS 7799 Part 1 into ISO/IEC JTC 1[1]. Not all member countries of JTC 1 that were in the position to vote approved of this course of action and after much debate it was decided that Part 1 would be published under the condition that an early revision of the standard should commence as soon as possible. Hence in 2000 BS 7799 Part 1 became ISO/IEC 17799:2000.

In 2005 a revised version of ISO/IEC 17799:2000 was published and in the same year BS 7799 Part 2 became ISO/IEC 27001:2005 and ISO/IEC adopted the numbering scheme based on an ISO/IEC 27000 series of numbers. Also in the same year the development of what is now referred to as "ISO/IEC 27000 family of ISMS standards" was adopted.

Today the international community is now adopting the ISO/IEC 27000 family as the *common language* for information security. This enables organizations worldwide to engage in securing their business using such a language, in demonstrating to their customers and business partners this are "fit for purpose" to handle information in a secure way whether it be on-line business or off-line business. The world is now opening up to this notion of a "common ISMS language" for the benefit of all organizations to manage their risks and to protect one of their critical assets information.

3.4 ISO/IEC 27001 ISMS REQUIREMENTS

3.4.1 Introduction and Scope

The international standard ISO/IEC 27001 is an information security management system (ISMS) set of requirements for establishing, implementing, deploying, monitoring, reviewing, maintaining, updating and improving a documented ISMS with respect to an organization's overall business risks.

It is based on the well-known PDCA (Plan-Do-Check-Act) process model as used by other management system standards such as ISO 9001(QMS), ISO 14001 (EMS) and ISO 22000 (FSMS).

---

1. JTCI (Joint Technical Committee 1) responsible for IT related standards.

ISO/IEC 27001 is suitable to all types and size of organization and the nature of their business and the market they operate in.

3.4.2 Mandatory Statements

The ISO/IEC 27001 uses the word "shall" in specifying the requirements and in ISO terminology any requirement, which includes this word, is mandatory to implement if an organization wishes to claim compliance with the standard. Therefore this makes this standard ideal for use in formal audits and third party certification, which is similar to the ISO 9001 case for quality management. ISO/IEC 27001 and its predecessor BS 7799 Part 2 are used for international certification of an ISMS using the same auditing processes as is used for ISO 9001 but focused on information security rather than quality.

3.4.3 Process Model

ISO/IEC 27001:2005 defines the processes needed to implement effective information security management in compliance with organizational objectives and business requirements (see Figure 3.3).

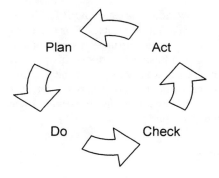

Figure 3.3 ISMS PDCA model

3.4.3.1 ISMS Plan Phase

During the PLAN Phase the organization needs to engage in the following processes:

- Specify the scope and policy for the ISMS,

- Define the risk assessment approach, risk acceptance criteria and the metrics and measurements,

- Carry out a risk assessment,

- Management decision making regarding how to treat and handle the identified risks,

- Select a set of controls to treat and handle the identified risks,

- Management to approve the remaining levels of residual risks and to authorize the implementation of the selected ISMS controls,

- Document a Statement of Applicability (SoA).

3.4.3.2 ISMS Do Phase

During the DO Phase the organization needs to engage in the following processes:

- Create a plan for the treatment of the risks,

- Implement the plan,

- Put into practice the implemented controls,

- Provide users with appropriate training,

- Manage the operation and deployment of the ISMS.

3.4.3.3 ISMS Check Phase

During the CHECK Phase the organization needs to engage in the following processes:

- Deploy operational procedures to monitor and review the ISMS,

- Carry out measurements on the effectiveness of the ISMS in operation,

- Carry out regular reviews to check that the ISMS is performing effectively,

- Carry out internal audits,

- Record actions and events relevant to effectiveness of the ISMS,

- Perform management reviews,

- Identify any improvements to the ISMS that might be necessary,

- Revise plans as a result of the ISMS reviews.

Examples of reviews:

- Review of incident handling results,

- User awareness and training records,

- Risk reductions,

- Audit trails showing access attempts.

Examples of revisions and improvements:

- Update business continuity plans,

- Incident handling procedures,

- Back up procedures.

3.4.3.4 ISMS Act Phase

During the Act Phase the organization needs to engage in the following processes:

- Implement and put into practice any identified improvements,

- Carry out corrective and preventive actions,

- Communicate to all relevant and interested parties the actions and enhancements that have been taken to improve the effectiveness of the ISMS,

- Ensure all actions and enhancements deployed to improve the performance of the ISMS do in fact achieve the expected effectiveness.

Employing this process approach enables organizations to establish a suitable level of information security to meet their business requirements and with regular reviews and monitoring of the effectiveness of the ISMS to be able to update and improve the ISMS to continue to meet their business requirements.

3.5 RISK BASED APPROACH

3.5.1 Risk Assessment

The standard adopts a risk-based approach and the specification is designed to take care of the information security aspects of business risks, corporate governance, protection of information assets, legal and contractual obligations, as well as the wide range of threats to an organization's information and communications technology (ICT) systems and business processes.

A high-level view of this risk-based process is illustrated in Figure 3.4. More details of the processes to be followed are given in Chapter 4.

3.5.2 Risk Management

Of course the management of risk is not just about assessing it and implementing risk controls. There are many other activities that an organization keeps update, with a well-informed knowledge of the risks it faces. There are many changes that are likely to occur during a 6-12 month period, which could change the risk profile of the organization. These changes include internal business changes: staff, operations and expanding/resizing/mergers, introduction of new products, services and technology; as well as external changes: market conditions, changes affecting clients, suppliers and business partners. Also, the threats and vulnerabilities relating to the organizations could change. All this means is that the organization needs to keep up-to-date it must reassess the risks it faces and thereby update and improve the risk controls it has. More details of the processes to be followed are given in Chapter 4.

The ISO/IEC 27001 specifies the requirements an organization should engage in to go through this risk management life-cycle.

3.5.3 Risk Controls

Annex A of this standard contains all the control statements from ISO/IEC 27002 (previously numbered as ISO/IEC 17799). The only difference between the two sets of control statements is that in ISO/IEC 27002 the word "should" used in statements whereas in ISO/IEC 27001 the word "should" is replaced with the word "shall". Therefore, ISO/IEC 27002 is not an auditable standard but ISO/IEC 27001 is.

ISO/IEC 27001 Risk assessment, risk treatment and selection of controls processes.

ISO/IEC 27001 Annex Best practice controls from ISO/IEC 27002.

Figure 3.4 Risk control selection

3.6 MANAGEMENT RESPONSIBILITIES

Another important aspect is the role that management plays in the establishment, implementation, monitoring and review, maintenance of an improvement to the ISMS.

3.6.1 ISMS Commitment

Commitment and action from management is essential to get support for the ISMS establishment, deployment and for its continual improvement. Information security is a management issue, which embraces most aspects of the organization's business: for example operational, personnel, legal, governance, customers and suppliers, delivery of products and services, and market positioning. Management has a responsiblity regarding the risks the organization faces and to ensure the appropriate management framework is in place to manage these risks. The ISO/IEC 27001 sets out the requirements that management needs to address regarding what it does in deploying an effective ISMS. For example the standard defines requirements as described in the following paragraphs.

3.6.2 ISMS Resources

Management has a responsibility to make sure there are adequate resources available to deal with all the processes outlined in Section 3.3.3. ISO/IEC 27001 sets out the resource requirements such as:

- Resources to establish, implement, deploy, review and update and improve the ISMS,

- Resources to carry out reviews,

- Resources to address the legal, regulatory, governance and contractual obligations and business requirements of the organization,

- Personnel resources have suitable competence to undertake the tasks and responsibilities they have been allocated,

- Personnel resources have the right level of training and awareness suited to the tasks and responsibilities they have been allocated.

Examples:

- Security officer/manager,

- Physical security manager,

- IT systems administrator.

3.6.3 Reviews

Management has a responsibility to make sure its ISMS continues to be suitable, adequate and effective for its business needs. This requires management to undertake regular reviews concerning the performance and effectiveness of its ISMS. ISO/IEC 27001 sets out the review requirements such as:

- Taking into account feedback from employees, customers, suppliers and shareholders regarding ISMS effectiveness, results from audits, reviews and assessments of the ISMS, the latest information regarding the threat, vulnerabilities and risks to the organization, and changes to the business,

- Review of the feedback and other inputs,

- Making management decisions of how to improve and update the ISMS,

- Establish and deploy an action plan to address recommended changes to the ISMS.

3.7 INTERNAL AUDITS

ISO/IEC 27001 sets out the review requirements for carrying out regular ISMS internal audits such as:

- Checking compliance with the requirements of the standard and the organization policy, objectives and business needs,

- That a system of ISMS risk controls has been implemented and is effective and achieves a suitable level of performance to what is expected.

3.8 ISMS IMPROVEMENTS

ISO/IEC 27001 sets out the review requirements for deploying ISMS improvement process, covering areas such as:

- Taking corrective actions to reduce the effects or remove the cause of the nonconformities and to prevent their reoccurrence,

- Taking preventive actions to reduce the effects or remove the cause of possible nonconformities and to prevent their occurrence,

- Taking account of the latest assessment and review of the associated ISMS risks.

3.9 LINKS

The standard is applicable to all types of organization irrespective of size of the business and the nature of their business. It also relates to other important aspects that might impact the information security of the business such as regulation and legislation. For example, corporate governance is concerned about the risk management and the deployment of an appropriate set of controls. The ISO/IEC 27001 standard is designed based on an information risk management approach and deployment of risk controls to manage the risks.

The standard also refers to the latest Organization for Economic Cooperation and Development (OECD) Security Principles, which emphasize the need to engender a "security culture" within an organization. This is especially important in helping the organization fulfill its corporate social responsibilities and for its overall well-being.

3.10 ISO/IEC 27002

"An ounce of practice is worth more than tons of preaching." Mohandas Gandhi

3.10.1 Overview

The international standard ISO/IEC 27002 (Code of Practice for information security management) was previously, from December 2000 to July 2007, numbered as ISO/IEC 17799. The standard ISO/IEC 17799 Code of practice for information security management was first published in December 2000. On the 15th June 2005, a revised edition of this best practice standard was published. Over the last five years, business has been gaining experience in using and road-testing this standard. In addition the growing number of diverse industries and markets adopting ISO/IEC 17799 is a clear indication of the increasing importance of managing and protecting information, one of the most important of business commodities.

The standard is a set of best practice measures that can be deployed by companies to help them protect their information whether it be on paper or in electronic form. It covers user and employee security measures, procedures and policies, asset management, IT security measures, physical security and many other areas to enable a company to build a management control framework for its information security. Such security controls whether implemented to protect information in IT systems, being processed in paper, or held in the heads of their employees, is covered by many best practice measures given in the standard. All versions of the standard set out the following information security purpose:

"To minimize the risks and impacts to business whilst maximizing business opportunities and investments and ensuring business continuity"

This has become the objective "Charter" or trade-mark associated with the ISMS standards.

3.10.2 Management Domains

ISO/IEC 27002 covers three major areas of enterprise and organizational security:

- Security management of people, processes and information,

- Legal, regulatory and contractual security, third party services,

- Technical and infrastructural security.

Figure 3.5 shows the management domains covered by 27002 that address these major areas. *In Annex A of I/O 27001 : 2005 standard*

A. 5 8	Information security policy
A . 6	Organising information security
A . 7	Asset management
8	Human resources security
9	Physical and environmental security
10	Communications and operations management
11	Access control
12	Information security acquisition, development and maintenance
13	Information security incident handling
14	Business continuity management
A . 15	Compliance

Figure 3.5 Information security management domains

3.10.3 Control Structure

For each of the management domains covered in ISO/IEC 17799 there is a set of control objectives and controls defined. At the control objective level the standard is structured in the following way:

- A control objective is defined to meet a certain security requirement,

- One or more controls are defined to satisfy this requirement,

- For each control there is a set of implementation guidance text,

- For each control there are references to further information.

This structure (with example) is illustrated in Figure 3.6.

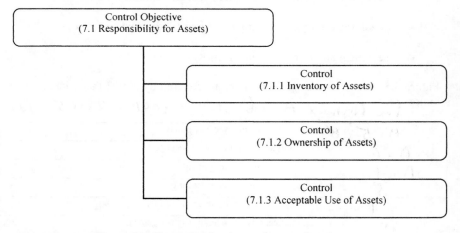

Figure 3.6 Control objective and control structure

3.10.4 Compliance with ISO/IEC 27002

The term "compliance" is often depreciated by overuse, misuse, bad use and inappropriate use. As a code of practice ISO/IEC 17799:2000 takes the form of guidance and recommendations which means it should not be quoted as a specification and care needs to be taken to ensure that claims of compliance are not misleading.

The idea of compliance with ISO/IEC 27002 is therefore very much a question of management requirements since this is a code of practice and not a mandatory specification. Hence if a customer requires an organization to apply ISO/IEC 27002 then this is a matter of a contractual arrangement between the organization and its customer. ISO/IEC 27002 has no recognition as a compliant standard as is ISO/IEC 27001, which is an internationally recognized standard for compliance and conformity assessments.

3.10.5 Applying ISO/IEC 27002

ISO/IEC 27002 is a catalogue of best practice controls, which users can select from to deploy security management controls in their business environment. When combined with ISO/IEC 27001 these two complement each other providing organizations with a set of tools for managing information security risks. Of course ISO/IEC 27002 can be used on its own but the management processes in ISO/IEC 27001 facilitate the management of an effective information security system with an inbuilt programme for continually improving an organization's security status. Chapters 4 through 6 provide more detailed information on the use, implementation and application of the ISO/IEC 27002.

3.10.6 Example Controls

same as the 11 "management domains"

The catalogue of best practice controls given in ISO/IEC 27002 covers many aspects of management controls that are particularly useful.

3.10.7 Access Control (Chapter 11)

This chapter includes various aspects of access control including access policies, access to information, applications and software and network services including specific control areas such as:

- User access management,

- User responsibilities,

- User identification and authentication,

- Network connections and routing controls,

- Controlling to the use of system utilities,

- Restrictions to information access,

- Access regarding the use of mobile devices and communications.

3.10.8 Backups (Clause 10.2)

Routine procedures should be established and deployed to ensure the protection of the information software an organization has, from loss of integrity and availability. The backup methods, devices and routines used should be regularly tested to ensure that information and software can be recovered in the case of an incident such as a system or media failure.

3.10.9 Third Party Supplier Contracts, SLAs and Service Delivery (Clauses 6.2 and 10.2)

These controls cover the risks associated with external connections with customers, suppliers and service providers. Given the growing dependence that organizations have on the use of external services from the provision of network and Internet services to the outsourcing of an organization's IT and information assets, this area of management security has become of critical and major importance. These controls cover, both the contractual and SLA aspects, as well as the management of service delivery. This last aspect is closely linked to ISO/IEC 20000 on IT Service Management.

Specific controls include:

- Identification of risks in relation to external parties,

- Addressing security in relation to dealing with customers and third party agreements, SLAs and contracts,

- Security aspects of service delivery,

- Monitoring and review of service provision,

- Managing changes to service delivery and agreements.

3.11 ISO/IEC 27000 AND 27003 TO 27005

3.11.1 Introduction

This group of ISO 27000 series of standards are at various levels and stages of development. All of these developments will conclude with standards published in the period of late 2007 to late 2008. Like ISO/IEC 27002 they all are to support the use and the implementation of the ISMS processes specified in ISO/IEC 27001.

3.11.2 ISO 27000 Overview and vocabulary

The scope of this standard is to specify the fundamental principles, concepts and vocabulary for the ISO/IEC 27000 (information security management system) series of documents. It provides an overview of all the ISO/IEC 27000 family of standards, the relationships among this family of standards and to specify the terminology applicable to this family of standards.

ISO/IEC 27000 is related to all standards within the ISO/IEC 27000 family and provides a single common point from which an introductory understanding of these standards can be obtained succinctly and effectively. Areas covered by this standard include:

- Published standards,
  - Generic/Terminology,
  - Supporting the PDCA model,

- Under development,
  - Generic/Terminology,
  - Requirements,
  - Guidelines,

- ISO/IEC 27000 Family Document Relationships,
  - ISO/IEC 27000 Overview and vocabulary,
  - ISO/IEC 27001 ISMS requirements,
  - ISO/IEC 27002 Code of practice for information security management,
  - ISO/IEC 27003 ISMS Implementation guidelines,
  - ISO/IEC 27004 Information security management measurements,
  - ISO/IEC 27005 ISMS risk management,
  - ISO/IEC 27006 Accreditation requirements for certification bodies,

- Control implementation guidelines,

- Other management system standards,

- Terms and definitions.

3.11.3 ISO 27003 ISMS implementation guidelines

This International Standard provides help and guidance in implementing the Information Security Management System (ISMS) requirements in ISO 27001. This standard will provide further information about using the PDCA model and give guidance addressing the requirements of the different stages on the PDCA process to establish, implement and operate, monitor and review and improve the ISMS. Areas covered by this standard include:

- Critical success factors,
    - Management commitment,
    - Governance,

- Guidance on using the "Plan-Do-Check-Act (PDCA)" Model,
    - The model,
    - Integration with other management systems,

- Guidance on the "Plan" processes,
    - Operational analysis,
    - Organizing the work,
    - Risk assessment,
    - Policy,
    - Applicability,
    - Guidelines and instructions,

- Guidance on the 'Do' processes,
    - Producing and implementing the risk treatment plan,
    - Advice on implementing controls,
    - Training and awareness requirements,
    - Implementing an information security incident management programme,
    - Managing resources of the ISMS,

- Guidance on the 'Check' processes,
    - Monitoring the ISMS,
    - Routine ISMS checking,
    - Self-policing procedures for the ISMS,
    - Reviewing the ISMS,
    - Internal ISMS auditing,
    - Carrying out management reviews,
    - ISMS measurements and effectiveness,
    - Undertaking trend analysis,
    - Controlling documentation and records,

- Guidance on the 'Act' processes,
    - Implementing improvements,

- Identifying nonconformities,
- Identifying and implementing corrective and preventive actions,
- Achieving continual improvement testing,
- Communicating changes and improvements,

- Guidance on documentation,

- Co-operation with other organizations,

Chapter 5 provides more details of applying 27003, implementations in practice and the controls, tools and methods organizations might like to consider to establish, deploy and maintain their ISMS.

3.11.4 ISO 27004 Information security management measurements

This international standard provides guidance on the specification and use of measurement techniques for providing assurance as regards the effectiveness of information security management systems. It is intended to be applicable to a wide range of organizations with a correspondingly wide range of information security management systems.

   This international standard provides guidance for measurement procedures and techniques to determine the effectiveness of information security controls and information security processes applied in an ISMS. A summary of the topics covered by this standard are:

- Measurement overview,

- Measurement process,
    - ISMS life-cycle integration,
    - Control objective and control improvement,
    - Roles and responsibilities,

- Measurement development,
    - Control selection,
    - Goal identification,
    - Object identification,
    - Measure development and selection,
    - Measure validation,
    - Data collection, analysis and reporting,
    - Documentation,

- Measurement operation,
    - Integrated procedures,

- Collect data,
- Store data,
- Verify data,

- Measurement analysis and reporting,

- Measurement outputs,

- Measurement process improvement.

Chapter 6 provides more details of applying 27004: the measurements in practice and the tools and methods organizations might like to consider to assess their performance and effectiveness.

3.11.5 ISO 27005 ISMS risk management

This standard provides techniques for information security risk management that includes information and communications technology security risk management. The techniques are based on the general concepts, models and management and planning guidelines laid out in Part 1 of this International Standard. These guidelines are designed to assist the implementation of information security. Familiarity with the concepts and models and the material concerning the management and planning of information security in ISO/IEC 13335-1, is important for a complete understanding of Part 2.

This document gives guidelines for information security risk management, which ISO/IEC 13335-1 of this International Standard specifies as one of the activities that information security management requires to be carried out.

ISO/IEC 27005 is applicable to any organization, which intends to manage risk that could compromise the organization's information security. A summary of the topics covered by this standard are:

- Information security risk management process,
  - Process elements,

- Information security risk assessment,
  - Introduction to information security risk assessment process,
  - Information security risk analysis,
  - Information security risk identification,
  - Information security risk estimation,
  - Risk estimation,
  - Information security risk evaluation,

- Information security risk treatment,
    - Information security risk treatment process,

- Information security risk treatment options,
    - Avoidance,
    - Transfer,
    - Retention,
    - Reduction,
    - Acceptance,

- Information security risk communication,

- Information security risk monitoring and review,
    - General considerations,
    - Monitoring and review of risk elements,
    - Information security risk management monitoring and review.

Chapter 4 provides more details of applying 27005, risk management in practice and the tools and methods organizations might like to consider, to assess and manage their risks.

3.11.6 ISO/IEC 27006 Requirements for the accreditation of bodies providing certification of information security management systems

This international standard specifies requirements and provides guidance for bodies providing audit and certification of an information security management system (ISMS), in addition to the requirements contained within ISO/IEC 17021 and ISO/IEC 27001. It is primarily intended to support the accreditation of certification bodies providing ISMS certification.

The requirements contained in this international standard need to be demonstrated in terms of competence and reliability by those organizations providing ISMS certification and the guidance contained in this standard provides additional interpretation of these requirements for those organizations providing ISMS certification.

A summary of the topics covered by this standard are:

- General requirements,
    - Legal and contractual matter,
    - Management of impartiality,
    - Liability and financing,

- Structural requirements,
    - Organizational structure and top management,

- Committee for safeguarding impartiality,

- Resource requirements,
  - Competence of management and personnel,
  - Personnel involved in the certification activities,
  - Use of individual external auditors and external technical experts,
  - Personnel records,
  - Outsourcing,

- Information requirements,
  - Publicly accessible information,
  - Certification documents,
  - Directory of certified clients,
  - Reference to certification and use of marks,
  - Confidentiality,
  - Information exchange between a certification body and its clients,

- Process requirements,
  - General requirements,
  - Initial audit and certification,
  - Surveillance activities,
  - Re-certification,
  - Special audits,
  - Suspending, withdrawing, or reducing scope of certification,
  - Appeals,
  - Complaints,
  - Records of applicants and clients,

- Management system requirements for certification bodies,
  - Options,
    - o Management system requirements in accordance with ISO 9001,
    - o General management system requirements,

- Annex A (informative) Analysis of a client organization's complexity and sector-specific aspects,

- Annex B (informative) Example areas of auditor competence,

- Annex C (informative) Audit time,

- Annex D (informative) Guidance for review of implemented ISO/IEC 27001, Annex A controls.

Chapter 7 provides more details of the ISO/IEC 27001 ISMS certification processes.

3.12 STANDARDS SUPORTING THE ISO/IEC 27000 ISMS FAMILY

3.12.1 ITU-T X.842|ISO/IEC TR 14516:2002 Guidelines for the use and management of trusted third party services

Associated with the provision and operation of a Trusted Third Party (TTP) are a number of security related issues for which general guidance is necessary to assist business entities, developers and providers of systems and services. This includes guidance on issues regarding the roles, positions and relationships of TTPs and the entities using TTP services, the generic security requirements; who should provide what type of security; what the possible security solutions are and the operational use and management of TTP service security.

This technical report provides guidance for the use and management of TTPs, a clear definition of the basic duties and services provided, their description and their purpose and the roles and liabilities of TTPs and entities using their services. It is intended primarily for system managers, developers, TTP operators and enterprise users to select those TTP services needed for particular requirements, their subsequent management, use and operational deployment and the establishment of a security policy within a TTP. It also identifies different major categories of TTP services including: time stamping, non-repudiation, key management, certificate management and electronic notary public. Each of these major categories consists of several services, which logically belong together.

This standard is a joint development with ITU-T and is applicable to the implementation of the controls in ISO/IEC 27002.

The objective of this Recommendation/Technical Report are to provide:

- Guidelines to TTP managers, developers and operations personnel and to assist them in the use and management of TTPs,

- Guidance to entities regarding the services performed by TTPs and the respective roles and responsibilities of TTPs and users.

Additional aspects covered by this Recommendation/Technical Report are to provide:

- An overview of the description of services provided,

- An understanding of the role of TTPs and their functional features,

- A basis for the mutual recognition of services provided by different TTPs,

- Guidance of interworking between entities and TTPs.

3.12.2 ITU-T X.843|ISO/IEC 15945 Specification of TTP services to support the application of digital signatures

Technical services definitions and protocols are required to allow for the implementation of TTP services and related commercial applications.

This standard focuses on implementation and interoperability, service specifications and technical requirements. It defines those TTP services needed to support the application of digital signatures in commercial applications. This standard also defines interfaces and protocols to enable interoperability between entities associated with these TTP services. This standard does not describe the management of TTPs or other organizational, operational, or personal issues. Those topics are mainly covered in TR 14516.

This standard is a joint development with ITU-T and is applicable to the implementation of the controls in ISO/IEC 27002.

3.12.3   ISO/IEC TR 15947 IT intrusion detection framework

This technical report defines a framework for detection of intrusions in IT systems. Many classes of intrusions are considered. These include intrusions that are intentional or unintentional, legal or illegal, harmful or harmless and unauthorized access by insiders or outsiders. The TR focuses on:

- Establishing common definitions for terms and concepts associated with an IT intrusion detection framework,

- Describing a generic model of intrusion detection,

- Providing high-level examples of attempts to exploit systems vulnerabilities,

- Discussing common types of input data and the sources needed for an effective intrusion detection capability,

- Discussing different methods and combinations of methods of intrusion detection analysis,

- Describing activities/actions in response to indications of intrusions.

This framework explains intrusion detection terms and concepts and describes the relationship among them.

3.12.4   ISO/IEC 18028-1, Information technology — Security techniques — IT Network security - Part 1: Network security management

This standard provides direction with respect to networks and communications, including on the security aspects of connecting information system networks themselves, and of connecting remote users to networks. It is aimed at those responsible for the management of information security in general, and network security in particular. This direction supports the identification and analysis of the communications related factors that should be taken into account to establish network security requirements, provides an introduction on how to identify appropriate control areas with respect to security associated with connections to communications networks and provides an overview of the possible control areas including those technical design and implementation topics dealt with in detail in ISO/IEC 18028 Parts 2 to 5.

This standard is applicable to the implementation of the controls in ISO/IEC 27002.

3.12.5 ISO/IEC 18028-2 IT network security - Part 2: Network security architecture

This standard defines a network security architecture for providing end-to-end network security. The architecture can be applied to various kinds of networks where end-to-end security is a concern and independently of the networks underlying technology. The objective of this part of ISO/IEC 18028 is to serve as a foundation for developing the detailed recommendations for the end-to-end network security. This standard is applicable to the implementation of the controls in ISO/IEC 27002.

3.12.6 ISO/IEC 18028-3 IT network security - Part 3: Securing communications between networks using security gateways

This standard provides an overview of different techniques of security gateways, of components and of different types of security gateway architectures. It also provides guidelines for selection and configuration of security gateways. Although personal firewalls make use of similar techniques, they are outside the scope of this part of ISO/IEC 18028 because they do not serve as security gateways. The intended audiences for this part of ISO/IEC 18028 are technical and managerial personnel, for example, IT managers, system administrators, network administrators and IT security personnel. It provides guidance in helping users choose the right type of architecture for a security gateway, which best meets their security requirements.

This standard is applicable to the implementation of the controls in ISO/IEC 27002.

3.12.7 ISO/IEC 18028-4 IT network security - Part 4: Securing remote access

This standard describes remote access a method to remotely connect a computer either to another computer or to a network using public networks and its implication for IT security. In this it introduces the different types of remote access including the protocols in use, discusses the authentication issues related to remote access and provides support when setting up remote access securely. It is intended to help network administrators and technicians who plan to make use of this kind of communications connection or who already have this type of connection in use and need advice on how to set it up securely and operate it securely.

3.12.8 ISO/IEC 18028-5 IT network security - Part 5: Securing communications across networks using virtual private networks

This standard considers the security aspects of using virtual private network (VPN) connections to interconnect IT networks and also to connect remote users to IT networks. It builds upon the IT network management direction provided in ISO/IEC 18028-1. It is aimed at those individuals responsible for the selection and implementation of the technical controls necessary to provide IT network security when using VPN connections and for the subsequent IT network monitoring of VPN security thereafter.

This standard is applicable to the implementation of the controls in ISO/IEC 27002.

3.12.9 ISO/IEC 18043 Guidelines for the selection, deployment and operations of intrusion detection systems

This provides guidelines to assist organizations in preparing to deploy an intrusion detection system (IDS). In particular, it addresses the selection, deployment and operations of IDS. It also provides background information from which these guidelines are derived.

This standard is applicable to the implementation of the controls in ISO/IEC 27002.

3.12.10 ISO/IEC TR 18044 Information security incident management

This technical report provides advice and guidance on information security incident management for information security managers and information system, service and network managers. This technical report is applicable to the implementation of the requirements in ISO/IEC 27001 and the controls in ISO/IEC 27002.

3.12.11 ISO/IEC 24762 Guidelines for information and communications technology disaster recovery services

This standard specifies the guidelines for the information and communication technology disaster recovery (ICT DR) services focusing on the desired disaster recovery (DR) facilities and services capability. It deals with the provision of fallback and recovery support to an organization's information and communication system, including test, implementation and execution aspects of disaster recovery. This standard primarily focuses on ICT DR services and does not include guidelines in other areas of business continuity management.

3.12.12 BS 7799 Part 3: ISMS risk management

This standard covers all the requirements relating to risk management that are specified in ISO/IEC 27001. It provides implementation guidance regarding compliance with these requirements: risk assessment, risk treatment and on-going risk management activities.

3.12.13 BSI ISMS guides

3.12.13.1 BIP 71 Guidelines on requirements and preparation for ISMS (information security management system) certification based on ISO/IEC 27001:2005

BIP 71 provides guidance on the requirements specified in the ISMS standard ISO/IEC 27001 and the best practice described in ISO/IEC 27002 to support the use of these standards. It gives guidance on the complete "PDCA life cycle" of ISMS activities required to establish, implement, monitor and continually improve a set of management controls and processes to achieve effective information security.
This guide is intended to be used by those involved in:

- Designing, implementing and maintaining an ISMS,

- Preparing for ISMS audits and assessments,

- Undertaking both internal and third party ISMS audits and assessments.

3.12.13.2 BIP 72 Are you ready for ISMS audits? - An assessment workbook for ISO/IEC 27001:2005

BIP 72 provides help to organizations trying to assess how prepared their ISMS is with respect to formal audits in accordance with the requirements specified in ISO/IEC 27001. It uses the following workbooks:

- ISMS Process Workbook to check the whether the organization has a set of systems and processes in place to satisfy the requirements specified in Clauses 4 to 8 in ISO/IEC 27001,

- Annex A Gap Analysis Workbook that can be used to check and record which controls have been selected from Annex A of ISO/IEC 27001 as part of the control selection process defined in ISO/IEC 27001 Clause 4.2.1 g). Organizations can also use this Workbook to document the reasons and justification why a particular control has not been selected or its requirements are not fully satisfied, which subsequently can be used in the production of the Statement of Applicability (see Clause 4.2.1 j) of ISO/IEC 27001). Note: For accredited certification this type of gap analysis has no formal status and should not be taken as a replacement for the Statement of Applicability (SoA).

3.12.13.3 BIP 73 Implementation and auditing of ISMS controls - Guidance for organizations preparing for certification

BIP 73 provides guidance on the implementation of ISMS control requirements for auditing existing control implementations to help organizations preparing for certification in accordance with ISO/IEC 27001.

The contents of this guide include the ISMS control requirements that should be addressed by organizations considering certification according to ISO/IEC 27001. Section 2 of this guide, describes each of the controls in Annex A of ISO/IEC 27001 in two different aspects:

- Implementation guidance: describing what needs to be considered to fulfil the control requirements when implementing the controls from ISO/IEC 27001, Annex A. This guidance is aligned with ISO/IEC 27002, which gives advice on the implementation of the controls,

- Auditing guidance: describing what should be checked when examining the implementation of ISO/IEC 27001 controls to ensure that the implementation covers the essential ISMS control requirements.

3.12.13.4 BIP 74 Guidelines on measuring the effectiveness of ISMS (information security management system) implementations

BIP 74 provides information and help on measuring the effectiveness of ISMS implementations, as required by the ISMS standard ISO/IEC 27001. This guide refers to two different types of measurement; one for the ISMS processes that are described in clauses 4 through 8 in ISO/IEC 27001 and other forms of measurements for the controls from ISO/IEC 27002 that have been selected to reduce identified risks. This guide introduces an approach to measuring the ISMS processes and controls that is aligned with ISO/IEC 27004 and several of the currently used methods and developments to support organizations in identifying the appropriate selection of metrics and measurement techniques. This guide also gives some examples of metrics and measurements used by leading organizations and interest groups in the field of information security. This is not a replacement for ISO/IEC 27004 but a useful complement to it supporting it with many example measurements and additional information.

Chapter 4

Managing ISMS Risks

4.1 IMPORTANCE OF RISK MANAGEMENT

"To do is to be." Socrates, "To be is to do." Plato and "The way to do is to be."
Lao-Tzu

4.1.1 Risk Factors

An organization and its operational systems and networks are vulnerable to a constantly evolving diversity of risks. If an organization does not know the information security risks it faces then its investment in resources and solutions may not be the best. An organization needs to be well informed with regard to the risks in order to make the best management decisions about how and how best to use its resources to manage the risks. Managing the information security risks is key to a successful implementation of an ISMS and the protection of the organization's assets.

Areas related to an organization's risk profile include:

- Governance and the compliance with legislation and regulations and contractual obligations,

- Organizational,
  - Strategy, policy and decision making and strategy: expansion, acquisitions, joint ventures in projects, development of new products or the provisioning of services, investments in emerging markets and new technologies, restructuring/downsizing, reducing costs,
  - Culture,
  - Corporate and brand values,
  - Human resources, skills and their operational deployment,

- Information and information systems,
  - Confidentiality, integrity, reliability, availability, and timeliness of management and operational information,

- Dependency on ICT to process and deliver such information,
- Non-ICT information systems,

- Business Processes,
    - Outsourcing arrangements,
    - Supply chains,
    - Customer interfaces,
    - Management processes,
    - Operational processes,
        - Accounting processes,
    - Supporting processes,
        - Recruitment,
        - ICT services,

- External influences such as,
    - Epidemics (e.g., SARS, Avian Flu, Ebola),
    - Physical and environmental conditions,
    - Technological developments and changes in information systems and networks,

4.1.2 Small, Medium and Large Enterprises

Risk is an important issue to all organizations irrespective of their size from a 1 to 2 person company to the super-large companies. Risk to the business is something that no manager can ignore as risks abound everywhere in the working environment. Everyone needs at least some protection against: physical threats, loss of data, noncompliance with the law, nonavailability of information to carry out job functions and this is irrespective of size or the nature of the business.

What is covered in the sections that follow apply to all. The SMEs (small-medium sized enterprises) should not be scared off or be apprehensive of what follows. All that is described can be scaled down, tailored and customized to all sorts of business and the resources to carry out this work for SMEs does not necessarily need to highly skilled people as most of what follows should be common sense once users are aware of the principles of what is involved. The cost of implementing information should also not be a barrier to the small companies as much can be done with the best practice controls contained in the ISO/IEC 27001 and ISO/IEC 27002 without spending a fortune. As we shall see in a later section it is all a matter of balance of what the business can afford to spend on security and what it can afford to lose without security.

So SMEs should read on and understand the basic principles of risk management and customize and deploy these to fit in with their business and its culture.

4.1.3 Informed Decision Making

The organization needs a clear understanding of the risks it faces and the nature and degree of risk it is prepared to tolerate and accept. This should enhance its means of informed policy and decision making as well to effectively manage its business and resources.

Information security treated as a management issue is a business enabler to take advantage of its investments and business opportunities.

The management of an organization is responsible for the management of the risks it faces. This includes operational responsibility as well as providing assurance that the risk management processes are adequate and effective. Risk management in general covers the assessment of the risks, the implementation and deployment of controls and processes by which the risks are managed and maintained at an acceptable level. The system of controls deployed by the organization should strictly depend on the considered risks.

4.1.4 What the Risk Management Process Covers

The overall process covers:

- Risk planning and screening *(ISO/IEC 27001 clause 4.2.1 a)-c))*,
  - Risk approach,
  - Critical business areas,
  - Priorities,
  - ISMS scope,
  - Levels of risk acceptance,

- Risk identification *(ISO/IEC 27001 clause 4.2.1 d))*,

- Risk assessment and evaluation *(ISO/IEC 27001 clause 4.2.1 e))*,

- Risk treatment and response *(ISO/IEC 27001 clause 4.2.1 f)-g))*,
  - Management decision making,
  - Selecting, implementing and deploying a system of controls and processes,

- Risk monitoring and reassessment *(ISO/IEC 27001 clause 4.2.3)*,
  - Changes to the risk profile,
  - Incident handling reports,
  - Changes affecting the organization (e.g., restructuring, mergers, supply chains and outsourcing, human resources, external systems, technology, market conditions, legislation).

4.1.5 Depth of Assessment

There are many risk assessment methods. ISO/IEC 27001 does not specify any specific methods or solutions to use. ISO/IEC 27001 states in clause 4.2.1 the common risk elements that are mandatory for assessing the ISMS risks to be compliant with the standard:

- Identifying the ISMS assets,

- Valuing the utility of these assets,

- Identifying the threats and vulnerabilities associated with these assets,

- Assessing the likelihood that the identified could exploit the identified vulnerabilities,

- Assessing the risks and impacts based on this information above.

Once the organization understands what risks it faces it is then in a position to select, implement and deploy controls and processes to manage these risks.

ISO/IEC 27001 clause 4.2.1 (c) requires the organization to decide on its risk assessment approach at the start of the planning phase of the ISMS project. The approach taken will need to take account of the size and nature of the business, any policy on risk and risk acceptance and any existing risk management approaches that are being deployed.

There are several levels of risk assessment that can be considered. A *high-level assessment* which:

- Focuses on a risk profile at the strategic and management level covering,
    - The information security threats, risks and impacts,
    - The critical macro areas of asset and process risk,
    - The context within the broader business risks it faces,

- Enables a generic information security policy to be defined,

- Provides the basis for an ISMS project plan of organizational actions and a more detailed risk assessment.

A *more in-depth assessment* which:

- Focuses on a more detailed risk profile at the operational level covering,

- Information systems,
- Processes,
- Human resource risks,
- Legal compliance,
- Business continuity,
- ICT,
- Physical aspects,

- Provides the basis for the development of more detailed policies and procedures such as,
  - Information classification and handling,
  - Access control,
  - Incident handling,
  - Backup,
  - Acceptable use of organizational resources,
  - Media handling,

- Provides the basis for the design, implementation and deployment of a risk focused ISMS architecture based on best practices.

4.1.6 Risk Measurements and Metrics

Different measurement systems can be used for the risk assessment based on quantitative or qualitative metrics.

Quantitative metrics and measurements are based on the use of statistical or historical data and monetary values. This includes assets where real quantities can be used to associate damage directly with some numerical value:

- Cost of replacing a damaged piece of equipment,

- Cost of recovering from a system failure, virus attack, denial of service and other incidents,

- Reliability figures of equipment or component failures (e.g., MTBF),

- Records relating to system downtimes, access attempts, network data (e.g., transmission delays, access delays, call and session drops, error rates),

- Statistics relating to earthquakes, tsunamis, volcano eruptions, flooding, typhoons and other natural threats.

Some assets are difficult to assign a quantitative risk measure and value to for example information itself, company image and reputation, the skills of its human resources, or the competency of the attacker and their resources for carrying out the attack. Quantitative methods have a degree of subjectivity and bias associated with them.

Qualitative metrics and measurements do not involve the use of statistical or historical data but use a grading system such as low, medium, high and very high to express the value of the threat, vulnerability, or risk. Although this may seem imprecise it is generally more objective than the quantitative method and can cover a broader range of asset types both varying, noncomplementary and discontinuous for example, information, hardware, corporate image and staff skills.

Qualitative methods are generally more suited to an ISMS since there is often more uncertainty in assessing the information security environment. In practice the complexity of information security issues require a combination of qualitative and quantitative assessment especially so as the assets will cover tangible and nontangible, technical and non-technical and management types.

Semi-quantitative methods address the need to express qualitative measurements in the form of numbers for example, low risk = 0, medium risk = 1, high risk = 2 and very high risk = 3. The numbers themselves can be further quantified in more meaningful terms such as monetary values, degradation in levels of service and availability, reduction in performance levels and decrease in efficiency and productivity output.

4.1.7 ISMS Scope

4.1.7.1 What to Include

The starting point for any ISMS development is to decide the scope of the ISMS. This is an important aspect to get right before the organization spends its resources in carrying out a risk assessment. This might sound like an obvious thing to do, but defining the ISMS can present a number of challenges.

The ISMS scope can cover part of the organization or all of the organization. The choice depends on the organization's business aims and objectives and the motivation for its particular choice of ISMS scope.

Experience and feedback of existing implementations around the world informs us that organizations are selecting the ISMS route and a particular scope of application:

- Minimise the business impact and financial costs of security incidents,
  - Delayed deliveries to customers,
  - Reduction in staff morale, productivity, effectiveness,

- Loss of contracts, sales, orders, or profits,
- Loss of customers,
- Loss of trust and confidence,
- Loss of market position,
- Loss of assets,
- e-risk insurance,
- Legal/contractual penalties/liabilities,
- Breach of operating controls,

- Reduce the number and frequency of incidents,
  - Human errors,
  - Service interruptions,
  - Misuse/abuse of company resources,
  - Theft, fraud and other related crimes,
  - Malfunctions, system failures, system downtimes,

- Complying with a set of laws and regulations such as data privacy directive in the European Union and its Member States, or for complying with the Sarbanes Oxley (SoX) regulations in the United States. Companies (e.g., in Europe and Asia) wanting to trade globally with organizations located in the United States are finding that SoX is in a number of cases applicable to them,

- As a market differentiator such as those companies that offer on-line (e.g., Internet banking service) or off-line (e.g., media disposal, data recovery) services,

- Enhancing customer and business partner confidence and relations and meeting contractual obligations of its customer(s) such as in the case of a company providing managed services to its clients,

- Enhancing corporate value to their business and as a business enabler,
  - Maximising business opportunities and investments,
  - Providing more informed decision making about security risks,
  - Improving risk awareness, risk control and information security, effectiveness for the organization's sensitive and critical assets,
  - Facilitating an organizationally information security risk culture,

- Public demonstration that they are "fit for purpose" by means of a third party independent audit such as providing a particular line or type of customer facing services (such as help desk and call centre facilities), as part of a supply chain, as a supplier of products, as a supplier of infrastructure supporting services (electronic signatures for secure payments and transactions).

Whatever the organization decides the size of its ISMS scope is, it must ensure that it is well defined and covers all that it should cover. The organization should not exclude things from within the ISMS boundary if they seem too difficult to deal with as such exclusions could affect the organization's ability and/or responsibility, to provide information security that meets the security requirements determined by risk assessment and applicable legislative and regulatory requirements.

The scope of the ISMS should include:

- The people operationally involved in the ISMS,

- The processes and services used within the ISMS area of work,

- The information and information systems necessary to carry out the business of the ISMS,

- The policies, procedures and documentation to be deployed necessary to carry out the business of the ISMS,

- The interfaces and connections to the ISMS,

- Supporting ICT infrastructure for the ISMS,

- The physical location(s) of the ISMS.

4.1.7.2 Scope Example

An example ISMS scope could be an Internet banking service provided by an international bank as one of the many of the other services it offers will in practice involve:

- The personnel providing the banking service,

- The procedures used by the personnel,
    - System operating manuals,
    - Security manual,
    - Banking procedures,

- The information used,
  - Customer details,
  - Internal banking data,
  - External data from other banks,

- The network services used to engage in on-line transactions,
  - Customer connections,
  - Other bank connections and interfaces (internal and external),

- Technology to facilitate the on-line services,
  - Desk top computers and other ICT equipment
  - Telephones.

This example illustrates an ISMS scope that is only part of the bank's operations and the banking services it provides.

Other scoping examples include:

- Internal services supplied by the ICT department,

- Call centre,

- Internal help desk support,

- An organization's claims and payments department for its customers,

- ICT based logistics support for shipping or airline company,

- On-line hotel booking system for an international hotel chain,

- Research and development group of a software company,

4.1.7.3 External and Internal Connections

An important aspect of the ISMS scope is that the connections to the ISMS be those with external customer or supplier systems or be they connections with other parts of the organization. In the example given above typical internal connections might be with the personnel department, those dealing with IT services and those dealing with physical security. External connections might typically be those with other banks, networks and ISP service providers (see Figure 4.1). It is important to consider these connection interfaces since it is across these interfaces that risks present themselves to the ISMS. Managing and control of the flows of information across these interfaces are important to protect the ISMS against these risks.

Managing these interfaces can be done in many ways through the use of contracts and SLAs, as well as through the use of operational procedures and technical controls. ISO/IEC 27002 (clause 6.2) provides a list of things to be considered when considering the inclusion of security aspects in contracts and SLAs.

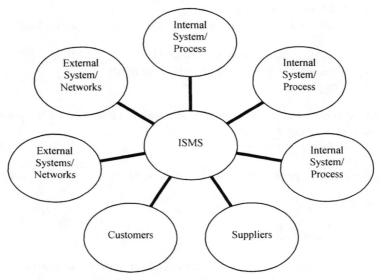

Figure 4.1 ISMS Scope and external connections

An example of an external connection is that of providing managed services through an outsourcing contract. Many organizations outsource parts of the operations such as help desk facilities, data management, IT services or ISP hosting.

4.1.8 Travel Company Case Study

This example concerns a travel company, which provides travel services to some of the world's top corporations and multinational organizations. It has offices in 11 different countries and its workforce is in the region of 3000 employees. It is a well-established travel business that has been in the travel market for more than 12 years.

The company's aim is to give confidence to its customers that its travel services are reliable, value for money, efficient and deliver the right end product on time, to the right requirements and at the right price. To achieve this it needs to ensure that its management system is effective enough to achieve these goals. This includes providing adequate information security assurance to protect its commercial interests in the highly competitive market as well as serving the best interests of its customers.

The company decides to outsource the management of its data to a managed services company as well as hosting its Web site for on-line travel services. The managed data services company process customers travel data and other related travel and company information and will look after the on-line payment side through the Web site. The contract and service level agreement requires the managed services company to provide high levels of service availability, quality and appropriate information security sufficient to meet the demands of its customers and the market and to protect all the information assets it is managing. The travel company therefore requires desired levels of confidence and assurance from the managed data services company that it can function correctly, reliably and effectively to deliver the services to its customers.

This is also an example of an important scoping problem concerning managing the risks across external interfaces. There are many real-life examples of this type of ISMS scope including several organizations that have achieved ISO/IEC 27001 certification.

A typical scope for this case study would be similar to that given in 4.2.1:

- The staff providing the managed services,
  - Management and operational staff,
  - ICT support staff,
  - Web support staff,
  - Help desk staff,

- The procedures, documentation and business continuity plans used by the staff including,
  - Backup,
  - Incident handling,
  - Media handling,
  - Operational,
  - Access control,

- The information used
  - Customer details, travel requirements, travel itineraries, payment details,
  - Travel company data,
  - Travel information from various sources,
  - Other details such as relating to banks,

- The network services used to engage in on-line transactions,

- Travel company's connections,
- Web site connections,
- Other connections such as to banks,

- The ICT systems to process and manage the Travel company's data and to support its Web site and the on-line travel services,

- Help desk facilities,

- Contracts and service level agreements (SLAs).

4.1.9 ISMS Certification

As regards to ISO/IEC 27001 ISMS certification, it is the responsibility of the organization to define its ISMS scope and it is up to the certification auditors to confirm that this scope makes sense with regard to the organization's structure, business and operations. The scoping exercise is the first step and is crucial to get right from the word go to ensure that the ISMS development get the best start and the organization does not waste its resources on work that may need to be redone in the case where the scope is found to be wanting or lacking on its coverage. Such a situation could arise as a result of the certification audit.

4.2 ASSETS

"Normally, we do not so much look at things as overlook them."
Alan Watts

4.2.1 Assets Management Controls

ISO/IEC 27001 Annex A specifies several asset management controls that need to be attended to and implemented, deployed and regularly reviewed, reassessed and updated. The main controls cover:

- Asset inventory,

- Asset classification,

- Asset valuation,

- Asset ownership,

- Assets handling and acceptable use.

4.2.2 Asset Inventory

Producing an asset inventory is a necessary part of the process. This should clearly identify all the important assets related to the ISMS. This inventory is drawn up by those responsible for the ISMS and should be regularly updated and maintained.

The asset inventory should indicate the type of asset, the location, the owner and its value/utility as a minimum set of information.

The types of asset that are within the scope of information security as specified in ISO/IEC 27001 and referred to in ISO/IEC 27002 are very broad and include:

- Information and Information Systems,
  For example, customer details, supplier details, company financial data, personnel data, research results, product designs, sales and marketing data, documentation systems, automated manufacturing systems, software specifications, software code as well as ICT and non-ICT systems for the processing, communication and storage of information.

- Processes,
  Organizations deploy a number of processes to keep their business operational and to deliver products and services. These range from generic processes for example, company accounts, invoicing and payments, purchasing, staff recruitment to more specialized process for example, for the manufacturing, retail, financial, communications, food supply, healthcare, transportation sectors and government applications,

- People,
  For example, specialist skills, knowledge and competencies,

- Policies and Procedures,
  Procedures for operational purposes, backups, incident handling, ICT systems access, business continuity, training.

- Services,
  Organizations employ a number of services to help their business be it network services, outsourcing, supply services, consultancy services, legal services, ICT infrastructure, financial and insurance services.

- ICT,
  The majority of organizations are highly dependent on the use of ICT. Hardware and software computer systems for communicating, processing and storing information. There is an ever increasing development and advancement of technologies for business and personal use with more and more emphasis on mobile working, remote access and home-

working. the range of ICT assets that an organization has is likely to be very diverse in for SMEs.

- Locations,
  Some organizations have high prestige premises or buildings that have been specifically designed for the business as might be in the case of a manufacturing company.

- Company brands, image, reputation and public standing,
  The organization's reputation is regarded as one of the most valuable of its assets. Its brand names, image and public standing give it the potential to continue its business in a profitable way, to gain new markets to affirm customer confidence in its reputation.

Typically organizations will have an inventory listing of their capital and tangible items such as their IT equipment typically for accounting purposes. Normally organizational inventories have not included items such as information and non-ICT information systems, process designs and other intangible items, however, with more awareness of the information security risks this situation is starting to change.

There are many business reasons why such an inventory is important including:

- Organizational reasons,

- Information security and risk management,

- Managing outsourcing arrangements,

- Business continuity,

- Aspects of governance and compliance (e.g., accounting, fiscal, due diligence, IPR and software licences).

The look and style of an inventory are entirely up to the organization to decide upon. The guidelines provided by the ISMS standards say no more than there are several aspects that need to be considered and recognized and included.

A typical template for an inventory might include items as illustrated in Table 4.1 as an example.

ASSET INVENTORY

Type	Itemization	IDs	Owner	Location	Value and notes	
Personnel	Personal data		Head of Human Resources	Human Resource Group		
	Employment records					
	Training records					
	Contracts					
	Contractors records					
	Employment manuals					
Purchasing	Supplier details		Head of Purchasing	Purchasing Group		
	Payment details					
	Invoices					
ICT	PC/laptop type I		Head of ICT	ICT Group		
	PC/laptop type II					
	PC/laptop type III					
	Software product X					
	Software Product Y					

Inventory Owner _____ Approved _____ Date _____

Table 4.1 Example asset inventory

The **Value** column can indicate the importance and utility of value of the asset. This may be in terms of the asset business requirements for confidentiality, integrity or availability or in terms of some other criteria, see ISO/IEC 270001 Clause 4.2.1 and Sections 4.3.3 and 4.3.4 for more information.

The **Notes** column might include information on date of acquisition/disposal, retention period, legal information, more descriptive information on the asset and its deployment and application and a hyperlink to other documents relating to the assets and so on.

This type of inventory does not need the use of any special application software, any office spreadsheet application will suffice for producing such a list of assets. This will provide an easy way of keeping track of the assets, as well as being able to update and maintain the list on a regular basis.

4.2.3 Defining Information Classes

There are many ways of defining the confidentiality of information for example:

- In Strictest Confidence: *For example information that is strictly accessible only to a limited closed group within the organization. This could be future plans for the business only shared between the directors and CEO. Another case could be information regarding a recent research discovery not ready to be disseminated to a broader group within the organization.*

- In Confidence: *For example information that is available on a 'need-to-know' basis. This could be personnel data (within the Human Resources Department), financial data (within the Finance department), or commercially sensitive such as marketing information, research results and design data related to new products, or information about a manufacturing process.*

- Restricted: *For example information that is generally available within the organization but not publicly accessible. This could be company-wide policies and procedures, operational manuals, or employee manuals.*

- Publicly Available: *For example information available on its company Web site or information given in product catalogues, advertising literature and any other documents, information, or brochures made available for public use.*

In the same way that information can be classified on the basis of its sensitivity/confidentiality (that is a "need-to-know" approach), information can also be classified in terms of its criticality/integrity (that is a "need-to-modify" approach), its availability, or authorized accessibility (that is a "need-to-have use of" approach).

Any piece of information will have requirements for the preservation of its confidentiality, integrity and/or its availability.

Protecting the asset value and taking account of these requirements is the essence and primary focus of information security and the avoidance of a business impact if and when these requirements cannot be preserved, see Section 4.3.4 for information regarding this and the asset value.

Class considerations regarding availability might be:

- Service accessibility (e.g., real-time services, diffusion or broadcast services, interactive services),

- Service levels (e.g., >99%, >95%, >85%, 24x7 and other level of business requirements),

- Performance levels,

- Coverage (e.g., voice, data, multi-media),

- Speed (e.g., uploading, downloading),

- Failure rate (e.g., network and service rates, error rates).

Class considerations regarding integrity might be:

- Data integrity (e.g., personal data, financial data, research results, operational data, automated production and manufacturing data),

- Network integrity (e.g., access points, routing, data loss),

- Service integrity (e.g., consistency, accuracy and validity of service features and attributes),

- Organizational and process integrity (e.g., data input, output results, process consistency, completeness and accuracy, human factors).

Of course, in practice an organization would not want or be expected to overburden its management systems with a wide plethora of classes and so it should focus its efforts on those that are critical to its business. Again it is all a sense of proportion and balance based on the business requirements.

4.2.4 Asset Values

The value of an asset can be very subjective and one individual's or organization's valuation can and does vary from another organization, as the value is closely tied to the organizational view of the asset. For assets such as computing equipment the situation is easier as this has a purchase value and replacement value as well as a depreciation value. However, the information stored on the PC or laptop is an entirely different matter. The value of this information can often be difficult to estimate and can vary from one organization to another depending how it views the importance, worth and/or utility of such information.

The value of company secret, sensitive and confidential information needs protection. How the company values this information is dependent on how it defines what is secret, sensitive and confidential and also its utility/value to the company to maintain its profitability and the impact in the case that security of the information was stolen or leaked.

One way of valuing information assets is in terms of qualitative and semi-quantitative values such as, for example, in Figure 4.2.

Qualitative Value	Quantitative Financial Values
Low	Less than $500
Medium	More than $500 but less than $10,000
High	More than $10,000 but less than $100,000
Very high	More than $100,000

Figure 4.2 Example asset value scales

Another organization might use the same qualitative scale for the same types of information assets but the numerical values might be very different depending on how they consider the importance of the information to their business. Also the number of qualitative grades that an organization might use may be more than just the four indicated above depending on the degree of granularity it requires to cover the range of assets it will be assessing.

Depending on the requirements of the business, the protection of the confidentiality, integrity and/or the availability of information will generally have different associated asset values. For example, availability of on-line services for information searching across Internet sites could be medium to high depending on the organization's needs but the confidentiality of this information is low as it is public information, whereas on-line payment services for the confidentiality of credit card details being sent across the Internet is considered to be high. Figure 4.3 gives an example of quanitative values for assets.

| Qualitative Value | Quantitative values | |
	Processing Capability *(loss in accuracy of results, productivity and/or performance)*	Service Level *(loss in availability and/or quality)*
Low	Loss < 5%	Loss < 5%
Medium	5% < loss < 25%	5% < loss < 35%
High	25% < loss < 75%	35% < loss < 90%
Very high	75% < loss	90% < loss

Figure 4.3 Example asset values

4.2.5 Asset Ownership

The ultimate responsibility for an organization's assets is at senior management level with roles and functions as directors and CEOs.   Often ownership is delegated down to particular groups, departments or functional units within the organization for the day-to-day management of the assets.

Custodians within these groups are then given the operational responsibility of being the owner, which means the need to manage these assets and to ensure they are afforded an appropriate level of protection.

For example, personnel information is handled and managed by the human resources group, financial information by the finance group, or research work by the research and development group. The same could apply to sales and marketing information, ICT software and documentation and information associated with a particular type of data, or application or service.

Whoever has the day-to-day custodianship and responsibility of looking after the assets the overall liability for managing the risk to these assets rests with those at the top of the organization. Ultimately, whatever operational structure and responsibilities and arrangements are in place to deploy and use the assets should not affect the organization's ability and/or responsibility, to provide information security that meets the security requirements determined by risk assessment and applicable legislative, regulatory, or governance requirements.

What needs to be in place is awareness across the organization of the management and employees risk responsibilities. Establishing an information security culture based on awareness, the employees and managers integrated with the organization's existing management culture is one means of achieving a good basis for protecting the organization's assets.

4.2.6 Travel company Case Study

The value of information assets is not always easy to quantify as already discussed above. In this case study the travel services company is handling various forms of information (see Figure 4.4).

Information Asset	Confidentiality/ Sensitivity	Integrity/ Criticality	Availability
Travel company staff records	Restricted - Confidential	High	High
Customer details	Restricted - Confidential	High	High
Credit card details	Confidential	High	High
Customer bookings	Restricted	High	High

Figure 4.4 Travel company information classifications

3 asset values for each asset

The travel company will also have information such as sensitive corporate information, yearly accounts and tax records and sales and marketing information, which will also need to be considered.

In addition the managed services company will also have information related to the Web site (see Figure 4.5).

Information Asset	Confidentiality/ Sensitivity	Integrity/ Criticality	Availability
Web booking forms with customer content	Restricted	High	Medium-High
e-tickets	Publicly available	High	Medium
Web content (e.g., flight, hotel and car rental information, latest offers,	Publicly available	Medium-High	Medium-High

Figure 4.5 Travel company Web site information

The managed services company has access to a range of information assets owned by the travel company, which it is responsible for on a custodian basis. The information security they deploy to protect these assets is its responsibility. Under some contractual and service level agreement the companies will have agreed terms and conditions in place including the levels of liability if information security is breached. However, the ultimate responsibility of managing the risks rests with the travel company, the owner of its assets. Of course, there is customer information that the travel company needs to protect on its site as well as the protection of this information via contractual means on the services company site (which we will see later comes into the risk management category of risk transfer).

4.2.7 Asset Usage

Rules for the handling and acceptable use of information and assets associated with information systems and processing facilities should be in place and used throughout the organization. For example, it is good practice to have a policy and/or procedure on information handling and email usage. This should provide guidance on the proper way of sending information either within the email or as an attachment. This policy could also be extended to cover the use of the Internet regarding uploading and downloading information, files and documents, the use of messaging services, on-line transactions, on-line bookings and accessing unknown Web sites.

Another example is the use of mobile computing devices such as mobile phones, BlackBerries, PDAs and similar devices, laptops and for sending information, their use in public places and/or client sites for remote access to company systems, email and Internet usage. In addition, the use of such mobile devices for the processing company and client information in public places needs to be carefully considered and managed. Not only arethe organization's information assets potentially at risk, but also those of your clients and business partners, which runs the risk of legal actions in the case of compromise of this information.

Also care needs to be taken on the use of any mobile storage devices that are able to store information from organizational information systems on the site of your clients and business partners.

4.3 THREATS AND VULNERABILITIES

"Things are not what they appear to be: nor are they otherwise."
Surangama Sutra

4.3.1 Incidents

Many threats that are present in the business environment however may not have any effect on the organization. The organization may never have suffered a virus attack, or its Web site may never have been defaced. This does not mean that the threat is not there, all it means is that the conditions have not been right within the organization to enable the threats to manifest themselves.

This is similar to many things around us in the world we live in which do not immediately affect or influence us such as radio waves. We can detect the radio waves if the conditions are right, for example, if we switch on a radio and tune it into a radio station then we are detecting the effects of the radio waves carrying music, conversations and other audio signals. The threat of many medical problems and diseases that can only manifest themselves within an individual if the conditions are right, for example, if there are certain features, characteristics and/or weaknesses about the individual that are conducive to catching the disease.

So if the conditions within the organization are appropriate then the threats can cause security problems, compromises and/or failures. This is the case when the threats are able to exploit vulnerable conditions within the organization and its information systems. The likelihood of this coming together of the threat and vulnerability is the situation the organization needs to assess and be able to manage to ensure it does not happen or at least reduce the likelihood of it being able to happen.

When this threat/vulnerability is allowed to manifest itself then the organization has an information security incident to deal with which exposes its assets to a risk and potential business impact that is:

Threat + Vulnerability = Security Incident

The spread of a computer virus is symptomatic of not taking adequate precautions to protect information systems against the introduction of a virus or not acting in response to virus update alerts. The same would be the case with other incidents such as the theft of information from an unattended laptop used in a public place.

Examples of this potential threat/vulnerability/security incident situation include:

- Unauthorized access to information which can occur through threats exploiting various weaknesses in the organization's information systems such as,
    - Compromise of user access control methods and procedures for example for logon to information systems,
    - Using out-of-date user accounts,
    - An attacker gaining access through insecure network connections and/or badly configured firewalls and gateways,
    - Lack of physical access controls,

- System failures of an organization's information systems for example due to the lack of,
    - Regular system testing and maintenance or software updates and patches to software being installed,
    - Adequate capacity planning resulting in excessive systems and network demands, overloads and downtimes,

- User errors, for example, due to the lack of,
    - Suitably skilled staff, appropriate staff training,
    - Adequate or ineffective deployment of operating procedures,
    - Stress related factors, work pressures.

4.3.2 Call Centre Case Study

The CEO and directors of an international call centre are placing ever increasing pressure on operational managers and staff to reduce costs in the face of increasing competition. It has decided to lay off 15% of its workforce, the remaining managers and staff should take on more responsibilities and that staff are given less support and supervision in order to streamline operations. After a period of time this situation affects the staff with increasing stress and strain to maintain a high standard of service provisioning to its customers.

Some of the work demands are driving some staff to such high levels of stress that one individual manager who originally was responsible for the centre's ICT support now has taken on additional work and he starts to break down under the strain. This manager is not only doing his job but is also doing some of the work of staff such as answering customers calls. Whilst doing this he ignores warning messages on his computer screen from his virus checking software, he forgets to backup his data, he sends out emails by mistake to the wrong recipients and many other errors occur whilst answering customer calls. This results in several operational errors, which escalate to major incidents including spreading of a virus, loss of data, embarrassment regarding the emails that were sent and many customer complaints.

The call centre is now in a crisis and management cost cutting plans have turned into a disaster. The threat of a virus attack, loss of data or customer complaints is always there but in this case any previous controls in place to counter these were allowed to develop levels of vulnerability to enable these incidents to manifest into real security problems.

Not only do we have weaknesses appearing in the capability of the manager to cope with the increasing stress and lack of control, for example, over the virus and backup of data but also management should have been more responsive to the growing levels of stress caused in all staff and for the lack of better management of its resources.

This case study example illustrates the relationship between threats, vulnerabilities and incidents but also that a chain of events and linkages between several weaknesses can cause more overarching and dire consequences. Again if the conditions are right and vulnerabilities remain unchecked then the consequences are that the organization leaves itself open to threat manifestation.

4.3.3 Types and Classes of Threat

There are many types of information security threats and the following is just one of several ways of categorizing such threats:

- Organizational,
  These might include threats resulting from bad decision making, bad financial or investment advice, changing competitive markets, changing legal conditions, supplier chain changes, sabotage, espionage, terrorism, industrial strikes, or criminal activities,

- Human Factors,
  Information disclosure, shortage, or unavailability of skilled staff, human errors, omissions or shortcomings, document and information theft, equipment theft, fraud, forgeries, unauthorized use of resources, unacceptable use or illegal use of resources, unauthorized acquisitions of resources, terrorist actions, strikes and civil unrest,

- Services,
  Security threats include those concerning the use of external services be they network services, outsourcing and managed services, as well as internal services,

- ICT,

Security threats include those concerning the access, proper usage, reliability, maintenance, connecting and networking, disposal, backups of ICT facilities and systems

- Physical and Environmental,
  Fire, water damage, pollution, flooding, earthquakes, volcano eruptions, tsunami, tornadoes, typhoons, lightning strikes, physical damage of buildings, physical failures, damage or destruction of equipment, thermal or electromagnetic radiation, pulses or interference,

- Electronic Radiation,
  The threat of electronic radiation can also be a problem for information security. This could be the bombardment of systems with radiation, electromagnetic interference, or the leakage from radiating wireless systems.

4.3.4 Types of Vulnerability

The scope of ISO/IEC 27001 covers many areas on management control all of which can present many types and sources of vulnerability, which the threats mentioned above could exploit. This would of course be the case if the implementation of the ISO/IEC 27001 controls are deemed to be: not adequate, insufficient or lacking in strength or in some feature or without the necessary capability to resist threats. The following is a small list of some vulnerabilities:

- Lack of effective procedures, inappropriate procedures, difficult to use procedures, out-of-date procedures,

- Inappropriate or insufficient training of staff,

- Inadequate control over the handling of computer media,

- Insufficient control of user accounts,

- Faulty equipment,

- Software bugs and flaws, coding errors and other coding problems.

In naming a particular threat, it should not be difficult to list ways in which the threat could exploit the system. The threat of unauthorized access might lead to a security incident if for example:

- Physical access to a building, office or computer room is lacking such as the locks are of poor quality and can be easily circumvented, door password controls can be guessed, the strength of the door is insufficient to withstand brute force, windows might provide easy access due to their particular resistance to force or the windows being left open or if easy accessibility is possible through other entry points (e.g., loading bays, ventilation ducts),

- Access to computer systems through poor passwords or insufficient user management of the passwords, accounts still open of staff that have left, identity theft, lack of control over scams, phising attacks, no control over the use of social engineering techniques, unattended equipment, badly configured network servers, firewalls or other network components and of course lack of user awareness and training.

4.3.5 Estimating the Threat Level and Its Likelihood

When we hear reports that the threat level is high or that likelihood of the threat happening is low it's not always easy to be clear about the precision of these statements. Some threat estimates are based on historical data, for example, prior evidence and data relating to the threat of earthquakes in a particular region of the world.

If we start asking questions like what is the threat of unauthorised access, user errors, denial of service, system failures, or fraudulent activities then we do not always have enough historical data to be precise as in the earthquake example to give an accurate answer as to the risk of exposure.

Of course if we had an effective incident handling scheme running then we will have records of past problems and so we can in some threat cases do better than a rough estimate.

For example if we have sufficient incident records or audit trails listing failed or successful attempts into a database server as indicated by an audit trial then we have information on the level of threat over a period of time and the weakness of the server to hold out against this threat. This might be the case in other incidents such as those related to the other threats given above.

The best we can do is to gather as much information as we can that relates to the organization's particular work environment to make estimates. This can be supported by similar information and reports relating to other organizations, to the Internet, about specific products and services being used as well as more general information about threats.

The organization needs to assess its risk of exposure levels primarily based on its experiences and incident reports and then secondly any other information, for example, from outside sources such as other organizations threat situation.

The organization needs to produce its own list of threats and vulnerabilities related to its business. Sources for this type of information should come in the first instance from the identification of such threats and vulnerabilities locally around the operational environment including:

- Brainstorming actives with staff across the business,

- Staff feedback (as well as from customers, suppliers and business partners),

- Audits and reviews,

- Scorecards, gap analysis methods and other information gathering techniques,

- Incident handing reports, fault reporting and audit trail analysis.

A second source of information would be the many Internet sites and publications that list threats and vulnerabilities. Of course, this information may not be directly relevant to the organization but nevertheless it is useful information for what might be relevant to the organization for the future.

4.3.6 Risk of Exposure

Figure 4.6 shows one way of estimating the "Risk of Exposure" (RoE) of a threat or threats exploiting one or more vulnerabilities. The higher the RoE, the greater the chance or likelihood of a serious incident occurring.

	RoE	Threat			
		Low	Medium	High	Very High
Vulnerability	Low	1	2	3	4
	Medium	2	3	4	5
	High	3	4	5	6
	Very High	4	5	6	7

Figure 4.6 Risk of exposure (RoE)

If the threat of online fraud is considered high, then depending on the degree of protection or the lack of protection (i.e., the vulnerability or susceptibility of the organization and its facilities) the organization deploys to stop identity theft, unauthorized access to credit card details, the protection of transactions across networks, or employee internet usage policy then the RoE could be high.

The threat of earthquakes is only a problem if the organization's premises and systems are geographically located in an earthquake zone. However the organization may have its premises and it facilities in a nonearthquake zone but it has outsourced it help desk and information processing to a company in such a zone. Therefore the threat to an organization is therefore on the low side but that of the outsourced company may be high or even very high. The vulnerability in this case is partly an organizational one where the organization's decision to contract to a company in an earthquake zone has raised the RoE to high. Of course there are other vulnerabilities that need to be considered such as what business continuity and contingency plans the outsourcing company has in place, the ICT readiness plans and arrangements it is able to deploy to cope with such emergencies. It is good to ask questions to help and guide how to assess the of risk exposure. Some high-level questions might include:

- Have the plans ever been tested? Any lessons learnt? Any follow-up action?

- Have the plans been able to effectively deal with real-life emergencies, incidents, or disasters? Any lessons learnt? Any follow-up action?

- Are the plans regularly reviewed and updated? Who provides input?

A similar scenario could be if the outsourced company is located in an area which is under threat from other environmental threats.

4.3.7 Call Centre Case Study

Continuing with the Call Centre scenario introduced in Section 4.3.2 we can consider the risk of exposure (RoE) levels. Figure 4.7 shows some example incidents.

Example Incidents	Estimated RoE
Threat of serious data loss due no backups being taken	5-6 region
Threat of virus infection due ignoring the warnings of the anti-virus software	5-6 region
Threat of incorrect results and advice being given to customers due to human errors in processing data caused by staff working under extremely stressful conditions and whilst multitasking	5-7 region
Threat of loss of business and customers due to infected ICT systems and consequential downtimes, bad image of reputation as a result of a degradation of services to customers and the consequential loss of market positioning in a highly competitive market	5-6 region
Threat of staff strikes, walkouts or resignations by disgruntled staff working under bad operational conditions.	4-5 region

Figure 4.7 Example incidents

4.4 RISKS AND IMPACTS

"There is no security in life. There is only opportunity." Douglas MacArthur.

4.4.1 Risk Levels and the Risk Matrix

Once we have identified and assessed the threats and vulnerabilities related to the
ISMS assets we can then go on to calculate the levels of risk the organization
faces. Figure 4.8 illustrates one method of assessing the risk.

Risk	Exposure to a security incident (unlikely to very likely)		
Consequence (insignificant to dire)	low	medium	medium-high
	medium	medium-high	high
	medium-high	high	very high

Figure 4.8 Simplified matrix method

Taking the method in Figure 4.8 one stage further we can include the level or
value of the risks. This process involves a calculation based on the level of threat
and vulnerability (or RoE) and the asset (or impact) value:

Risk level = f(asset value/impact, threats, vulnerabilities) = consequential
value/impact value*susceptibility/risk of exposure

Note the product operation * can take on several meanings such as addition (+) or
multiplication (x), or some other operation.

Figure 4.9 illustrates the matrix method for displaying the various risk levels
according to the risk formula: Risk Level = Impact Value + Risk of Exposure and
where low through to very high take on the values from 0 through to 3.

[handwritten: p.72 Table of threats vs vulnerabilities]

Risk Level	Risk of Exposure			
	Low	Medium	High	Very High
Low	0	1	2	3
Medium	1	2	3	4
High	2	3	4	5
Very High	3	4	5	6

[left axis label: Asset or Impact Value]

[handwritten: RISK LEVELS]

Figure 4.9 Simplified risk matrix

Figure 4.9 shows the level of risk increases in degrees of severity from 0
(lowest) to 6 (highest). There are variants of this, for example, if it is desired to

[handwritten note at bottom: See p. 65. You will/can have 3 asset values for every asset — one each for the value/impact of losing confidentiality, integrity, availability]

have the risk, RoE and impact ranges start with the value 1 then we just use the formula:

Risk Level = Impact Value + Risk of Exposure − 1.

4.4.2 Risk Register

Compiling a risk register is a good idea as it brings together the complete list of risks and associated business impacts that have been identified. It enables the organization to categorise the risks in a way that is appropriate to the business (e.g., listed in terms of risks to department, projects, applications, or types of information), as well as being ordered according to their risk level. The register could also contain details of the risk conditions that contribute to a particular risk level: associated threats, vulnerabilities, incidents and RoE. It then provides a good picture of the organization's risk profile at a particular point in time.

The risk register could be compiled using a standard office spreadsheet application such as the Excel product. This enables the register to be easily revised and updated. This is very useful for tracking trends and the organization's risk management performance and responsiveness to achieving effective information security. Figure 4.10 gives an example of a partially complete risk register.

Risk Category	Risk Type	Risk Level	Conditions	Business Impact
Accounting Group System	Loss of confidentiality and integrity of payment details	6-7		Very high
	Loss/damage/destruction of purchase orders			
	Loss/damage/destruction of invoices			
	Availability of accounting applications			
Web Content Dev. Group System	Loss/damage/destruction of Web designs and browser code			
	Defacing of Web site pages			
	Loss/damage/destruction to Web content			
	Loss of protection of Web design tools and design group's ICT			
Software Dev. Group System	Loss/damage/destruction of software source and object code	6-7		Very high
	Loss of protection of developer tools and ICT			
	Compromise of test routines			
	Risks related to protection of documentation and manuals			
Register Owner _____	Approved _____	Date _____		

Figure 4.10 Example risk register

4.4.3 Call Centre Case Study

A simplified risk register for the Call Centre Case Study, based on a risk level scale 1-7 using the matrix in Figure 4.9, might be as illustrated in Figure 4.11.

Risk Category	Risk Type	Risk Level	Business Impact
ICT	Virus infection (1)	4-5	High
	System failures and downtimes (2)	3-4	Medium
	Data loss (3)	3	Medium
Operational	Human errors and mistakes processing customer data and call enquiries (4)	6	High
	Adherence to procedures concerning backups, viruses and email usage	5	High
	Email errors (5)	4	Low to Medium
	Staff strikes, walkouts or resignations (6)	4	Low to Medium
Corporate	Image and reputation loss (7)	5	Medium
	Market position loss (7)	3-4	Medium
	Legal liabilities (7)	3-4	Medium

Figure 4.11 Case study example risk register

Notes (these are all based on example judgments):

(1) This would be the case if the virus was not dealt with and eradicated.

(2) This would be the case if the virus spread itself across the company.

(3) The lack of backup was isolated to the single individual.

(4) This was the cause of too much stress on the individual involved and the fact that multitasking was also taking place.

(5) This risk could be damaging to the organization depending on what the emails contained.

(6) These risks are all considered low to medium in the short term but become high in the future if management fails to take actions to improve the working conditions.

(7) These risks are all considered medium in the short term but become high in the future if management fails to take actions to manage this risk in case of a similar incident occurring.

4.5 TREATING THE RISKS

"Don't go backwards, you have already been there." Ray Charles

4.5.1 Management Options

Once the organization has carried out its risk assessment and produced a risk register the next step is to consider the options for treating the risk (ISO/IEC 27001 clause 4.2.1 f). It is helpful to be reminded that the purpose of this exercise is to protect the organization's sensitive, critical and important assets from the risks that have been identified and assessed. This eventually involves making management decisions of how to manage these risks in a way that meets the demands and strategic and financial objectives of the organization. Typically this will involve deploying a system of controls and processes. There are several options management can consider:

Risk avoidance includes making the decision to not carry out or perform an activity that could cause the risk. Also risk avoidance might involve changing:

- Company policy or strategy,

- Location or relocating,

- Methods, procedures or processes used,

- Operational conditions,

- Objectives of new projects, developments or technology being used.

An example might be the relocation of the business to an area that is found to be less environmentally hazardous in order to not take on the liability that comes with the likelihood of these hazards occurring and interrupting or destroying the business and its operations. It might be that the site for relocation is a less dangerous area of a city to avoid serious incidents involving criminal activities and civil disorder. Avoiding this risk may seem a way of dealing with this problem but could also mean losing out on the benefits of relocating.

Management thinking needs to weigh up the pros and cons of either avoiding the risk in order to take the opportunity of safer operating conditions or taking the risk in order to take the opportunity of other business benefits that may be afforded by the current location such as its customer base. The same avoidance strategy might be taken regarding the risks of taking on new research projects, selecting backup sites for business continuity purposes, embracing new technologies such as digital accounting or on-line business.

Transferring the risk is a method or means that can be used to employ another party, such as insurance companies, suppliers, venture capital business and external parties, to accept the risk. Typically this could be by contract, insurance or by some form of hedging. Insurance is one type of risk transfer that uses contracts and in recent times e-risk insurance protection has started to emerge on world markets. Other means of transfer might involve the use of contract language that transfers the risk to another party without the use of an insurance premium. Such a contract might set limits of liability on contractors or service suppliers and are very often transferred this way. Of course in the financial world there are many other transfer instruments for financially managing risks such as taking offsetting positions in order to hedge, for example, against investment losses.

Reducing the risk involves control methods that reduce the severity of the impact or loss caused by an incident. In the area of physical security computer rooms need to be protected against the threat of fire. Using water sprinklers designed to put out a fire to reduce the risk of loss by fire is not generally a good idea in this application since this method may cause a greater loss by water damage. Various solutions on gas based fire suppression systems can help to mitigate this risk problem e.g., the use of Halon system. However management, in making the decision, needs to consider the cost of such systems as this solution may prove to be prohibitive as a strategy and course of action.

In the area of online business there is a need to protect transactions against fraud or identity threat, with systems dealing with personnel records there is a need to protect an individual's data for inaccuracies, misuse and abuse, with patient records an individual's medical record needs to be protected against unauthorized disclosure and with ICT equipment there is a need to protect against failures. These and many other incidents cause risks that could be reduced by the appropriate selection of controls.

Knowingly and objectively accepting the risk means the organization is able to tolerate and retain the risk within its business risk management strategy by accepting the impact or loss when it occurs. Management must be fully knowledgeable and objective about this course of action. At the end of the day perhaps there is no other course of appropriate action to take. By default, all risks that are not avoided, reduced, or transferred are retained.

Risk sharing within a group of individuals or companies is also a risk retention option. This involves spreading the risk across the group by transferring the risk liabilities and losses to all those members involved in the group. This is not the transfer by insurance option.

When the risks are small, acceptance or retention is a viable strategy and financial option. Of course we need to bear in mind what might be small to one organization may not be small to another in terms of the costs and financial impact it is able to sustain. Acceptance of risk is especially the case where the cost of reducing or transferring the risk could add up to be greater in the long run than the total losses sustained.

At the other extreme when the risks are catastrophic in nature, uninsurable or so large to make reduction or transference financially infeasible, then acceptance becomes a fact of life.

4.5.2 Travel Company Case Study

In outsourcing its ICT and Web site activities to a managed services company the travel company has made a decision to transfer the risks via contractual means. This would have been primarily on economic grounds. The resources to run an effective ICT infrastructure to meet the demands of customers both on-line and off-line can be quite a management challenge. This strategy leaves the travel company time to concentrate on what it is good at: providing travel services.

Again, as stressed before, the senior management of the travel company still has the overall responsibility for the information security risks. However the business benefits and opportunities to be gained by this outsourcing strategy are very appealing to many organizations as demonstrated in the dramatic rise in this type of activity over the last 10 years or so.

The travel company needs to satisfy itself in taking this strategic option that the service provider is able to offer a sufficient level of information security and this needs to be discussed with whoever wins the contract for this work. In Chapter 5 we will return to this issue of service contracts.

4.5.3 In Summary

The opportunities for *risk avoidance* are limited but if the risk of avoiding the situation that causes the risk far out weighs going ahead with the risk taking activity and the associated business benefits then this could likely be the best or only course of action. There is also the opportunity to modify the business activity to be less risky.

Risk transfer also has its limitations. Contractual transfer is quite common in areas engaging the use of third party services whereas transfer by insurance at the moment is not so common (although the trend is slowly changing) in the area of information security with the exception of a few areas.

Risk acceptance/retention is necessary and unavoidable in some areas of business and information security risk. Again the business benefits and opportunities to be gained need to be assessed with taking the risk versus reducing the risk.

Risk reduction is a very common approach and one that is most emphasized in standards and texts on risk assessment but information security comes at a cost and the extent of reduction needs to be carefully assessed against the business benefits gained.

In practice a combination of the above options will be used as no single one can cover all possible business scenarios.

4.6 MANAGEMENT DECISION MAKING

"Not everything that can be counted counts and not everything that counts can be counted." Albert Einstein

4.6.1 Basic Ideas

The process of informed decision-making is key to good risk management. There are many ways, methods and analytic tools available to help management in this task. Before deciding on what method or approach to take it is important to review some of the basic ideas as well as the objectives and goals of the decision making process.

Making decisions regarding information security risks in general is no different than any area of business where management needs to go through a decision making process. The following are some points of consideration:

- The corporate culture of the organization is a powerful element in the decision making process. For example, Is the organization risk averse or risk opportunist? Is the decision making a democratic process or an oligarchic process? Organization style, policy and the nature of its business are all factors regarding its culture. Does it have an information security culture? Knowing the corporate culture is an important step as it effects the risk treatment options it takes,

- Decision making styles, methods and approaches do vary from organization to organization, for example:

  - Rational (logical) thinking versus intuitive, creative and innovative thinking (or hunches),
  - Previously successful risk management scenarios and precedents can lead to future workable solutions but changes in the business could require more innovative thinking,

- Decision making team, Who should get involved? Who should be consulted? Those responsible for the corporate information assets and governance hence with managing the risks should be senior management, in particular the directors and CEO of the organization. The team should also involve any other employees that can provide input to engage in an effective decision making exercise. They may delegate parts of the risk decision process to others with specialist skills in certain areas of the business. However senior management need to take ultimate responsibility for making the final decision on managing information security risks and the approval of a risk treatment plan,

- Decision making process,

    - Gather information from recent risk assessment reports, using previous decision making results, current and future business objectives and targets,
    - Assess the treatment options, assess the consequences, impacts and trade-offs, generate ideas and scenarios based on these options and judge their validity, consider the alternatives,
    - Make the decisions and before implementing these run over the details checking and vetting that they make best business sense,
    - Establish approval and commitment to go ahead with the decisions,
    - Document the decisions that have been made,

- Develop an implementation plan and then go ahead with the implementation,

    - Funding and resources need to be committed,
    - Prioritise the implementation of the decisions where necessary,
    - Responsibilities need to be allocated,
    - The decisions need to be communicated to all those involved in the implementation and deployment of the decisions,
    - New policies and procedures maybe need to be produced or old ones updated,

- Monitor, review and keep track of progress on the implementation,

    - Measure progress,
    - Modify decisions if necessary,
    - Build on lessons learnt.

4.6.2   Risk Financing

Even after the risk has been treated there will always be a residual risk, unless of course the risk has been avoided, as the organization can only go so far in reducing the risk.

The organization could invest more and more money in reducing the risk further and further but the business benefits to be gained tend to be less attractive and economically viable after a certain cost-benefit threshold is crossed (see Figure 4.13).

Cost of reducing the risk (CR) versus financial benefits (FB) to be gained	
CR < FB	Economically good/sound
CR = FB	Economically even
CR > FB	Economically bad/unsound

Figure 4.13 Example cost/benifit comparison

Of course other factors might come into play here such as a piece of legislation, which requires information security to be in place such as data protection/privacy laws. But again the organization still needs to be financially and economically sound for its business so it needs to do its best to achieve the correct balance of reducing the risks with financially sound solutions whilst complying with the law.

Living with a set of residual risks also requires some thought if, for example, the organization is still compromised at some point in time due to even these residual risks. In such cases are the costs funded from the area of the business where the risks cause a compromise say a department's operating costs or is there a company-wide corporate fund for such as "rainy day" events as they occur?

Does the company take the strategy that if and when such an incident arises they will seek a financial loan to cover such incidents or does its current insurance policy cover such an incident?

However the organization addresses this question of risk financing it ends up with the risk acceptance/retention scenario if appropriate funding is not available or even risk avoidance in some extreme cases, for example, cancelling a project. Of course this can also be influenced by whether or not the organization is risk averse or risk opportunistic.

4.6.3   Decision Methods

Some of the methods that can be deployed are covered in the sections that follow. It is essential that the organization uses whatever method or methods that suit its area of business interest and the specific objectives of the decision making exercise.

4.6.3.1   Basic Objective

The general objective is to apply information security in a way that helps the organization but the cost of implementing, deploying and maintaining information security makes good economic sense to the company.

The following are some examples.

a. The Case of the Stolen Laptop

An organization would not pay £700 in the physical protection of a laptop if the laptop only costs say £500. It would be cheaper to buy another laptop and save the organization £700. However when we consider what the user has on the laptop in terms of information then the situation becomes a little more complicated. Theft of the laptop means theft of hardware, software applications and the information contained on the laptop. The hardware and software costs are easy to calculate but the value of the information is something more difficult to estimate.

A salesman's laptop which he uses when seeing clients might contain a range of information including company restricted information, other clients information, personal information or even worse, company confidential information. Opportunities for the theft of this information outside the organization's premises are quite high. The laptop may be used on trains and planes, in various open and public places as well as on client sites. So the cost of protecting this laptop becomes a little more involved.

Simple solutions to this problem are available which do not involve large costs. One simple best practice approach is to restrict what the salesman can have on his laptop however for practical and operational reasons the organization might consider this overkill as it might hamper potential business opportunities. The user should ensure he uses all the in-built software security on his laptop such as system start-up passwords, password screensavers and various other password mechanisms available.

Another solution would be to install an access control system to protect the folders, files and documents on the laptop. There are many affordable encryption products that are available that will do this job.

b. Back It Up Before It's Lost

What would it cost an organization if it lost some of its critical business data during a system failure or a virus attack assuming it has not been backed up? Depending on the volume and proportion of data, its value, sensitivity and criticality the impact might range from a few hundred to millions of pounds or dollars. All users of ICT face the same problem protecting the valuable data from accidental loss (recall the Call Centre Case Study example). The solutions to this are very affordable and avoid the disaster happening. Even if it is not a major loss any loss can impact productivity due to the lack of data and the time wasted in regenerating or reassembling the lost data. The solutions are a combination of technology to backup, CDs, DVDs, stand-alone hard drives, USB sticks and other storage media and a process and procedure for carrying out the backup.

In addition best practice stresses that backed up media should be stored off site, of course this is advisable for the organization's corporate and operational data. Other less critical data, from say the PC of a member of staff, might be stored locally but this should also subject to a risk assessment and the use of organizational procedures for backups.

So the path to success is affordable but requires management discipline and regular practice in deploying the backup process. So the cost is relatively marginal compared to the potential business impact of losing the data.

c. To Err is Human (errare humanus est ...)

Everyone makes mistakes but some can be catastrophic. Staff processing data in an organization making data entry errors on financial spreadsheets, for customer bills, for invoicing and payment reclaims can and does cost industry millions of pounds and dollars every year if errors are made.

Even though more data processing uses advance ICT systems there are still errors made and most of these are made by humans by accident through lack of management controls.

So it is clear what the business impact could be but what is the risk of this happening? The threat is always there but data processing incidents occur if, for example, the user is untrained in using the ICT system, a software accounting package or maybe is not motivated to do it right, is stressed or overburdened with other tasks (recall the Call Centre Case Study example).

Of course there is always the intentional case of the disgruntled employee or someone carrying out an inside job for personal gains. So if these weaknesses are allowed to be present then the risks are high. So it would benefit the organization to ensure its staff had adequate training, were sufficiently aware of the risks and that the staff working conditions, were conducive to avoid stressful or emotional incidents. These examples illustrate some of the analytic thinking that may need to be applied in making the decision on reducing information security risks.

4.6.3.2   SWOT Analysis

The SWOT (strengths, weaknesses, opportunities and threats) method of analysis is a strategic planning tool. It can be used prior to any cost-benefit analysis as it outlines the opportunities the organization has if appropriate action is taken to exploit its strengths whilst at the same time weighing up the organization's weaknesses or vulnerabilities against external threats of not achieving its goals.

To use this method effectively the organization should start with defining a business objective to be aimed at, for example in the case of developing an ISMS, for say, the travel company. The information the organization gathers its strengths, weaknesses, opportunities and threats can then be laid in a SWOT table as illustrated in Figure 4.14:

	Useful/Helpful	Barrier/Harmful
Internal	**Strengths** signify those attributes of the organization that are helpful to achieving its ISMS objective. What strengths can it exploit?	**Weaknesses** relate to attributes of the organization that may reduce its capability to achieve its ISMS objective. What weaknesses does it have that it needs to address?
External	**Opportunities** relate to any external conditions beneficial in achieving its ISMS objective. What opportunities can it exploit?	**Threats** relate to those external conditions that are detrimental to achieving its ISMS objective. What threats does it need to defend against?

Figure 4.14 SWOT analysis table

4.6.3.3   Travel Company Case Study

Figure 4.15 relates to the travel company discussed earlier in this chapter and its future objectives to both expand its business to offer Web-based travel services and also to outsource its ICT infrastructure to take advantage of the benefits to be gained by using technology.

Strengths	Weaknesses
• Well-established customer base • Good relationships with key players in the travel industry • Good image and reputation • Well located for international business • Intellectual property related to the travel industry • Quick and eager to expand its business • Good internal corporate culture • Efficient and effective customer services • Qualified staff with travel industry skills	• Lack of information security procedures • Ineffective information access control measures • Lack of business continuity arrangements and an incident handling process • Lack of resources to control management and maintenance of ICT systems • Lack of resources for information asset management and protection • Lack of qualified staff to develop a Web site for the travel business
Opoortunities	Threats
• International travel market • Exploiting the use of ICT • Better integration of off-line and on-line travel business • Increase in Internet for on-line booking • Better use of customer information • More time to focus on the travel business without the need to manage the ICT	• ICT security • Competitors and competitive actions • Increasing customer demands and expectations • Expectations of stakeholders • Possible downturn in economic conditions affecting travel industry and/or increased costs such as airport taxes and fuel costs • Legal and/or contractual requirements

Figure 4.15 SWOT Analysis for the travel company

4.6.3.4   Cost-Benefit Analysis

This method involves doing a monetary calculation based on initial and ongoing costs of deploying information security controls versus expected business benefit, opportunities or return on investments from such deployment of controls.

What constitutes plausible cost and benefit measures is often very difficult to assess without resorting to estimations, which in practice might involve making assumptions or drawing inferences based on other sources of information.

The accuracy of the results of a cost-benefit analysis is clearly dependent on the authenticity, correctness and realism of these assumptions as well as how accurately the costs and benefits have been estimated.

In practice cost-benefit calculations will also need to cover nontangible assets and the related risks and less tangible impacts and effects on the business. For example, risks related to information itself, to the image, branding and reputation of an organization, new research results or new methods and processes.

Overall the results of any cost-benefit analyses should be treated with care regarding estimates and inaccuracies. If the analysis results are inaccurate it could be argued that this might present substantial risk to the risk treatment decisions made consequently leading to bad or ineffective management actions and solutions.

Another issue that needs to be considered in the cost-benefit analysis is which costs should be included in an analysis. Different interest groups may have different views and different requirements may dictate several aspects that need to be considered.

For example an information security decision analysis is likely to need to take account of health and safety needs, legal and/or contractual requirements as well as other business needs. This is not just the case with cost-benefit analysis but all decision making processes.

If, for example, an ISMS solution was to used in an area which involved the processing and supply of information for the manufacture of medical components then design flaws, software problems and processing errors could all have a serious business impact. The same could be said in the case of a managed data services company providing ICT services for the processing of patient records.

Information security should be treated as an integral part of any business decision. If viewed as a business enabler and an integral part of the corporate culture then decision making concerning ISMS developments will naturally take account of business requirements in general as well as these other more specific requirements such as health and safety, environmental, legal and contractual.

4.6.3.5 Travel Company Case Study

The ISMS costs of the travel company will involve those related to its own ISMS arrangements as well as the cost of outsourcing activity. Considering one area of concern say the protection of customer booking details the Company would need to do a risk assessment on the information assets related to customer bookings made via the telephone through one of its offices (see assets values given in

Section 4.10.6). A simple version of this assessment might arrive at the results in Figure 4.16.

Threat	Vulnerability (examples)	RoE	Risk
Unauthorised access to booking information	Lack of suitable management and control over the use passwords	5	5-6
	User system accounts not in use	4	4
	Lack of security training	4	5
	Lack of physical protection	4	4
Unauthorised changes to booking information	Lack of suitable control over the processing, management and modification of booking details	4	4
	Software application failures or errors	4	4
Human errors	Lack of training	3	4-5
	In appropriate, disorganised and/or stressful operating conditions	3	3
Loss, damage or destruction of bookings	Insufficient backups	4	5-6
	System failures	4	5-6
	Disgruntled staff	3	3
	Lack of anti-virus protection	4	5
ICT failures	Lack of maintenance	4	5-6
	Lack of software updates e.g., patches	4	5-6

Figure 4.16 Travel Company: A simplified assessment

In addition the managed services company would need to do a risk assessment for this travel company and other organizations it provides outsourcing services to.

4.6.3.6   Other Methods

There are many tools and methods available to help management in the decision making process. There is much information regarding these various methods available on several Web sites.

A word of caution is do not get too absorbed in trying to sort out what is the best method to use as this could take some time as some of these are highly mathematical tools and possibly over the top given the granularity of data on threats, vulnerabilities and risks are working with.

If the organization already uses a particular method or approach then try this first, otherwise consider the methods looked at earlier on in the chapter and especially taking account of the basic principle given in 4.6.1.

4.7 SELECTION OF CONTROLS

"The difficulty lies not so much in developing new ideas as in escaping from the old ones." John Maynard Keynes

4.7.1   Objectives and Selection Considerations

Once decisions have been made regarding the treatment of risks then a system of controls need to be selected, implemented and deployed to manage the risks. There are several important considerations that should be looked at when selecting controls:

- What is the organization's criteria for tolerance/acceptance?

  - How much residual risk can it live with or sustain taking into account all likely impacts?
  - What is the organization's levels/thresholds of risk tolerance/acceptance?
  - It should be noted that these levels and thresholds are likely to vary over time in accordance with the changes to the business and as it gets richer/poorer, it becomes more risk averse/less risk averse.

- What existing controls and measures are in place?

  - Legacy systems, existing policies and procedures, well-tried and tested measures that still work and do not need to be replaced. It is useful to carry out a gap analysis to establish what is already implemented or partially implemented,

- Is a combination of controls needed? Examples might be,

  - A combination of operating procedures and technical measures is likely to be needed to control unauthorised access to rooms, theft of information and use of system applications, services and processes,
  - Combinations of measures related to human resource training and procedures are quite common and necessary to reduce the risk of fraud and/or processing errors. Social engineering attacks are a particular type of attack that exploit the weaknesses of staff and users and lack of awareness of such attacks is a sure way of ensuring a risk will occur,

- A combination of procedures, technical measures and user training and awareness could be used to reduce the threat of noncompliance of data protection/privacy legislation,

- What is the likely level of risk reduction, a control, or combination of controls, is able to achieve?

  - What level of reduction does an incident handling process make?
  - What level of risk reduction does a strong authentication technique make to the threat of ID theft, on-line fraud, unauthorised access to personal records, patient records or customer information? Does the technique need to be combined with other measures to achieve the desired level of reduction, for example, the use of encryption technology?
  - What level of risk reduction relating to human errors is made with the use of procedures and user training?

- Are there any business, legal, or regulatory requirements that need to be considered?

There may be a need to go through the selection process several times in order to reduce the risks to an acceptable level before coming to a final decision on what controls need to be implemented. It is important that the selection process is carried out as a team effort with as much consultation as is necessary.

4.7.2   Control Lists

ISO/IEC 27001 4.2.1 (g) refers to the selection of controls based on those provided for in Annex A, covering:

- Policy, procedures and processes,

- Human resources security,

- Asset control management,

- Physical and environmental controls,

- Operational and communication measures and management,

- Various levels of access control,

- Systems acquisition, development and maintenance,

- Business continuity and incident handling,

- Legal and regulatory requirements.

It is important to note that not all the controls in Annex A are expected or need to be selected and implemented. SMEs should pay particular attention to this since only those controls that reduce their risks and impacts need to be considered for selection. The reduction should be to acceptable levels in accordance with the organization's risk strategy, acceptance/tolerance criteria and the decisions it has made. For example:

- An SME may not do any software development work, therefore, those controls in Annex A such as A.12.4.3 and A.12.5.5 would not be applicable,

- An SME does backup its data in a very informal way. It does not have in place any formal process and procedures for doing backups. The SME will need to carry out a risk assessment to identify how much of a problem this is and then subsequently decide what controls are applicable to improve its current approach.

With such a wide range of controls the organization should be able to establish an appropriate ISMS implementation to suit most of its management needs. However there will also be occasions when other controls might be needed that are not in Annex A. The standard suggests that such requirements for additional controls that need be considered should be the subject of a risk assessment and account needs to be taken of these additional measures in the selection process. For each of the controls given in Annex A there is guidance on the implementation of the controls in ISO/IEC 27002.

4.7.3   Travel Company Case Study

Before embarking on the plan to contract with a managed services company to provide ICT services the travel company would have needed to have a number of controls in place of the type ISO/IEC 27001 Annex A in order to deal with the risks highlighted in Sections 4.6.3.3 to 4.6.3.5. Typically the travel company would need to go through the selection process and based on what measures it already had in place, select new controls to reduce the risks and/or modify/update existing controls (e.g., in the case where possibly a procedure was not provided effective protection). In outsourcing its ICT some of these controls would be deployed by services companies (such as ICT maintenance, software updates). Figures 4.10 and 4.17 illustrate some of the control examples appropriate to the travel company.

| | Annex A Controls (sample selection) | Gap Analysis | | Risk Reduction |
		Pre-risk Assessment	Post Selection	
Policy	ISMS information security (Annex A.5.1)	Partial (60%)	Yes	55%
	Access control (Annex A.11.1)	Partial (40%)	Partial (60%)	15%
	Acceptable usage, for example concerning email usage	No	Partial (60%)	45%
Procedures and processes	Asset management (Annex A.7)	Partial (40%)	Partial (65%)	30%
	Operations (Annex A.10.1)	Partial (40%)	Yes	55%
	Backups (Annex A.10.5) *	Partial (30%)	Partial (40%)	10%
	Data processing (Annex A.12.2) *	Partial (45%)	Partial (50%)	7%
	Media handling and disposal (Annex A.10.7) *	Partial (30%)	Partial (40%)	
	User access and password management (Annex 11.2) *	Partial (40%)	Partial (50%)	
	Incident handling (Annex A.13) *	No	Partial (35%)	
	Business continuity (Annex A.14) *	No	Partial (45%)	
Human resources	Recruitment process (Annex A.8.1)	Yes	Yes	-
	Training and awareness (Annex A.8.2)	Partial (50%)	Partial (70%)	40%
	Disciplinary process (Annex A.8.2)	Partial (70%)	Yes	60%
	Termination of employment (Annex A.8.3)	Partial (50%)	Yes	45%
	User responsibilities (Annex A.11.3)	Partial (40%)	Yes	40%
	Confidentiality agreements	Yes	Yes	-
Legal and contractual controls	IPR and copyright issues (Annex A.15.1.2)	Partial (60%)	Partial (75%)	20%
	Data protection/privacy (Annex A.15.1.4)	Partial (70%)	Partial (80%)	40%
	Computer misuse (Annex A.15.1.5) *	Partial (30%)	Partial (60%)	35%
	Customer and supplier contracts and SLAs (Annex A.6.2) *	Partial (65%)	Partial (80%)	45%
Technical measures	ICT maintenance (Annex A.9.2) *	Partial (25%)	Partial (35%)	15%
	Access controls (Annex A.11) *	Partial (35%)	Partial (45%)	20%
	Network access and services (Annex A.11.4) *	Partial (20%)	Partial (30%)	10%
	Software controls (Annex A.12.5) *	Partial (20%)	Partial (25%)	10%
Physical	Offices, rooms and buildings (Annex A.9.1) *	Partial (45%)	Partial (55%)	20%
	Equipment and media (Annex A.9.2) *	Partial (35%)	Partial (40%)	20%

Figure 4.17 Example selection of controls

Notes:
1) The percentages under the gap analysis columns represent the degree of implementation.
2) It is expected that risks related to items marked * will be further reduced as and when the travel company outsources in ICT.

3)   The travel company concludes that any risk reduction less than 40% will require further improvements in the information security measures which they intend to consider over the next 12 months or so once the managed mervices contract and operations is fully functional.

4.8   ONGOING RISK MANAGEMENT ACTIVITIES

"It takes less time to do things right than to explain why you did it wrong." Henry Wadsworth Longfellow

4.8.1   Risk Responsiveness and Commitment

Taking suitable action and being responsive to manage the information security risks an organization faces has been the topic throughout this chapter. The processes of risk assessment, risk treatment and selection of controls constitute the first phase of the risk control procedure. The second phase encompasses implementing the action to put in place a system of controls and getting them deployed in the ISMS and the third phase involves keeping ahead, being present with the latest changes, being responsive to changes that were appropriate and maintaining an effective information security regime. At all stages of the risk management process there needs to be commitment from senior management, operational managers and staff. All have a part to play to ward off the threats and vulnerabilities turning into incidents resulting in unwanted business risks and impacts. Figure 4.18 shows a simplified view of typical levels of commitment and responsibilities.

Human Resource	Level of commitment and example responsibilities.
CEO, Directors, Senior Management	Commit funding, staff and other resources for the management of information security risk control and mitigation. Set corporate policy, strategy and business objectives for risk management. Establish an information security culture.
Staff and Users	Being aware and responsible for information security risk management in their area of work. Report security incidents and feedback on effectiveness of security procedures. Be responsive and work as part of a collective team throughout the organization to manage the risks.
Operations, human resources and management functions	Implement operational risk management policies and procedures. Measure operational performance, and effectiveness. Management of operational staff and their deployment of risk controls. Recruit staff. Set operational risk control responsibilities, facilitate staff awareness and training where necessary. Monitor, review and report back to senior management risk related issues, incidents and risk management performance.

Figure 4.18 Management and staff responsibilities

4.8.2   Management and Staff Communications

Key to any critical action senior management might need to take, in this case with regard to information security risk, it must engage in effective communication with all its managers and staff: awareness and training and deployment of procedures. Users and employees need to be aware of the risks related to their own job functions and the work responsibilities they have been assigned. Indeed they need to practice deploying the procedures and processes they need to follow regarding the management of risk in their areas of work.

Communications of course need to be two-way. Management sets the policy and strategy, makes decisions and provides risk management resources. Users and staff on the other hand, should be reporting back to management incidents, giving feedback and providing information on potential risk situations to management that are valuable input for the organization itself to make informed decisions on how best to manage risks and the most appropriate course of action.

4.8.3   Call Centre Case Study

What happened in the case of the call centre? There are many questions that could be asked regarding conditions before, during and after the incidents occurred.

- Was there sufficient communications between management and the staff? Were management and staff sufficiently risk aware? Did staff know their risk control responsibilities? Had a sufficient review of working conditions and associated security risks been carried out?

- How did the staff respond when the security incidents occurred? Were there any procedures in place for dealing with the incidents? What level of incident reporting took place? Who took responsibility for dealing with the incidents? How did management react?

- What lessons were learnt?   What was the overall business impact? What were the costs for recovery?   What follow-up on actions did management take? Will it happen again?

It is clear from the case study scenario that insufficient precautions had been taken to guard against the incidents that happened. This may have been due to lack of risk awareness and assessment of the risks or bad decision making.

4.8.4   Monitoring and Reviews

Monitoring the ISMS environment is crucial to be able to know when and how to update the ISMS. In designing and deploying the ISMS we need to ensure that it is maintained and improved to achieve an effective level of information security in keeping with any changes that might affect the organization's ability and/or responsibility to provide the protection necessary to manage its risks.

Changes to the risk profile of an organization occur constantly so if an organization is to be successful at protecting its assets it needs to keep up to date.

Not all changes will require the updating of the ISMS: the organization needs to reassess its risks and update its risk profile then follow through with actions necessary to deal with those changes where the risks are critical to its business.

Gathering information concerning changes should be part of a monitoring and review process, in which the organization engages in a regular way. The organization can get information from:

- Incident handling records,

  These records can provide information on the organization's ability to resist and respond to threats to its information systems. These records are a valuable source of information regarding the effectiveness of the organization's ISMS. Regular reviews of this information are essential to keeping up to date regarding the organization's responsiveness and preparedness for threats and attacks. Incident handling is key to the ISO/IEC 27001 ISMS process.

- ISMS measurements,

  Setting up metrics, a measurement programme and performance indicators is key to the ISO/IEC 27001 ISMS process. How effective is the incident handling process? How well does the ICT backup process perform? How good is the performance of the access control system to withstand attacks from external networks? Is the training and awareness programme effective? These and many other questions can lead us to judge how effective our ISMS is at managing risks based on what we measure. More on this topic of measurements is covered in Chapter 5.

- Scorecards, gap analysis and benchmarking processes, tools and exercises,

  These methods, if used on a periodic basis across the organization and by an appropriate number of staff, can provide a valuable source of information. They give a relatively easy way of determining if security is being deployed, is working and whether target levels are being met.

- Internal audits and reviews,

  These are important to determine if the ISMS is: conforming to the requirements of ISO/IEC 27001, whether the system of controls to manage the risks has been properly implemented, deployed and maintained; to review other audit results; and to provide reports to management on the status of information security within the organization.

- Feedback from users, employees, customers and suppliers,

Often valuable information on the effectiveness of the organization can be obtained from staff. Of course this should be the case since they are in daily contract with the system of risk controls in place. They are using the procedures that underpin the management and application of the information security measures in place. Also customers and suppliers can sometimes provide useful information both positive and negative about the effectiveness of the organization's measures to protect information.

4.8.5   Risk Reassessments

From time to time the organization's risk profile needs to be reviewed. Updating the risk profile is essential to achieving an effective ISMS. It is a key part of the continual improvement process.

The risk reassessment needs to review the status, update and reconsider all those elements given in Sections 4.3 to 4.5 that is:

- The asset inventory,
    - Review current inventory to check its appropriateness,
    - Add, modify and/or delete asset entries taking into account the changes,

- The list of threats and vulnerabilities,
    - Review the status of previously identified threats and vulnerabilities
    - Identify new threats and vulnerabilities,
    - Recalculate the risk of exposures commensurate with any changed conditions and any new risk relevant information,

- The list of risks and business impacts,
    - Reassess and recalculate where necessary the previously identified risks,
    - Assess newly identified risks.

4.8.6   Improvements and Changes for the Better

Gathering information, evaluating and analyzing it with respect to the effectiveness of the organization's ISMS implementation leads to the next phase of the risk management process, that of deciding whether improvements need to be made. For any changes that are considered to have an influence and impact on the business the effectiveness of the ISMS may need corrective actions to resolve existing problems. It is also opportunity to take pre-emptive actions to prevent further problems occurring, either old problems reoccurring or the anticipation of new problems occurring.

The work in Sections 4.8.4 and 4.8.5 is aimed at identifying what problems need to be resolved, fixed and prevented. The corrective and preventative actions to be taken to make the required ISMS improvements require management commitment and support.

An action plan needs to be produced with a prioritization of the work. After implementing the action plan, it needs to be confirmed that the new improvements are working effectively and are being deployed correctly in the working environment. Reworking, revising and updating of policies and procedures may need to be instituted. The improvement phase might need to confirm whether certain processes need to be improved and/or modified accordingly.

The process of ISMS measurements might require changes to be made as the existing one may not have been as effective or efficient as it needs to be. New measures and performance indicators may need to be defined, or existing ones changed or replaced. The methods for taking measurements may need to be changed.

All staff and managers need to be made aware of the changes. Retraining may need to take place if the improvements involve totally new controls or upgrades to existing controls in particular with those staff who are directly impacted by these changes.

The organization should see this phase of the ISMS PDCA cycle not as an end but leading onto a continuing process of improvement always striving to have effective information security: a continuous life cycle of risk management.

4.8.7   Call Centre Case Study

As was indicated before the Call Centre has many security problems that need fixing. One area that needs to be improved is staff adherence to procedures. Failing to do backups and taking action regarding the virus warning help towards the problems occurring. What could be improved? A review of the procedures would reveal whether they were sufficient, were easy to use and to what extent was staff familiar with their content. Was staff training and awareness sufficient? These are all areas where improvements could be made to reduce the risk of a reoccurrence of this incident.

Another area of improvement would be the management of staff such as their job responsibilities and duties. A review should be undertaken of the operating conditions and the multitasking activity that contributed to the incidents that occurred. Managing the ICT as well as doing other work of a different nature at the same time does not bode well for an error-free environment.

Management could improve the situation by ensuring a better balance of duties to avoid conflicts in multitasking between operational work and ICT support work. An element of this problem could of course be lack of training as well as duty of care on the part of the employees. However management also plays a part in ensuring that the working environment is not so weighted down with stress and pressure that it makes the adherence to procedures impossible to enforce.

4.9 RISK TOOLS

"Do the difficult things while they are easy and do the great things while they are small." Lao Tzu

4.9.1 Software Tools

There are many software tools on the market for doing risk assessments. These range in price, features and capability. Some tools provide high-level assessments and some are very mathematical in the techniques they use. The big advantage of having an automated tool is that the assessment can easily be updated. Throughout the lifetime of the ISMS the assets, threats, vulnerabilities and impacts will change which will require a reassessment of the risks.

Also business and legal requirements can change which may have an effect on the risks the organization needs to deal with. So a tool is beneficial in this respect for regular review and reassessment of the risks as required by ISO/IEC 27001.

Now it is not always necessary to purchase a special software tool. Some organizations use an office spreadsheet application such as Excel to do the assessment. Also the organization may already be using a piece of software, which could be considered for doing an information security risk assessment.

Whatever the organization decides to use there are a number of considerations that need to be borne in mind:

- Does the tool allow for the assessment of all the different risk management requirements covered in ISO/IEC 27001 as well as the asset and control types given in Annex A? So does the tool support,

    - Risk assessment 4.2.1 d) and e)?
    - Risk treatment 4.2.1 f)?
    - Selection of controls 4.2.1 g)?
    - Statement of Applicability 4.2.1 j)?
    - Monitoring, review and reassessment of risks 4.2.3?

- In particular does it cover,

    - Identification and valuation of assets?
    - Identification and valuation of threats and vulnerabilities associated with these assets?
    - The impacts concerning the loss of confidentiality, integrity and availability of these assets?

- All necessary legal, regulatory, contractual and business requirements, which might impact the assessment of risk?

- Does the tool provide a means of being easily updated and refreshed as of the ongoing risk management process and for reassessment activities?

- Does the tool have the capability to produce risk assessment reports, lists of risk treatment actions, a list of the selected controls and the Statement of Applicability?

- Is it easy to use and does it have a help facility that provides information on the requirements of ISO/IEC 27001?

4.9.2   Use of Scorecards, Gap Analysis and Benchmarks

4.9.2.1   Measurements

There are many ways of gathering information and measuring performance which helps in the risk management process. It is frequently said that an organization only gets "what they measure" so if they do not measure the right things, set the most suitable performance indicators or ask the most appropriate questions they may not arrive at the right answers to tell them how effective their information security is.

Of course, this is easier said than done hence the reason for continual improvement helps to monitor, review and improve processes including those used for measurements. Therefore, care and attention in the design of these methods for measurements will avoid unnecessary work and provide more appropriate decision making results. The topic of ISMS metrics and measurements is discussed in more detail in Chapter 5.

4.9.2.2   Scorecards

Scorecards (especially balanced scorecards) provide a means of measuring the performance of key business processes against business strategy and objectives. In the case of ISMS scorecards it would be the business objective of managing information security risks through the effective implementation and operational deployment of suitable cost-effective and efficient security measures.

For example, the scorecard could be used to measure the performance of the incident handling process against the ISMS objectives referred to above. This might consider score questions related to:

- Incidents reported and resolved over a period of time relating to unusual Web site behaviour, adware, spyware, phishing and other similar issues across different parts of the organization and how long it took,

- The time spent recovering from system downtimes, failures and/or unavailability of network services,

- Possibly the time spent in correcting user errors in data entry and processing activities.

The result of using scorecards provides management with a snapshot of how effective their risk management controls are. It is a tool that can be used alongside other methods that have been mentioned to complement the contribution of information gathering during the monitoring and reviewing process.

Scorecards should be used on a regular or periodic basis to get the most benefit and to support the continuing pursuit of effective information security through the process of continual improvement.

4.9.2.3 Benchmarking

Benchmarking is a useful tool as it can provide a means of comparing different parts of the business as regards the effectiveness of their information security and their level of compliance and progress. It can also be used to evaluate and check how a company is doing as regards its information security with respect to other companies working in the same line of business or in the same industry sector. Benchmarks provide an innovative way of viewing information security as a business enabler across different areas of the business identifying areas for improvement, integration, streamlining and greater efficiency and productivity.

4.9.2.4 Gap Analysis

Gap analysis is another assessment tool which enables an organization to compare its actual information security profile with what it needs to be compliant with and/or the security objectives and targets it wants to achieve. This provides the company with insight into areas where there is room for improvement. The gap analysis process involves determining and documenting the variances between current ISMS business requirements and implementations. There are many uses of gap analysis:

- Pre-risk assessment to check what controls and processes are currently in place,

- Post risk assessment, treatment and selection of controls activities, actions,

- Check status of implementations, actions and status related to improvements,

- During ongoing risk management activities such a risk reassessments,

- Pre-certification audits as well as internal audits and reviews.

Figure 4.19 illustrates a simplified gap analysis table.

Control Item	Ranking			Action to Be Taken	Date of Closure
	F	P	N		
A.10.3.1 Capacity management			✓		
A.10.3.2 System acceptance			✓	Carry out risk assessment to identify the business impact	
A.10.4.1 Controls against malicious code		✓		Carry out risk assessment to identify areas of improvement	
A.11.2.3 User password management	✓			Existing measures are in place to comply with this control requirement. However a risk assessment should be taken into account to assess whether these measures are still adequate.	
A.12.5.5 Outsourced software development			✓	No action to be taken as the organization does not involve itself with software development. It only uses off-the-shelf software products.	

Figure 4.19 Simplified gap anaysis table

The granularity of the analysis can vary in several ways, for example:

- The number of compliance/implementation ranking classes Full (F), Partial (P), or No (N) could increase,

- The number of questions asked to establish the level of compliance can also vary.

The greater the granularity of analysis the more precise the results are likely to be. A single question to assess the compliance/implementation ranking of A.10.2.1 Service delivery could be: Has the organization made certain that what is specified in the third party service agreement is being implemented, operational deployed and maintained by the service provider?

Alternatively three questions in relation to A.10.2.1 could be asked:

- Has the organization made certain that what is specified in the third party service agreement is being implemented by the service provider?

- Has the organization made certain that what is specified in the third party service agreement is being operational deployed by the service provider?

- Has the organization made certain that what is specified in the third party service agreement is being maintained by the service provider?

Chapter 5

Implementing and Deploying the ISMS

5.1 IMPLEMENTATION PLAN

"Knowing is not enough, we must apply. Willing is not enough, we must do."
Johann von Goethe

5.1.1 ISMS Project

In Chapter 4 the tasks and processes that need to be done in the Plan Phase of the PDCA cycle were addressed. This chapter takes forward the results of this work to discuss the work to be done on the Do Phase of the PDCA cycle that is implementing and utilizing the ISMS design.

An implementation/risk treatment plan (ISO/IEC 27001 4.2.2. a) and b)) needs to be produced to take forward the decisions made to treat the risks and to implement the selected controls as described in Chapter 4.

The implementation phase should focus on the prioritization of the actions to be taken, have control over the project budget and resources, establish effective communication and reporting links with all those involved, manage the ISMS project roll-out in a systematic way and not lose sight of the business objectives and mission for the ISMS project.

5.1.2 Project Plan

The implementation plan for the ISMS project should cover all the normal things that plans would contain for other business projects. The ISMS Project should have a project manager responsible for the oversight and coordination of the work.

The ISMS Project needs to especially include:

- Actions, activities, priorities and delivery dates for the implementation and deployment of the ISMS selected controls specified in and selected from ISO/IEC 27001 Annex A,

- Any business and legal requirements that need to be complied with,

- Any interfaces and interdependencies that need to be considered to ensure effective integration of the ISMS within the organization and the proper management of the risk in the ISMS scope,

- Allocation of staff roles and responsibilities for the deployment of the ISMS,

- Roll-out of ISMS training and awareness activities.

5.1.3 ISMS Control Framework

There are different ways of viewing a control framework based on ISO/IEC 27001 Annex A. Figure 5.1 is one way that has been adopted by business:

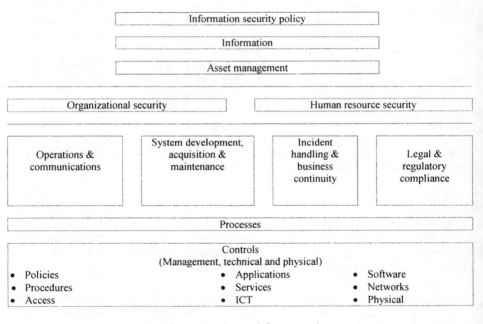

Figure 5.1 Control framework

5.2 INFORMATION SECURITY POLICY

"A policy is a temporary creed liable to be changed, but while it holds good it has got to be pursued with apostolic zeal." Mohandas Gandhi

5.2.1 General Aims

There are information security policies that provide either a high level of information or a more in-depth level of information. ISO/IEC 27001 refers to both these types of policy. Equally there can be procedures at different levels of detail. Both policies and procedures are needed. An information security policy (ISO/IEC 27001 Annex A.5.1) is intended to be a high-level directive and mission statement from management setting objectives and stating their commitment and support from the organization:

- It should define the scope of information security, its importance to the business and make it clear what the business information security objectives are (e.g., regarding the confidentiality, integrity and availability of its information assets),

- Make staff aware of their duties and responsibilities to protect the assets (e.g., their responsibility to handle and process company restricted and confidential information in a way that it is protected from being compromised),

- Set out what is acceptable and not acceptable as regards behaviour and use of its resources (e.g., acceptable use of the company email system),

- Make clear its obligations to carry out its business in compliance with the laws and regulations, contractual obligations, best practices and standards that staff need to comply with (e.g., compliance with laws on copyright, data privacy/protection and computer use/misuse/abuse),

- It should give reference to any other documents that staff need to be aware of and comply with, for example, more detailed security policies and procedures as well as any other relevant proceedings not directly related to security. This could be industry specific policies such as those businesses that need to deal with environmental issues, aspects of healthcare, production of pharmaceutical products, or food safety.

This information security policy should be written in a way that the style and content are independent of any particular skill, process, or technical knowledge.

For example, the content should be understandable by someone that is not an IT specialist, someone not trained in company finances or someone who does not have human resources skills. In other words it should state information security objectives that are generally understood by all staff not just someone with a highly technical background or certain professional qualifications or skills.

The number of pages is not specified in the standard. Some organizations produce such policies having any where between 1 to 3 pages. It is up to the organization to decide the volume of text. What is more important is that it contains enough information to convey in a clear way the objectives and ideas referred to above.

5.2.2 Approval, Communication and Awareness

The information security policy (ISO/IEC 27001 Annex A.5.1) needs to be approved and signed by the CEO (or someone of similar management standing and accountable status) since the aim is to indicate management commitment and support. Another important task is the production of a high-level management statement.

The information security policy should be clearly communicated to all staff. This could be in a paper form or by electronic means or both. Some organizations display their policies on the walls of offices, computer rooms and other areas to ensure they are continually accessible and visible. Other organizations resort to using ICT to distribute and have available their policies and procedures via their internal network. Others may choose to distribute in paper only for staff to keep at their place of work. Whatever the method used the policy should not be hidden away and forgotten. Staff need to read, understand and refresh their memories every so often of its contents.

Staff need not only be aware of the policy, but also understand its content and what it says about their specific information security responsibilities and duties.

5.2.3 Policy Review

Like most things in business there will be changes, such as how the organization operates and how it does its business. Therefore changes should be reflected in the information security policy. A review should be made of the policy whenever it is most appropriate, possibly after identifying changes to the business, after an incident, or as part of a regular management review on its ISMS.

5.2.4 The Risk of Not Having a Policy

There are a number of real-life scenarios that illustrate the problems that can and do occur if an organization does not have an information security policy. The following Sections present a few of these examples.

5.2.5 Case Study on Acceptable Use of Company Systems

One of the junior administrative staff of a law firm compiled a list of indecent jokes covering aspects of sex and racism during work time. The member of staff broadcasting this list on the Internet included pod-casting them, sending them by emails and publishing them on chat forums. The firm's email and contact details were appended at the end of the emails. The firm's clients and other law firms soon became aware of what was going on and started to complain. Senior partners and management of the law firm concerned were able to have the posts deleted from several Web sites and discussion groups. However, they were unable to stop copies of the list that had been sent via email and pod-cast to friends and colleagues of the staff member. A printed copy of the list also got into the hands of various other members of staff as well as a journalist. Various staff objected to the jokes on the grounds of sexual and racial harassment and discrimination. The staff involved threatened legal action which the senior partners and management were able to subdue by an out-of-court payment to the staff in compensation.

What went wrong? It was discovered that there was very little in the way of an information security policy. What could avoid this problem? As mentioned in Section 5.2.1, an information security policy should define what is acceptable and not acceptable as regards the staff behaviour with respect to the use of its resources. This includes acceptable use of the company email system. Section 5.2.1 also draws attention to compliance with legislation and in this case there seems to be a legitimate case regarding the offensive sexual and racial jokes and their impact on staff and those outside the law firm.

5.2.6 The Case of "It wasn't in the policy"

If an organization forgets and leaves something important out of the policy, is this a problem? Well, quite clearly, yes, as illustrated by, for example, the case of a member of staff that spends many hours a day surfing the Internet whilst in his office. The organization does not have any policy in place that makes it clear what staff can or cannot do regarding use of the Internet such as:

- How much time they can spend, if any, using the Internet for personal use during working hours using company resources,

- What they can or cannot download whether it be software of the share/freeware kind, pirated software, executable files, booking holiday trips or acquiring undesirable and offensive materials,

- Running a private business and/or using the resources for personal gain,

- Sending out company restricted or confidential information,

- Running private chat forums, doing pod-casts, messaging sessions, blogging and other similar activities.

Again this is possibly a case of "unacceptable use policy" similar to that described in Section 5.2.4. In this case, however, the member of staff in this particular instance is using the Internet to download software for personal use, both pirated and illegitimate freeware/shareware. His company has no policy covering acceptable use of the Internet and also does not have any policy on downloads or any guidance on the dangers of software downloads.

The company is running a risk because of this lack of policy as software may contain malicious code such as a Trojan horse or a virus and also it is a potentially serious criminal offence regarding the pirated software.

5.3 SPECIFIC DETAILED POLICIES AND PROCEDURES

"Lose no time; be always employ'd in something useful; cut off all unnecessary actions." Benjamin Franklin

5.3.1 General Remarks

5.3.1.1 Scope and Purpose

Policies, procedures and processes are types of control that appear in ISO/IEC 27001. They are necessary to define the rules, instructions, series of actions and practices that need to be in place to get things done and get things done correctly. They support management control of risks and deployment of other ISMS controls. They can range from high-level and specific to more detailed and specific. For example:

- Acceptable user policy (AUP),

- Backup procedures,

- Incident handling procedures,

- Procedures of handling and processing sensitive information,

- Software management policy and procedures,

- Policy on the use of laptops and other mobile equipment off-site,

- Access control procedures.

Policies, procedures, and processes should always be aimed at doing the right things to ensure the efficacy of information security risk management by getting things right by the efficient deployment of risk measures to achieve the desired level of risk control.

5.3.1.2 SMS Organizational and Operational Processes

ISO/IEC 27001 refers to a diverse set of policies, procedures and processes. The following illustrates the main processes dealt with in this chapter (as indicated by the numbers in parenthesis) focused around the subject of ISO/IEC 27001 information security and the secure and proper handling of information assets as shown in Figure 5.2.

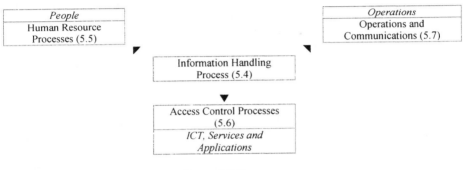

Figure 5.2 Processes

5.3.1.3 Approval, Sign-Off and Dissemination

All policies and procedures need to be approved by someone in management who is accountable, they should have an owner and/or custodian.

It is essential that there is timely dissemination of policies and procedures to staff for their immediate deployment and use. Of course some more detailed policies that are targeted for the technical tasks of the ICT Group or System administrators then would be of little necessity to distribute to all staff.

Equally important is user awareness and training in the use of these policies and procedures. Without such awareness usage may not be effective and the utility of such procedures is devalued with possible dire consequences of a security compromise.

5.3.1.4 Review and Updates

Policies and procedures need to reviewed and updated as and when necessary to maintain and/or improve the efficacy of the risk treatment process. When major changes have occurred in the organization then out dated procedures might be no better than having no procedures. Any updated procedures need to be approved and signed-off, disseminated to users and appropriate training need to be provided. The following section discusses by example one specific type of policy.

5.3.2 Acceptable Use Policy

5.3.2.1 Basic Idea

Many organizations do allow their staff to have access to the Internet for personal use as a goodwill gesture to improve employee relations. In such cases it is a very good idea to put in place "acceptable use policy" (AUP) with regard to the use of the organization's resources, in particular its ICT systems that are deployed for email, Internet access and services. The AUP policy is addressed in ISO/IEC 27001 A.7.2.3 under Assessment Management.

The basic intent of such a policy would be to protect the organization, its staff and management, its business partners, customers and suppliers from individuals involved in any illegal, incriminating and/or damaging actions, whether knowingly or unknowingly. The consequences of such actions could expose the organization and its staff, its business partners, customers and suppliers to a range of risks, impacts and possibly civil and criminal legal proceedings, actions and lawsuits.

The following is a word of caution regarding the content of the AUP. An organization that does not explicitly state what is not acceptable and what is prohibited might face some staff relation issues.

For example, a member of staff is dismissed for unacceptable use of the Internet for personal use. The organization faces the risk that the member of staff takes legal action for unfair dismissal and is claiming compensation since the activities they were engaged in were not expressly prohibited.

It is always good practice to make it clear to staff that access to the Internet and email facilities for personal use are a privilege and not a right.

5.3.2.2 General Policy Provisions

In producing this type of policy following are some notes should that be considered. The policy should:

- Apply to all levels of staff, as well as contractors, consultants and other individuals the organization might employ on a short term or temporary basis,

- Provide a clear definition of what is considered personal use including information on how much access time is acceptable and when personal access is allowed, as well as expressly stating that the user should exercise good judgement regarding the reasonableness of personal use,

- Provide a clear warning of what is not allowed and strictly forbidden and prohibited including the following,

  - Accessing pornographic or indecent Web sites and downloading material from these Web sites,

  - Using chat rooms or on-line messaging services in particular for the exchange of information, comments or opinions that are sexist, racist or anything that will cause offence and this includes the use of offensive and indecent language,

  - Any activities or transactions that are fraudulent or meant to deceive, or where the user masquerades as another user,

  - Any activities or behaviour that might provide unauthorised access to other organizations information, their systems and the network services they use as well as causing, for example, disruption or denial of services and damage to or loss of information assets and processing resources,

- Provide warnings regarding the need to comply with any copyright, digital rights and licensing requirements and restrictions related to material on Web sites,

- Provide instructions regarding the downloading of material from the Internet including warning of the cautionary measures to be taken to avoid downloading malicious code such as viruses, worms and Trojan horses and executable programs,

- Provide a clear statement of what disciplinary actions are to be taken if staff do not comply with the policy,

- State what the organization's rules are regarding its right to audit and monitor networks and systems on a regular or periodic basis. Staff should be advised that their access to the Internet and use of email may be monitored in accordance with the laws in whatever jurisdiction the organization operates.

A note of what this might include might be useful to staff as a cautionary measure. For example, the fact that Web sites that have been used can be traced, the frequency and time spent at sites will appear in an audit trail and the situation regarding using the Internet resources for personal transactions (on-line banking, bookings and orders).

5.3.2.3 Specific Policy Provisions

These might include:

- Warning users not to reveal their account password to others or allowing use of your account by others and this includes those outside of the organization such as family or friends in the case of a laptop being used off-site,

- Warning users to make statements regarding warranties, licences or any other statements that might legally commit the organization, expressly or implied, unless it is a part of the user's normal job duties and prior authorisation to carry out this action has been given,

- Reflect the organization's requirements for protecting the information that staff create on their systems and what is deemed to be the acceptable (and legal) use of encryption for information that is considered sensitive or especially vulnerable,

- Monitoring and/or intercepting a communication network or service monitoring for the purpose of intercepting data unless of course this activity is a part of their job function and prior authorisation has been given and it is allowed in the jurisdictions covered by these activities. For example, the UK Regulatory Investigatory Powers Act (RIPA) covers some such activities.

5.3.2.4 Travel Company Case Study

Figure 5.3 is a sample policy of that used by the travel company. Use of this policy will require an organization to customize the contexts to match their own requirements and legal obligations and liabilities.

Policies such as this one should always be checked by someone that has some knowledge of the law and contracts especially since what is in this example may not match the business rules and requirements such as the use of emails for personal use.

Travel Company Email Use Policy
Email Usage Policy Ref; TCP 3 version 2.0

Scope and Objectives: The purpose and objective of this policy is to prevent damaging the image of the travel company. This policy covers appropriate use of any email sent from the travel company email system and applies to all employees, service providers and agents operating on behalf of the company.

Policy Prohibited Use: The travel company email system shall not to be used for the creation or distribution of any disruptive or offensive messages, including offensive comments about someone's race, gender, religion, disabilities or age. Also prohibited is the use of emails of a sexual and pornographic nature, religious and/or political beliefs. Staff who receive any emails of this type from any other member of staff or from outside sources, should report the matter to their manager immediately.

Personal Use: The Travel company allows a reasonable amount of its email resources to be used for personal use as long as such use does not interfere with the users normal work tasks and the companies day-to-day operations and customers services. Any nonwork related emails and attachments, shall be saved in a separate folder from work related email. However the sending of chain letters or joke emails from the travel company email account is prohibited. Before sending mailings via a distribution list from the travel company shall be approved by the head of the travel company operations. These restrictions also apply to the forwarding of mail received by a travel company member of staff.

Monitoring Email Usage: The travel company reserves the right to monitor email system usage and to check anything that is stored, sent or received via the email system without prior notice. Therefore members of staff should not expect any privacy protection from the company's email system.

Disciplinary Action: Any member of staff violating this policy may be subject to disciplinary action. Depending on the severity of the resulting security policy violation the action may include the termination of employment.

I have read and understood this Email Policy and I agree to comply with its contents:
Staff name _____ Signature _____ Date _____

Approved _____ Dated _____

Figure 5.3 Email acceptable use policy

5.4 INFORMATION HANDLING

"Knowledge itself is power." Sir Francis Bacon

5.4.1 Basics and Objectives

The aim of these procedures for information security is to ensure that all staff know what they should do to handle company information in way that protects its confidentiality, integrity and availability: be it the processing, storage and archiving, distribution, copying or disposal of information.

5.4.1.1 Road Map

The subject of information handling is pervasive across the whole of the ISO/IEC 27000 family of ISMS standards since information is the core asset being protected. The processes referred to in Figure 5.1 covers the parts of ISO/IEC 27001 as shown in Figure 5.4.

Process	ISO/IEC 27001 Annex A
Information Asset Management (5.5.3.1)	Primarily Sections A.7, A.8, A.10, A.13
Information Processing (5.5.3.2)	Sections A.7 to A.15
Information Storage (5.5.3.3)	Primarily Sections A.9, A.10, A.13, A.14 and A.15
Information Distribution (5.5.3.4)	Primarily Sections A.9, A.10, A.13, A.14 and A.15
Information Backups (5.5.3.5)	Primarily Sections A.9, A.10, A.13, A.14 and A.15
Information Destruction (5.5.3.6)	Primarily Sections A.9, A.10, A.13, A.14 and A.15
Information Retention and Archival (5.5.3.7)	Primarily Sections A.9, A.10, A.13, A.14 and A.15

Figure 5.4 Process road map

5.4.1.2 Processes

Figures 5.5 to 5.11 illustrate the various processes involved in information handling. Information about such processes and instructions and rules for carrying out such process as part of the daily operations should be contained in a set of procedures or operating manual.

Information asset management

Asset inventory (A.7.1.1)

As discussed in Chapter 4 producing an asset inventory is a necessary and important part of managing risk. The inventory should:

- Clearly identify all important assets related to the ISMS, in particular the information assets,
- Be drawn up by those responsible for the ISMS,
- Have an owner who is responsible for it being regularly reviewed, updated and maintained,
- Indicate the type of asset, the location, the owner and its value/utility as a minimum set of information.

Example information assets includes:

- Customer details, supplier details,
- Company financial data, sales and marketing data, personnel records, invoices, orders, contracts,
- Research results, product designs, IPR, software specifications.

Ownership, accountability and third party custodianship (A.7.1.2)

Information assets that are generated and/or created using the organization's resources (money, staff, ICT systems and other information, especially that owned by the organization) is generally deemed to be their property and the organization becomes the owner. As the ultimate responsibility for all organization's assets are the senior executives, directors and CEOs they are accountable for these information assets.

Often responsibility for the day-to-day management of the information assets is delegated down to particular groups, departments, functional units and/or individuals within the organization. Custodians within these groups are then given individual operational responsibilities of being the owner/custodian, which means they need to manage these assets and to ensure they are afforded an appropriate level of protection. In the area of data protection with the roles of data controller and data user, both these roles are associated with different information asset responsibilities. It might also be the case that information assets are managed and processed by an outsourcing contract to a third party. In all cases of delegation, custodianship and outsourcing the ultimate accountability of these assets rests with the directors and executives and it is their responsibility to ensure their safe-keeping and the organization's well being.

Use and misuse of information assets (A.7.1.3)

The ISMS involves an ongoing process of practicing the right things to do for the business with due care and diligence to protect information, from a range of threats and risks. This means that staff must use the organization's assets in an acceptable and proper way to avoid security comprises and/or legal complications and actions, see Section 5.6.2 "Acceptable Use Policy."

Information classification (A.7.2.1)

Information assets should be graded appropriately according to their level of sensitivity and/or criticality. This enables an organization to be able to deploy the right amount of protection to the assets commensurate with these sensitivity levels. There are many names and levels of grading that can be assigned to information assets. Chapter 4, provides an example of a classification scheme:

- In Strictest Confidence (requires the highest level of protection especially for sensitivity and in practice this grade normally represents the lowest volume of information the organization might have),
- In Confidence (requires the next highest level of protection and in practice this grade normally represents the lowest volume of information the organization might have),
- Restricted (requires medium level of sensitivity protection and high levels of criticality protection and in practice this grade normally represents the highest volume of information the organization might have),
- Publicly Available (normally requires no sensitivity protection and medium-high levels of criticality protection and in practice this grade can represent the low-high volume of information the organization might have).

Figure 5.5 Processes for information asset management

Information gathering, creation and processing

Gathering and collecting

Gathering and collecting information is a normal function of most organizations. Maybe through market research, research on customer activities (types of spending, seasonal fluctuations), customer surveys and feedback and other forms of research. There are some legal, contractual and security implications about collecting information which organizations should be aware of and pay attention to. The most prominent one, of course, is personal data: what can be collected, what be done with this data and what controls are needed to protect it against abuse or misuse. Indicative of another area of attention is that of intellectual propriety and copyright related to both electronic and non-electronic information and of course "digital rights," DRM (digital rights management) and the rights of individuals.

ISO/IEC 27001 deals with this issue at many different levels such as:

- Policy (A.5.1.1),
- Confidentiality agreements (A.6.1.5),
- Contractual agreements (A.6.2.2-A.6.2.3),
- Asset inventory (A.7.1.1),
- Exchange of information (A.10.8.1-A.10.8.2),
- Audit logging (A.10.10.1),
- Collection of evidence (A.13.2.3),
- Legal aspects (A.15.1.2-A15.1.4)

Processing efficacy, effectiveness, efficiency and correctness

The activities of processing information can mean many things but all have information security requirements to ensure that the confidentiality, integrity and availability of information is preserved. This means doing the "right" things at the "right" time (efficacy of processing), getting these things done (efficiency of processing) and doing these things "right" (effectiveness of processing).

Information that is processed by organizations is vital to their business whether it be processing customer orders, accounts and statements, on-line transactions for buying and selling products, formal company accounts and tax records or other business processes it is important to get it right to avoid losing money, time, productivity, credibility and possibly customers through incorrect data entry and processing of this data through to subsequent results with mistakes and errors. Some of these problems are caused by human errors, lack of training in using processing applications, software flaws, system malfunctions and failures, data corruption and data loss, or unauthorised modification.

It is estimated that a high proportion of business losses and security compromises result from the people who handle information. The correct processing of information is a major area of security problems resulting in customer dissatisfaction, business losses, inefficient and ineffective business operations as well as legal action for failure to honour contracts or to be compliant with legislation.

ISO/IEC 27001 deals with this issue at many different levels such as:

- Responsibilities for information assets (A.7.1) and Acceptable Use Policy (AUP),
- Information handling procedures (A.7.2 and A.10.7),
- User training (A.8.2) in the use of procedures, ICT and application,
- Physical protection (A.9.1) of information processing facilities,
- ICT maintenance, off-site use and disposal (A.9.2) of information processing facilities,
- Operational procedures (A.10.1),
- Third party services processing information (A.10.2),
- Ensuring system capacity (A.10.3) is adequate to ensure against system failures and overloads,
- Backups (A.10.4) to maintain the integrity and availability of information and the systems that process this information,
- Media handling (A.10.7),
- Electronic commerce services (A.10.9),
- Monitoring of unauthorised information processing (A.10.10),
- Access control over applications and information (A.11.6),
- Correct processing of information (A.12.2) to prevent errors, loss, misuse or abuse, or unauthorised modification of information,
- Use of cryptographic tools (A.12.3) to protect the authenticity and integrity of information,
- Legal aspects (A.15) of information processing.

Off-site processing

Some information and data might be processed off-site such as a member of staff using a laptop to process information whilst out on business at a client's office, at home, or in a public place. A managed services company, under an outsourcing contract, might process the information. Whatever the business case the protection of this information during processing should be afforded at least the same level of protection, as it would receive on-site.

ISO/IEC 27001 deals with this issue at many different levels in addition to the control areas listed, the following off-site specific controls need to be considered:

- Contractual agreements (A.6.2.2-A.6.2.3),
- Off-site equipment (A.9.2.5),
- Network security management (A.10.6),
- Exchange of information (A.10.8),
- Network access (A.11.4),
- Mobile computing (A.11.7).

Figure 5.6 Processes for information gathering, creation and processing

Information storage

Electronic storage

With today's technology, organizations and users have many ways of storing information:

- Network servers,
- Hard drives (internal and external),
- Optical disks (e.g., CDs and DVDs),
- Flash memory devices (e.g., USB sticks, SD cards, memory cards) and CompactFlash cards,
- IPods and MP3 players and other memory technologies.

Whatever means and methods of storage are used security should be addressed: ensuring that confidential information is protected to prevent unauthorized disclosure, the integrity of the information to ensure the information does not get changed, modified or flawed whilst in storage and that the information is available to all those that need it.

A clear policy needs to be established on what protection measures need to be in place to protect its confidentiality, integrity and availability. The more sensitive and/or critical information should be stored using memory segmentation or paging, cryptographic technology and/or a strong access control system.

ISO/IEC 27001 addresses this issue in many different ways both for on-site and off-site situations.

Specific controls include:

- Contractual agreements (A.6.2.2-A.6.2.3),
- Information handling procedures (A.7.2 and A.10.7),
- Off-site equipment for stored information (A.9.2.5),
- Operating procedures (A.10.1),
- Third party services (A.10.3),
- Backups (A.10.4),
- Media handling (A.10.7),
- Use of cryptographic tools (A.12.3) to protect the authenticity and integrity of stored information,
- Legal aspects (A.15) of information processing.

Paper-based

Information in paper-based form requires just as much attention as information in electronic form. This should include:

- Physically protect sensitive and/or critical information by locking papers, documents and reports in lockable filing cabinets, desk drawers or in safes which is reduces the risk to an appropriate level, as well as the normal physical security to building, offices and rooms,
- Physical separation of papers having different information

classification,

- A clear desk policy should be established to ensure papers and documents are put away when unattended,
- Papers and documents should be protected from physical or environmental threats and damage, fire and water,
- Papers and documents kept off-site should have the same level of physical protection.

On-site and/or off-site

The decision of whether information should be on-site or off-site depends on circumstances of the organization. Whether off-site storage is a better option whether it affords a better level of risk management taking into account the cost of such storage and the availability and convenience of accessibility to such storage.

Off-site storage should always have the same level of protection as given to on-site storage.

Information might be looked after by a managed services company who store and process information on behalf of the organization. Access to this information is facilitated by use of networking, as is the situation with the travel company case study discussed in Chapter 4.

Of course in the case of backups off-site storage is quite the norm.

Figure 5.7 Processes for information storage

Information sharing, exchange and distribution

Electronic

With today's technology organizations and users have many ways of distributing information.

Information can be pushed out (such as Web casting, broadcasting or server-push) to users or pulled down from a Web site or server.

Whatever methods are used, security should be addressed that:

- Distribution of sensitive and/or critical information is kept to a minimum and the information should be clearly marked to indicate its classification,
- Ensures confidential information is protected to prevent unauthorized disclosure or interception,
- The integrity of the information to ensure the information does not get changed, modified or flawed whilst on route,
- The information is available to all those that need it,
- A clear policy needs to be established on what types of information can be sent electronically (e.g., via email, email attachments) and what protection measures need to be in place to protect the more sensitive and/or critical information,
- If confidential information is sent by those with the right level of authorisation then cryptographic technology should be used,
- The use of anonymous remailers and other technologies should be forbidden.

Fax	Sending information by fax machines can sometimes cause security problems:

- Make sure steps are taken to ensure faxes are indeed sent to the right destination often as it has often been the case that the sender has typed in the wrong telephone number or the redial button has been hit and the fax arrives at the wrong place,
- If sending sensitive business information, also make sure the fax machine is physically secure, that an authorized person is attending the receiving fax machine and get the person to telephone or email to confirm that the fax has been securely received.

Post and courier services	If sending information by post or by courier services there needs be a clear policy stating what types of sensitive and/or critical information can be sent and the means and methods for doing this:

- Information at the highest level of sensitivity should use the technique of double enveloping with the outer envelope not indicating the classification of the contents but the inner enveloped marked,
- It is generally accepted practice that materials containing restricted information could be sent in an single envelope as long as it doesn't indicate the classification marking but is marked with the words "to be opened by the addressee only",
- The use of tamper proofed containers or boxes, or such containers that makes it obvious that an attempt at access has been made,
- Using registered or recorded mail services, or accredited couriers.

Figure 5.8 Processes for information sharing, exchange and distribution

Information destruction

Erasure and deletion from ICT systems	Once information has gone past its "sell by date" and no longer needs to be kept it should be destroyed and/or deleted from the system:

- Electronic files and folders on PCs, laptops and servers should be deleted, this can be done using the standard O/S commands or application functions or by using an appropriate piece of software technology that wipes clean the information,
- A word of caution in most systems, although they have a delete command, the information is not actually deleted it is only the link to the directory system that is deleted or disconnected, which means it still is possible to recover part or all of the information if you know how to locate in the system. This is covered again in Chapter 6 on information forensics. There are ways of improving this situation other than by physical destruction of the storage media,
- Deletion of information should also apply to all copies as well as backups of the information,
- Having an orderly file directory system helps to facilitate the location of files and any copies or backups.

The asset inventory should be revised to record the deletion of information assets.

Disposal of hardware and storage media

Disposal of ICT systems poses the problem of information contained in their memory systems

Disposal of paper-based information

Again as with electronic information once paper documents and files have gone past their "sell by date" and no longer need to be kept, they should be suitably disposed of:

- Paper documents, reports and other paper-based information should be appropriately destroyed using approved shredding or other physical destruction methods and technology (e.g., burning, pulping),
- Destruction of paper documents should be carried out by a trusted person or an approved external organization,
- Copies and backups of all information being disposed of should also be destroyed.

Figure 5.9 Processes for information destruction

Information backups

Identification of information to be backed up

All information should be backed up one way or another. Backup information on staff PCs and laptops, information on servers and on other ICT equipment. As regards backing up software see Section 5.10.

Method of backup

How, when and where backups need to be done needs to be defined. Backups can be done centrally using a network of one or more servers, servers at a specific department level or locally at a user's computer. The policy should define which information applies to which type of backup.

For example operational information is commonly done via a central networks server whereas locally processed information on someones PC, which is not critical, would be done locally. It must not be forgotten that it is not only electronic information that needs to be backed up but also paper-based information systems since all information systems, ICT or non-ICT suffer from the risk of physical or environment damage or loss as well as theft.

How frequent backups should be taken should be related to the criticality value or level of the information. Daily overnight backups are quite common in many organizations especially the large ones.

End-of-week backups should be the norm and may be combined with the routine overnight process. Backups need to be done often and regularly and the more often the better, of course within reasons of practicality. The more time information is left not backed up the more risk the organization runs of it being lost or damaged.

Protection of backups

Critical and/or sensitive information should be secured to:

- Protect its confidentiality and integrity such as the use of cryptographic technology or strong access controls,
- The backup systems should be physically protected to ensure the integrity and availability of the information.

Test restoring backups

There should be a procedure for checking the backup systems and restoring backed up information to make sure the backup process and system are working properly and the backed up information can be read and is a faithful copy of the original.

Storage

Storage of the backups is another issue that needs to be addressed by the policy. The normal best practice for this is to store the backups off-site somewhere away from where server and processing of the information takes place.

The reasons should be quite clear if such backups are kept on the same site then they face the same risks the originals are subject to.

For example damage and loss by office fires, physical destruction, theft and other threats. Hence backup means not only backup the information but also backup the information somewhere else.

Store some backups away from home (or "offsite" to use the jargon) in case your backup data gets stolen or damaged along with the computer it is backing up.

Storage media

The type of media used for backups is also another policy issue. There are many types of media for this purpose including tapes, DVDs/CDs, USB sticks, SD cards and other removable memory devices as well as removable or external hard-drives.

Backup records

Accurate records should be kept of what is backed up, where the backups are kept, date/times and other information that might be necessary for incidents, disasters and system failures, as well as for auditing purposes and other information handing processes.

Figure 5.10 Processes for information backups

Information records management

Records

Keeping records appears many times in ISO/IEC 27001. Records provide a vital link between past events and activities and the effectiveness and efficiency of the ISMS to preserve information security and to manage the organization's risks.

Retaining or archiving information

Certain documents an organization has will need to be kept for a certain period of time as required by law such as tax records and company accounts.

For documents outside of the legal and regulatory category an organization

 may have both business and technical reasons for the retention of information such as:

- Protecting its IPR, trade secrets and research results,
- Audit trails, system and network configuration files and other records especially if they are required to be used as part of an incident handling or a forensic and/or criminal investigation.

Figure 5.11 Processes for information records management

5.5 HUMAN RESOURCES

"An investment in knowledge pays the best interest." Benjamin Franklin

5.5.1 Basics and Objectives

An organization's human resource (or personnel) group is generally there to recruit, develop and utilize its personnel for the purposes of meeting the organization's operational and business needs.

It has been shown many times in surveys and through work experiences that the biggest threat to information systems originates from people.

The people threat could be accidental (e.g., errors in entering customer information into an ordering system or the unintentional deletion of files on a PC) or intentional (e.g., the abuse of organizational ICT systems for personal gain or destroying critical data as might be the case with a disgruntled employee).

Therefore management should focus its effort on getting the people aspect of information security right. This involves several things:

- Achieving an internal security culture,

- Awareness and training,

- Human resource management support,

- Regular updates on security issues,

- Getting staff involved in discussions, user feedback and reviews.

5.5.2 Processes

Figures 5.12 to 5.14 illustrate the processes that the human resource group needs to consider regarding the security aspects of employment.

Before employment	
Recruitment	The human resource group is responsible for facilitating the recruitment of the right people to fit the job vacancies. The defining of the skills, qualities and competencies of the right people is an organizationally determined aspect. The area of information security applies to those specialist jobs such as a security officer, risk manager, ICT expert as well as those staff that are not specialists but will need to take into account the requirements of information security policies and procedures in the day-to-day work.
Screening	This process involves assessing the applicant's suitability for the job advertised. This normally involves screening applications based on their work experience, skills and training for the described job. This normally involves a two or three-stage process. Screening at a general level, for example, reviewing applications and requesting a CV, followed by getting letters of reference from previous employers and from educational establishments, as well as checking certificates as proof of their qualifications. Depending on the type of job being applied for, further screening stage might need to be carried out. For example, for some security specific jobs there may need to be more detailed assessment of their previous work and/or social background. This could go as far as checking whether they have a criminal record or checking their financial state by doing a credit reference check.
Interviews	Like most recruitment drives the interview activity is a critical part of the process involving the human resource group, representatives from the department involved in the vacancies and the candidates themselves. The more detailed screening process normally comes after the interview relating to those that have been short-listed.
Signing documents	The new employee will be expected to sign a contract of employment with the employer's terms and conditions. They will also be asked to sign a nondisclosure or confidentiality agreement, as well as various forms for their salary payments and whatever security forms are deemed necessary, for example, an acceptable use policy.

Figure 5.12 Prior employment processes

During employment	
Employee responsibilities (A.8.2.1)	Staff will be assigned certain roles, responsibilities and duties during their employment, which are related to the organization's information security policies and procedures. These include general security duties and responsibilities as well as more specific security duties and responsibilities.
Employee system account (A.11.2.1)	During employment users would normally be given a system account to allow them to access the organization's ICT systems and networks. What they can access and what rights they have to read, write, print, copy or execute files on the system will largely depend on their specific job role. It is good practice for the human resource group to keep a record of this on their system.
Provision of training (A.8.2.2)	Staff needs to be given training according to their job function and needs. The objective of this should be to provide: • Awareness of information security and risks, • Instruction on how to use security related policies and procedures, • For career development. There are various forms training can take such as on-the-job training, formal training courses, on-line training and at the desk self-instruction using training software.
Review of training	As business needs change, staff development and/or staff get moved to different job functions and/or responsibilities then training needs will likely change. This will entail reviewing staff training, providing additional or new training and updating the staff records. It is important that staff keep up-to-date with the organization's developments in information security.
Disciplinary process (A.8.2.3)	Security compromises involving staff can and do lead to disciplinary action depending on the severity of the incident.
Legal representation	Some information security incidents can involve civil or criminal activities. Members of staff who are named as being the perpetrators or being involved in any way could face legal action against them as individuals and possible action against the organization itself.

Figure 5.13 During employment processes

Termination of employment	
Termination responsibilities (A.8.3.1)	Termination of employment occurs for various reasons: voluntary termination, say, if the member of staff wants to move or he/she needs to move for domestic reasons, or involuntary termination such as being fired or sacked for disciplinary reasons or maybe he/she are made redundant. For these different types of circumstances the responsibility of handling the termination process should be assigned to someone in the organization's human resources group with the appropriate seniority level. This role should involve making sure the process is handled correctly to ensure that all business, legal and personal issues are concluded in a proper and effective way appropriate to the circumstances of the termination. Some terminations can be the result of disciplinary action relating to the activities of a severely disgruntled employee with bad feelings and indignation towards the organization. These types of situation need to be handled in a sensitive way (and with extreme caution taking cognizant of what damage the employee might cause before leaving). In some organizations employees may be asked to leave the premises immediately without serving the normal period of notice if there is a risk of a security compromise. This is very sound policy. This is also the case of "garden or gardening" leave where the employee is asked to serve out their period of notice at home and is often used to prevent the employee from working for one of the organization's competitors.
Return of assets (A.8.3.2)	Staff is normally expected to return all assets that belong to the organization. This should especially be the case with all computing equipment, storage devices, software and applications, as well as paper documents, files, reports, manuals and/or procedures containing the organization's information, in particular that which is sensitive, confidential, restricted, or related to personnel.
Removal of access rights (A.8.3.3)	To avoid the risk of unauthorized access to buildings, offices and rooms, pass cards, identity cards and other devices should be collected from the member of staff. Also any physical entry PIN codes should be removed from the system. All access accounts to information systems, in the name of the member of staff, should be removed from the system. This is to avoid unauthorized access by the ex-member of staff or a colleague or accomplice at a later date. This applies to all ICT equipment from system servers, PCs, laptops, mobile service accounts and any other device that allows a user to gain access to the organization's information assets.

Figure 5.14 Termination of employment processes

5.5.3 More on Training

Information security training needs not just to achieve knowledge transfer and understanding of security policies and procedures but should also aim at getting staff involvement and commitment to adopting the procedures. Just knowing the procedures without practice does not lower the risk of loss or damage to the organization's information assets. Some specific information security training and awareness aspects (for which the content should be as a minimum: the information security and business risks, rules and guidelines, roles and responsibilities, commercial and legal aspects) include:

- Processing of personal data and/or the organization's confidential information,

- Information processing activities,

- Use of ICT systems and software, the Internet and email, mobile and wireless services,

- Reporting incidents, system malfunctions and failures,

- Backup of data,

- Physical protection,

- Dangers of social engineering.

5.6 ACCESS CONTROL

"It is easy at any moment to resign the possession of a great fortune; to acquire it is difficult and arduous." Livy

5.6.1 General Ideas

Access control is a very broad subject and encompasses various types of methods and means of access such as having:

- The rights and means of access to enter buildings, offices and computer rooms,

- The right, privilege or opportunity of access to use or deploy something like a ICT system,

- The right, means and ability of access to approach, see or talk with someone such as might be the case with using the organization's ICT resources including laptops for on-line telephone calls and video-messaging,

- The right and means of access to action and/or process information: obtain, retrieve, copy, store, or destroy to prevent unauthorized access or accidental damage to or compromise of information,

- The ability to be reached such as having access to someone at anytime via a mobile computing device.

Access is given to information or other assets and resources to enable staff to carry out their particular job function. Hence access should not be given to specific information if it is not necessary for the conduct of the staff's official business duties. Normally the "principle of least privilege" is used to grant users/staff permissions they need to do their jobs thus not providing additional permissions that are not necessary to minimize the risk of compromise. This principle should not be mistaken for the other principle of segregation or separation of duties even though this latter principle employs the idea of giving limited or least privileges.

Of course this does not mean compromises will not occur with those users that have been given access permissions and rights as there is always the case of those authorized to have access doing damage to the system and its contents. This can be the case with insider trading, staff involved in internal fraud, theft by staff and other incidents where the culprits did have authorization. Hence ISMS measures need to protect against those not having sufficient access rights and permissions and those owners of the information assets to control those that do.

Although access control is primarily about ingress rights, permissions and privileges to gain entry, there is also a dual protection aspect and that is the egress situation where exiting from a building or system does not leave it in a condition that could be compromised.

It is important from the word go to have a clear understanding of the business requirements for access: access to what and by whom and the means of gaining access. What are the requirements for access to the different information systems the organization has? Are there requirements for access to different applications and processes? What are the physical access requirements for staff, contractors, maintenance engineers or visitors?

5.6.2 ISO/IEC 27001 Access Road Map

Figure 5.15 is a high level overview of the ISO/IEC 27001 Annex A, which covers some aspects of access control. Not all of these may be applicable to every organization since it will depend on the extent and nature of its business, the complexity of its systems and processes as well as the risks it faces and the controls they need to implement to reduce these risks.

Measures (*Annex A*)
Human resources
Access staff during employment *(Annex.8.2)*
Removal of access at termination of employment *(Annex.8.3)*
Physical security
Building and office access *(Annex.9.1)*
Equipment access *(Annex.9.2)*
Operations and communications
Operational access *(Annex.10.1)*
Third party service access *(Annex.10.2)*
Access related to backups *(Annex.10.5)*
Access for network service management *(Annex.10.6)*
Access related to media handling *(Annex.10.7)*
Access related to the exchange of information *(Annex.10.8)*
Access for electronic commerce services *(Annex.10.9)*
Access to monitoring process *(Annex.10.10)*
Access control
User access management *(Annex.11.2)*
User access responsibilities *(Annex.11.3)*
Network access control *(Annex.11.4)*
Operating system access control *(Annex.11.5)*
Application and information access control *(Annex.11.6)*
Mobile computing and teleworking access *(Annex 11.7)*
Information systems acquisition, development and maintenance
Access related to correct processing in applications *(Annex.12.2)*
Access to system files *(Annex.12.4)*
Access to vulnerability management process *(Annex.12.5)*
Information security incident management
Access to information on incidents, weaknesses and information security events *(Annex.13.1)*
Access to evidence *(Annex.13.2)*
Business continuity management
Access to business continuity process, plans, test results and backup facilities *(Annex.14.1)*
Legal compliance
Legal aspects regarding the access to information *(Annex.15.1)*
Access to system audit processes and audit results *(Annex.15.3)*

Figure 5.15 Access road map

5.6.3 Access Rights and Information Classifications

The organization needs to decide what access rights are given to information and by whom. Some may be given access to information at different levels of classification (recall from Chapter 4 Annex A.7 an example of such classifications). Staff will be given access to information that is on a "need to know" basis.

The higher the classification (most sensitive information) the smaller the group that have "need-to-know" rights, hence the biggest group of users would be those having access to restricted information (less sensitive). In addition, information can further classified, for example a confidential marking might a caveat attached to it such as in Figure 5.16

Marking	Rights
In-Confidence	"Need-to-know" rights covering information without a caveat.
Medical-In-Confidence	"Need-to-know" rights with the caveat medical information restricted to those working in the healthcare field such as doctors and nurses.
Personnel-In-Confidence	"Need-to-know" rights with the caveat personnel information restricted to those working in Human Resources.
Financial-In-Confidence	"Need-to-know" rights with the caveat financial information - normally restricted to the Finance Department/Group, the CEO and directors.

Figure 5.16 Information classifications

In addition to "need-to-know" rights which are a means of allowing users to read information, there is also "need-to-modify" rights which give users permission to modify, delete and/or generally to create information.

An example of these different types of access is that referred to as "read" and "write" access. There are of course other access rights such the right to be able to execute a particular piece of software code. The following is a list of these rights found in applications. Some applications do not offer all these options or restrictions, see Figure 5.17:

Access Right	Access: subject → object
Read (R) access	The subject can: • Read the contents of a file, • List directory contents.

Write (W) access	The subject can change the contents of the information contained in a file or directory with these tasks:
	    • Add,
	    • Create,
	    • Delete,
	    • Rename.

Print (P) access	The subject can print a copy of the file.
Copy (C) access	The subject can make a copy of the file.
Execute (X) access	If the file is any software program or executable code, the subject can cause the program to be installed and run.

Figure 5.17 Access rights

5.6.4 Authorization, Accountability and Ownership

In ISO/IEC 27001, Annex A.7.1, the topic of asset ownership and accountability for asset protection, was discussed. Access to information needs to be controlled by the owner of this information.

The owner is responsible for making sure the information is appropriately protected and thus accountable for whatever measures and actions are taken to ensure such protection is suitable and effective.

Authorization for access is also another aspect of ownership and for granting or denying access and the appropriate access rights.

5.6.5 Access Control Processes

5.6.5.1 General

The implementation of access control does have many variants depending on the type of access, the methods of access and the technology being used. There are, however, some common elements, which should be considered when producing access control procedures.

The overall process should start by registering the user onto the system and then setting up an account for them. Once this has been established the user can use the account to access resources on the system according to the rights and permissions that have been given. This also applies to the access of services, for example, telecommunication services and Internet services.

The management and maintenance of access policy and procedures, the rights, permissions and privileges, the control measures and methods for access are not necessarily trivial and can sometimes prove to be quite an administrative burden and overhead, if not managed correctly, especially in large organizations with thousands of users and system accounts.

Systematic properly implemented ISMS processes and the effective deployment of the ISMS measures can reduce this workload.

From the point when a user is first registered and given an account on the system until the time when that account is cancelled and the user's access rights need to be revoked there needs to be management measures in place to ensure the access process is secure, effective and robust.

This process involves a number of measures both non-technical and technical, all of which should work in harmony and without compromise.

5.6.5.2 Processes

Figures 5.18 to 5.23 illustrate the processes related to access control.

User Registration (Annex 9.2)	
Selection of user attributes: name and other credentials	The user attributes need to be linked together to form a unique combination. For example, a user name and password should be a unique pair of user credentials.
System authorization	Access to each of the systems which the user needs access should be authorized by the owner/custodian/administrator of that system.
Allocation of rights, privileges and permissions for user access to information assets	Authorization and approval of a user's rights of access to the system contents such as information assets. This approval needs to be given according to what is appropriate and necessary for the user's job function based on the principle of least privilege. Approval might be given by management and/or the owner of the information assets.
Recording the user details on the system	The details of the registered user and the user's rights and privileges should be recorded and documented on the system to allow for auditing purposes, tracing events relating to incidents and various other security purposes.
User acknowledgement	The registered user needs to acknowledge having read and accepted the conditions under which access has been given. Sometimes this is an on-line process, which is quite common when a user signs up to some Internet service or access. Another way is to get the user to sign an internal written statement of acceptance, which does happen in a number of organizations.

Figure 5.18 User registration

System Logon/Login	
Identification and authentication of the user	This could be a simple login process involving a username and password. There many other ways of identifying the user, for example, using cards and tokens, biometric devices and many others (see Section 5.10 for more details).
Check and verify user attributes	The user attributes are checked and verified against those recorded on the system.
Grant or deny access	Dependent on the success or failure of this identification and verification process.

Figure 5.19 System login

Access to Specific Information Resources	
Identify and authenticate the user	The system will request the user to present access credentials in order to identify him/herself and to be authenticated.
Check and verify user attributes	The user attributes are checked and verified against those recorded on the system.
Check the access rights of the user	The system needs to check the user's access rights: for example, to access folders, files and documents. This could be a simple access control list which details which user has access to what and with what rights, for example, user A may have both "Read" and "Write" access but user B may only have "Read" access to the same file. This type of access control list can be set up using many office software operating systems and applications available today. There are other more sophisticated methods, which offer a lot more security features and user access capabilities.
Grant or deny access	Dependent on the success or failure of these activities the user is given access, for example, to read or even process a document.

Figure 5.20 Access to information resources

Physical Access	
Buildings, offices and computer rooms	There are many well tried and tested physical access controls available to secure buildings, offices and rooms. For example locks, keypads, swipe cards and many more. There is also monitoring equipment such as CCTV, which is commonly deployed in many organizations.
ICT and other equipment	Again there are many technologies for protecting equipment. One area that is very critical is the physical protection of laptops and other mobile computing devices when used outside of the office, especially in public places.

Figure 5.21 Physical access to information resources

Updating User Accounts	
Review of user accounts	As changes happen in the organization that are deemed to be security related, user accounts need to be reviewed. Some accounts may no longer be needed and therefore these need to be cancelled.
Changing access rights	In addition if a user changes their job or extension of responsibilities regarding his/her existing job function changes of the corresponding access rights of the user will need to be reflected in the access control system by appropriate changes. For example, a user may no longer need to have write access to a certain set of files as it is no longer part of his/her job but he/she can still have read access. This needs to be reflected in the system as well as being communicated to the user.

Figure 5.22 Updating access accounts

Removing User Access	
Removal and de-registration of a user from the system	Whenever a user terminates employment any user accounts (to systems and services) he/she had need to be closed.
ICT equipment, buildings, offices and computer rooms	Also any physical access rights need to be removed including the handing back of employee passes and removal of any door entry access devices and/or passwords.

Figure 5.23 Removing/terminating access

5.6.6 Complying with the Laws on Access

Many countries have legislation that deems unauthorized access as a criminal offence. For example, the UK Computer Misuse Act (1990) makes unauthorised access to computer systems a criminal offence as defined in the following extract from this Act:

1(1) A person is guilty of an offence if:

    a)   He causes a computer to perform any function with intent to secure access to any program or data held in a computer;

    b)   The access he intends to secure is unauthorised; and

    c)   He knows at the time when he causes the computer to perform the function that this is the case.

In the United States the Computer Fraud and Abuse Act of 1986 was intended to reduce hacking of computer systems. This Act has been subsequently amended in 1994, 1996 and in 2001 by the US Patriot Act. The following is an extract from this Act:

1. Knowingly accessing a computer without authorization to obtain national security data,

2. Intentionally accessing a computer without authorization to obtain,

   - Information contained in a financial record of a financial institution, or contained in a file of a consumer reporting agency on a consumer,

   - Information from any department or agency of the United States,

   - Information from any protected computer if the conduct involves an interstate or foreign communication,

3. Intentionally accessing without authorization a government computer and affecting the use of the government's operation of the computer,

4. Knowingly accessing a computer with the intent to defraud and thereby obtaining anything of value.

Other countries either have laws, regulations or decrees on unauthorised computer access, hacking and SPAM or are developing laws or directives including:

- Australia Commonwealth Cyber Crime Act (2001) and the Spam Act (2003),

- Canada CAN-SPAM Act (2003),

- India Information Technology Act (2000),

- Singapore Computer Misuse Act (2003),

- As well as many others such as China, The European Union and Japan.

Many countries also have legislation that governs access to personal data. For example, all the Member countries of the European Union have this type of legislation as do countries such as Australia, Canada, China, Japan, Malaysia, Singapore and many others.

There are also laws in some countries regulating:

- Access to telecommunication networks and communication services such as in the United Kingdom and other parts of Europe, the United States and parts of Asia,

- Corporate governance and financial systems, processes and services such as Basel, the US Sarbanes-Oxley Act (SoX) and the US GLB Act,

- Healthcare such as the US Health Insurance Portability and Accountability Act (1996),

- Freedom of information such as the UK Freedom of Information Act.

The important point about all this is that any access policy must recognize and take heed of the laws that apply to the organization and its information systems. Of course, the organization may need to be cognizant of the various legal systems as its business may cut across different jurisdictions depending on the nature of the business, the geographical locations, their market position and the Internet presence and the countries to whom it offers its on-line services. Whatever rules and conditions of access are laid down in law need to be taken into account when devising the access control policy and subsequently the control mechanisms themselves.

5.6.7 Policy Production

The access control policy needs to address all the aspects of access presented in Sections 5.3.1.1 through 5.3.1.5 and more specifically the areas defined in Section 5.4.8 where applicable to the organization. How it organizes and implements its compliance policy is entirely up to them, there are no standard ways of doing this. The organization may decide to cover all aspects of access in one policy. It might otherwise decide to produce several policies and procedures covering one or more of these topics, or maybe one set devoted to management and deployment of access control measures and the other set devoted to the more technical aspects of access control.

It is also important to note that many ICT platforms and products have built-in policies based on software controls integrated into the products. For example, most modern operating systems have degrees of access control security built into them and the same goes for database products. However, all these platform and product policies do need to come under the overarching management level for access policy and supporting procedures for the deployment of this policy.

5.6.8 Access Policy for SMEs

5.6.8.1 General

SMEs should not be discouraged or put off by such a long list of access items. Again it should be reiterated that all of what is in the ISO/IEC 27001 is scalable to the size of the company.

Some aspects of access are either common sense aspects that could already be in place such as physical access or they may be mandated by law such as data protection/privacy, which addresses access to personal data of staff, customers and others.

5.6.8.2 SME Case Study

For example, take the case of a small accountancy firm supplying services to local SME businesses. The firm consists of three partners who are qualified accountants, four assistants, an office administrator, two office clerks and a receptionist.

Their business involves processing their clients' information to provide them with annual accounts and statements, financial reports and various other office services.

All employees have a PC and these are all networked together. All PCs are password protected at system start-up. The case files of the firm's clients are located on a network server in folders that each partner and the assistant have access to using an access control application residing on the server. A general outline of an SME policy for this firm could be as follows.

All members of staff shall abide by the following rules for information access:

- All sensitive, personal, confidential and restricted company information contained in filing cabinets, folders and files and on all PCs and servers on the internal network shall be subject to access control on a "need-to-know" basis,

- It is the responsibility of all staff to protect the information they are handling to avoid any unauthorised access by anyone that does not have the right of access to such information. Such access can lead to loss, damage and leakage of this information.

Figure 5.24 is a simplified access control list defining the allocated rights of staff regarding information access.

	Company Confidential information	Client Case Files	Company Policies/ Procedures	Restricted Information/ Documents	Generally Available Information/ Documents
Partners	R/W Access	R/W Access	R/W Access	R/W Access	R/W Access
Assistants	No access	R/W Access	R/W Access	R/W Access	R/W Access
Administrator	R/W Access	No access	R Access	R/W Access	R/W Access
Office clerks	No access	No access	R Access	R/W Access	R/W Access
Receptionist	No access	No access	R Access	R Access	R Access
	Financial records, personnel records, business plans			*Invoices, payments, letters, staff diaries, work schedules*	*Publicly available newsletters, brochures, leaflets and guidelines*

Table 5.24 SME access control list

5.6.9 Example Check List

Figure 5.25 illustrates a typical checklist an SME might use.

User Responsibilities
- All access to information will be protected by the use of a username and password
- Users must change each of their passwords every two months and a different password must be selected each time a change is made.
- Passwords must be 6 to 10 characters in length and be composed of both numbers and letters.
- Users must keep their passwords safe and secure. They must not be left on pieces of paper, stick-on notes or anywhere that might be visible to other people such as visitors.
- For the purposes of UK Data Protection compliance the firm's administrator is the Data Controller. All queries regarding personal data should be addressed to the Administrator.

PC and Network Access
- User passwords for PCs are required at system start-up and for logon purposes.
- Staff must be careful when using the firm's email system and Internet that company- and client-sensitive information is sent on. Staff sending such information without the firm's authorization shall be appropriately cautioned and disciplined since such action could compromise the firm and result in legal action.
- No staff should attempt to gain access to information they have no right to access.
- Reasonable personal use of the email system and the Internet is permitted. This should be restricted to lunchtimes and at time when the work is very slack. Staff must exercise a sensible level of what is considered as reasonable as such access is a privilege and not a right. Under no circumstances should staff allow such access to interfere with their work.
- Under no circumstances should staff get access to undesirable sites or download undesirable material (e.g., pornographic literature or photographs). All staff should be aware of the criminal offences and legal action such access might result in.

Figure 5.25 SME Check list

Physical Access
• All staff can have access to the firm's offices between 8 am and 6 pm each weekday unless otherwise authorized for work purposes (e.g., evening or weekend work to finish high priority client assignments). Partners have access at any time.
• All visitors must sign-in at the reception desk, be given a pass and be escorted by a member of staff when in the offices.
• Unless by prior authorization and arrangement with a partner no company folders or files shall be taken off the office premises. If a member of staff has such authorization for the purposes of visiting and/or delivering such files to a client, a local government office, a lawyer or tax office on behalf of a client then the documents need to be held in a secure briefcase.
• Access to laptops of those members of staff that are allowed to use such equipment off-site.
• Policy and guidance on the handling of personal data, illegal downloading and/or copying any copyright material, downloading undesirable material from the Internet.
Disciplinary Process
• Any member of staff that fails to abide by these policy rules could face disciplinary action and also dismissal.

Figure 5.25 SME Check list (continued)

5.7 OPERATIONAL AND COMMUNICATIONS SYSTEMS

"If you don't know where you are going, you'll end up someplace else." Yogi Berra

5.7.1 Operational Systems

5.7.1.1 Running the Business

Information processing systems and services that support the day-to-day operations of an organization need to be functioning properly and correctly; the information driving these operations needs to be protected. Again it is a question of efficacy, efficiency and effectiveness of the operations and information security, which makes things happen in a way that the organization benefits: ensure its profitability and survivability in the market place, achieve customer (and employee) satisfaction and future proof the well-being of its business.

When an organization is hit with a severe denial of service attack its information processing systems could either grossly underperform or fail/stop functioning completely. Disaster has struck and the accessibility to that information driving operations is then no longer available in electronic form. Whilst the organization has no operations to support its business then the inevitable impacts start to kick-in such as loss of production, customer services, deliveries, revenue and possibly its established position and reputation in the market. Its on-line shop is hit by disaster or system failure and it is out of business for several days - What can they do?

The business, of course, might be able to continue using manual methods or maybe its business continuity process will facilitate resumption of operations at another location or using a backup system. It may be that this is possible with some organizations whose line of business allows these alternative options to be implemented. However, not all businesses will have these options, clearly an automated manufacturing plant, certain types of travel and transportation systems, healthcare delivery systems and several others may not be able to easily switch options.

5.7.1.2 Controlling Operations

From an information security perspective procedures and processes for doing the "right" things and getting the things done "right" is at the heart of secure operations. ISO/IEC 27001 Annex A cites many examples of procedures that need to be considered to support both operations and communications within the organization. The examples include procedures for handling of information, secure use of ICT, correct and secure use of Internet and email services, system and software acceptance, incident reporting and handling, back ups, management of networks, using e-biz/commerce applications, monitoring the effectiveness and performance of information security measures, monitoring and audit trails, as well as many others.

5.7.1.3 Capacity Planning

In the context of ISO/IEC 27001, capacity planning is the process of adjusting the capacity of an organization's ICT systems to do work in response to changing current demands and/or predicted future demands. The objective of capacity planning is to avoid the problems of overloads, reduction of performance levels due to the lack of capacity commensurate with the demands of users and customers. The capacity planning helps to minimize this discrepancy between capacity and demands.

An organization's information processing and/or networking demands will and do vary due to various reasons:

- Extending the processing operations of the business, for example, due to increase in sales and production, increase in customers, expanding supply chains,

- Additions or modifications to current Internet services it offers, its outsourcing services,

- The introduction of new working practices and/or methods of processing such as allowing staff to work from home and giving them remote access,

access,

- New computer systems being networked together or new networks being introduced,

- Redeployment of staff, large increase in the staff count.

The term capacity, for the purposes of capacity planning, can be taken to mean, for example, the amount of information processing that an organization is capable of completing in a given period of time or the amount of emails and Internet transactions an organization needs to engage in over a period of time. A simple capacity calculation of this is (number of computer systems and/or users) x (number of processing activities) x (utilisation of the systems) x (efficiency).

Capacity planning is essential to ensure that the organization's information processing systems are available to meet the demands of business operations and to avoid problems such as system overloads, downtimes, or degradation in system processing capability. ISO/IEC 27001 states this as an important and critical management control in any risk management strategy and one that the organizations need to pay careful attention to. In addition, capacity plans do need to be reviewed on a regular basis. The ISO/IEC 27001 best practice control A.10.3.1 addresses this issue.

5.7.1.4 System Testing and Acceptance

Any new information systems facilities, upgrades, new versions or improvements to existing facilities need to be tested before being commissioned for operational use. These new facilities need also to be approved and accepted for utilisation in the operational environment. For example, new software, upgrades or new versions of software should be approved and tested before use on the operational applications and processes. The reasons should be clear without such management control unauthorized and untested software might be installed on a user's system and cause a security compromise. Also untested software might cause system failures and cause conflicts with other applications due to incompatibility problems. The ISO/IEC 27001 best practice controls address some of these issues (see A.10.1.4 and A.10.3.2). System acceptance and capacity are essential management activities to minimize the risk of exposure to system crashes, failures, conflicts or degradation in performance and quality.

5.7.1.5 Malicious Software

The computer virus attack is a worldwide headline catching piece of news. The virus is an example of a piece of malware or malicious software, which is designed to infiltrate or damage a computer system. This class of software also

- The *worm* is generally not intended to cause damage or loss, however, depending on how far and/or deep it penetrates it can have a dire impact on systems leading to the overloading and slowing down of computer systems by its self-replicating nature, filling up system storage memory with copies of itself. The business impact of this is loss of availability and performance. Supposedly the first of its kind was known as the Internet Worm, which spread around the world like a forest fire slowing down computer networks in thousands of companies,

- The virus, on the other hand, is a more hostile piece of malicious software whose intent is to vandalize, damage or cause data loss,

- A Trojan horse is a file that claims to be something it is not, it deceives and can be thought of an imposter by giving the impression it is desirable or needed but, in fact, it is something malicious. It does this by appearing to do one thing when in fact it is doing something else, such as could be the case with downloaded screen savers, wallpapers for desk tops or other seemingly harmless and attractive items. They might be advertised as a screen saver but when installed they do something else, something undesirable and potentially malicious to the computer system. Some Trojan horses provide a back door into the computer system allowing unauthorized access to the system and, for example, files containing passwords, PINs and other information linked to the legitimate users of the system. The Trojan horse does not automatically replicate itself as a virus does but can do so when allowed to enter the system, for example, by a user downloading and opening an email attachment or running/executing a file download from the Internet,

- Spyware is a piece of software that collects personal information about users from their computer system. It does this without the users informed consent by secretly recording personal information. Recording Web browsing history, scanning user's documents and logging keystrokes all can provide information about the user (e.g., for overt theft of passwords and/or credit card details and other financial details) and their activities (e.g., for targeted consumer advertising, or collecting information about user's Web searching habits including their buying and spending interests),

- Adware is a piece of software which automatically plays, displays, or downloads advertising material to a computer after the software is installed on it or while the application is open.

5.7.1.6 Monitoring

Monitoring the use, performance, effectiveness and efficiency of the ISMS and the ICT systems and network services it deploys is essential to:

- Assess and review of the current utilisation and demand of ICT resources to help reduce the likelihood of system overloads, bottlenecks, downtimes, disruptions or failures,

- Review system logs and records of activities to avoid potential system abuse or misuse,

- Detect suspicious activities, malicious attacks, intrusions, failed access attempts and other threats and events that could compromise the information security policies and procedures.

Monitoring work can be carried out using automated tools, collection of user feedback, observation of working practices, review of incident handling records, regular inspection of audit logs, usage reports from service providers, performance checks and measurements and many other sources.

As this illustrates there are many important requirements of ISO/IEC 27001 that need to be attended to that are all interrelated which help to monitor ISMS performance, effectiveness and the provision of availability of business processes, systems and services:

- System and usage monitoring,

- ISMS measurement process,

- ISMS audits and reviews,

- Incident handling process,

- Capacity planning,

- Maintenance of ICT systems.

5.7.1.7 Documentation System

All operational procedures and processes need to be well documented and be accessible to all those that need them for their jobs and in some cases this could be all members of staff.

All operational procedures and processes need to be well documented and be accessible to all those that need them for their jobs and in some cases this could be all members of staff.

To be effective, the use and deployment of ISMS policies and procedures need to be supported by an easy to use, efficient documentation system.

Many organizations take advantage of ICT and Web technology to have their documentation system on-line and accessible on their internal network. This has the benefit of:

- An easy means of getting new documents, revisions and updates to users immediately as they are released,

- Immediate access by staff and easier to search for documents,

- Avoids having a pile of paper documents to search through,

- Facilitating easier record keeping, completing security forms such as reporting incidents or problems,

- Facilitating on-line learning through self-assessment and teaching.

Whether the organization's ISMS documentation system is all electronic or paper there are certain things that need to be done:

- Make sure the documents are reviewed on a regular basis,

- Make sure that documents are always up to date, they have been approved and signed and the latest versions are available and distributed to all staff,

- All old versions should be removed from the system on the arrival of new versions,

- They are secured from unauthorized modifications and other security compromises.

5.7.2 Third Party Services

5.7.2.1 Addressing Information Security

More and more organizations are using third party services:

- Outsourcing call centres and help desks,

- Recruitment of staff taking over from the activity of a human resources Group,

- Managed data backup and data recovery services,

- Hosting Web sites,

- Development of software,

- Recovery of debts, goods relating to unpaid invoices and payments,

- ICT support services.

Whatever the purpose is for using external services, information security is an issue that needs to be addressed and be the subject of contractual and service level agreements. At the core of this are the information outsourced and its protection. The organization is giving custodianship to a third party of its information assets.

This "transfer of risk" does not obviate the accountability of these assets on the part of the organization, it just adds to their risk problem. Having said this there are many business benefits to using third party services, which as we have addressed in Chapter 4, the organization needs to weigh up the pros and cons as part of its risk decision making process.

Considering information security the organization should ensure that its information assets are given information security measures that are commensurate with the organization's business risks and to its business interest.

5.7.2.2 Service Agreements

The main aspects that need to be dealt with in third party service agreements are:

- A clear definition of security roles, responsibilities and obligations of both parties for fulfilling the information security requirements of the organization,

- The process for dealing with information security incidents,

- The access arrangements to ensure the confidentiality and accessibility of the organization's information assets,

- Backup and business continuity arrangements to ensure the integrity and availability of services and of the organization's information assets,

- Regular reporting,

- Provisions for management changes,

- Right to review and audit the third party arrangements.

5.7.2.3 Selecting an Outsourcing Company

In deciding whom to outsource to it is important to consider a company with:

- Reputation and image in the market place,

- Financial viability, Is it likely to have financial difficulties in the near future?

- Size of its systems and processing capabilities, capacity and robustness,

- Costs, What does it charge for what it can offer? Are the costs comparable with other providers?

Geographical location concerning offshore versus on-shore arrangements:

- Environmental hazards Is the outsourced company located in an area which is prone to threat of volcanoes, earthquake, tornadoes, flooding, tsunamis?

- Stability of the offshore region, Is it economical or politically stable?

- Local jurisdiction of the outsourced company and compliance with legislation from the organization's country.

5.7.2.4 Publishing Company Case Study

A small publishing and printing company decides to outsource the day-to-day technical support for its ICT. This will include off-site diagnosis of faults, on-site engineering support, help desk support and temporary on-site staffing cover.

The publishing company requires ICT support services during the normal working week from 8 am to 6 pm and sometimes to support its production group which occasionally need to work out of normal working hours to meet certain customer delivery times.

A draft of the publishing company's SLA is illustrated in Figure 5.26.

Scope
This SLA covers the technical management, maintenance, supply and installation of ICT hardware and software resources by the "ICT Support 4U" company.

Range of Services
The company "ICT Support 4U" shall supply the following service:
- Telephone technical support for reporting of faults and to discuss technical problems using a help desk/call centre,
- Off-site remote diagnosis of faults,
- Supply of new or replacement ICT hardware and software,
- On-site technical support for installating and maintaining ICT resources, trouble shooting,
- Temporary on-site staffing cover.

Service Availability
The "ICT Support 4U" company shall supply services as follows:
- Every working weekday between the hours of 08:00 and 19:00,
- Outside normal working hours as arranged and agreed between both parties on a call-off basis.

Service Response Times
The "ICT Support 4U" company shall respond to reported major faults within 1 hour with off-site remote diagnosis and support or 3-4 hours with on-site support. Minor faults shall be responded to within 24 hours after the fault has been reported.

Escalation Procedures
To ensure faults and problems are addressed in a timely and satisfactory way the "ICT Support 4U" company shall make available the resources to deal with this by escalating from off-site support to on-site support and fault resolution in the shortest possible time. This includes making available enough resources to focus and intensify the investigation and resolution efforts without further delay. This escalation effort should be coordinated by someone at the senior level in the company who can take responsibility of the staff's progress.

Record Keeping
The "ICT Support 4U" company shall keep proper records giving details of reported faults, problem and solution analysis and the closure of the actions being taken.

Performance Review
There shall be regular reviews of service delivery against the requirements to maintain acceptable levels of service over time in accordance with this agreement. This shall be every three months or sooner if necessary.

Supplier and Customer Obligations
The supplier shall make provision for spare parts, the qualifications of support staff and the need to meet response times. Responsibilities of the customer to provide information regarding any changes in scope of the contract and the cooperation of staff with the supplier.

Termination of agreement
A formal process shall bein place, which defines the specific terms and conditions under which the contract may be terminated.

Signed and approved by _____ on behalf of ICT Support 4U   Date _____
Signed and approved by _____ on behalf of Publishing Company Date _____

Figure 5.26 Example SLA

5.7.3 Communications

5.7.3.1 Access to Communications

In today's high-tech, mobile, multi-media world the means of getting connected
and to communicate with anyone, anywhere, with anything at any time is getting
easier. Fixed networks, terrestrial mobile networks and satellite broadcasting and
mobile networks are globally connecting organizations and citizens.

As greater connectivity is now possible and the mobile and wireless
technologies are shaping the way we do work, the traditional boundaries of an
organization are rapidly changing, becoming fuzzy and in some cases almost
disappearing. The traditional defence in depth and physical protection strategies
are becoming outdated and are being replaced with a more open, continually
shifting communications space where a user can, in theory, log-on to a network
anywhere.

The market has also had the emergence of Internet voice services such as
voice-over-IP (VoIP). This is also being offered as a package with other Internet
services integrating together many different media: voice and data, for example.

This all presents benefits and challenges to organizations wanting both
information security and the maximum business advantages these communications
technologies can offer.

5.7.3.2 Wireless and Mobile Technology

Over recent years mobile technology has been developing by leaps and bounds.
Merging various multi-media offerings alongside traditional telephony capability
users can listen, see, talk, send messages, tune-in to radio, send emails and surf the
Internet and these are just some of today's mobile technology attractions, with
many extensions promised for tomorrow. Combine this with the advances in
wireless technology and the information security issues start to become an
interesting challenge for industry.

Any user within range of an open, unencrypted wireless network can gain
unauthorized access to an organization's internal network and the resources
connected to this network as well as to the Internet. The user may just want to gain
Internet access through some broadband link without paying for the privilege.
However the user may have other things in mind: information theft, bringing down
the organization's system, sending viruses, spam or doing other illegal actions
using the owners IP address.

Users can gain access via several different types of mobile computing devices,
which have a wireless capability built in: laptops, Apple computers, palmtops,
PDAs, BlackBerries, mobile phones and many other devices.

Bluetooth is an industrial specification for wireless personal area networks
(PANs). Bluetooth provides a way to connect and exchange information between

devices such as mobile phones, laptops, PCs, printers, digital cameras and video game consoles via a secure, globally unlicensed short-range radio frequency.

5.7.3.3 ISO/IEC 27001 Communications Security and Management

All of what has been covered so far in this and previous chapters is relevant to communications and the management of communications systems and services. Communications security covers the protection of information in transmission to allow communicating parties to share and exchange information to ensure the information is not modified in transit and any interception of the network traffic does reveal the contents of the information. In addition, communicating parties need to be assured that the intended recipient of the information indeed gets the information and it is not rerouted to some other destination.

Some of the information security required for communications can be provided by the use of cryptographic techniques to give the confidentiality, integrity and authenticity of the information. Similarly we can use these techniques for authenticating end users and for non-repudiation purposes.

However these techniques do not cover communications scenarios. For example, a member of staff using a mobile phone or other mobile device in a public place, such as on a train, at an airport or at a conference, transmitting sensitive business information by voice, can be easily intercepted by listeners located in the public place.

Also, faxes can be accidentally sent to the wrong destination. These all require appropriate policies and procedures to be in place and for staff to trained in the use of these facilities.

Some of the relevant best practice controls highlighted in ISO/IEC 27001 Annex A are included in Figure 5.27.

Equipment security (A.9.2)	
A.9.2.1	Equipment and siting
A.9.2.3	Cabling security
A.9.2.5	Security of equipment off premises
Network security management (A.10.6)	
A.10.6.1	Network controls
A.10.6.2	Security of network services
Exchange of information (A.10.8)	
A.10.8.1	Information exchange policies and procedures
A.10.8.2	Exchange agreements
A.10.8.3	Physical media in transit
A.10.8.4	Electronic messaging
A.10.8.5	Business information systems
Electronic commerce services A.10.9	

Figure 5.27 Communication controls

Monitoring (A.10.10)	
A.10.10.1	Audit logging
A.10.10.2	Monitoring system use
A.10.10.3	Protection of log information
A.10.10.4	Administrator and operator logs
A.10.10.5	Fault logging
A.10.10.6	Clock synchronization
Network access control (A.11.4)	
A.11.4.1	Policy on the use of network services
A.11.4.2	User authentication for external connections
A.11.4.3	Equipment identification in networks
A.11.4.4	Remote diagnostics and configuration port protection
A.11.4.5	Segregation in networks
A.11.4.6	Network connection control
A.11.4.7	Network routing control
Mobile commuting and teleworking (A.11.7)	
Cryptographic controls (A.12.3)	
Information security incident management (A.13)	

Figure 5.27 Communication controls (continued)

5.8 NETWORK SECURITY

5.8.1 Risks

For the majority of organizations and users the Internet and other networks are the artery system for business. As industry and commerce are so dependent on ICT systems and the communications infrastructure that supports the connectivity of the systems, it is essential that the security of these networks is properly addressed. Depending what part the organization plays in the communication chain (e.g., consumers, customers and subscribers, service providers and ISPs, broadcast media companies or network carriers) means attending to a number of information security topics. ISO/IEC 27001 is aimed at all these types of users.

So on the one hand, a commercial publishing company that is using ISO/IEC 27001 might be using an Internet service provider (ISP) which may or may not be different from a company providing it with telecommunication services. On the other hand the telecommunications company may or may not be using ISO/IEC 27001. How it applies the standard will of course be different due to the services it offers, for example, securing a national communications backbone is different from securing an organization's internal LANs. They are all dealing with security risks and security controls but there are essential differences in some of the specific problems they need to deal with. ISO/IEC 27001 provides an information security framework for all needs for all these different types of organizations.

Security problems in networks can present themselves at the logical or physical level, different transport levels as well as the higher application levels. Some of the issues that have security implications at the network and infrastructure level include:

- Network management,

- Resilience and reliability,

- Quality and availability of services,

- Incident handling,

- Emergency and contingency aspects,

- Traffic-flow security,

- Application, transport and physical level security, emissions and emanation security,

- Integration of networks,

- Routing,

- DNS systems, name and addressing and directory systems and services.

These security areas are generally covered in ISO/IEC 27001 primarily in:

- Equipment Security (A.9.2),

- Network Security Management (A.10.6),

- Exchange of Information (A.10.8)

- Electronic commerce services (A.10.9),

- Monitoring (A.10.10),

- Network Access Control (A.11.4),

- Mobile Commuting and Teleworking (A.11.7),

- Cryptographic Controls (A.12.3),

- Information security Incident Management (A.13).

5.8.2 Network Management

Whether it is a PAN (personal area network), LAN (local area network), WLAN (wireless LAN), CAN (campus area network), MAN (metropolitan area network) or WAN (wide area network), network security will always be an issue.

Like other information security aspects the solution lies in a combination of good management controls with the appropriate security technology to achieve the desired levels of protection. A firewall is a good access control device but is of little use if it is not configured properly and regularly maintained and updated. A highly qualified and skilled person network or systems administrator needs to be supplied with sufficient tools to do this effectively.

Network management involves the maintenance and administration of computer networks and services, telecommunications networks, services and infrastucture to facilitate the controlling, planning, managing, deploying and monitoring the resources of a network.

Dealing with networking issues is a specialist job. It requires expertise, having the knowledge and experience of a range of communications and networking topics, security issues, ICT and cabling to name but a few areas.

There should be someone assigned, a network owner, whose task it is to be responsible for all network activities. In addition there may be a need, depending on the size of the organization and the complexity of the computer network system, for a network team that has the responsibility of running, configuring network components, dealing with network problems and being able to handle the "peaks" and "troughs" in network usage.

5.8.3 Configuration of Networks

5.8.3.1 Objective

Configuration is vital to maintain security technology to withstand business systems against malicious attacks. For example, a firewall is configured by the ingress and egress of traffic such as between the Internet and an organization's internal networks.

5.8.3.2 Best Practice

There are several configuration tasks that need to be done to facilitate network security such as:

- Overloads and/or exceptional network conditions should be detected and highlighted,

- Network logs should be produced and available,

- Incorrect and/or unauthorised updates and modifications should be prevented,

- Disable access to services that are not used and are not necessary for business operations,

- Access control methods and technology should be integrated with network devices to restrict access,

- Routing information should be protected from unauthorized disclosure, modification or incorrect updates in the system and being exchanged and communicated.

Configurations should be reviewed on a regular basis and updates should be made as and when necessary and appropriate.

5.8.4 Network Robustness and Resilience

5.8.4.1 Objective

Network availability is vital to the delivery of continuous services that most organizations are highly dependent on alongside the dependency of ICT systems for processing information.

To ensure the network is available and accessible as and when required, the network needs to be robust and highly resilient to withstand failures, disasters and malfunctions of its software and components.

5.8.4.2 Best Practice

Security risk controls include:

- Using backups and duplicated systems,

- Using alternative network administration points,

- Timely replacement of key network components, software and devices,

- Providing and arranging a fall-back process to facilitate, duplicate and/or alternate points of connection,

- Using alternative network carriers,

- Using more than one switch or exchange to re-route critical links and connections,

- Monitoring, managing and maintaining a properly configured firewall,

- Using backup/alternative firewalls for the rerouting of traffic,

- Regular testing and maintenance of network equipment and devices.

5.8.5 Network Capacity

5.8.5.1 Objective

The organization's networks should be able to cope with the current and future demands for user services, volumes of traffic, response times and levels of availability and other business requirements.

5.8.5.2 Best Practice

It is important that an organization carries out a regular capacity planning activity to assess current and future demands (Annex A.10.3.1).

5.8.6 Network Monitoring

5.8.6.1 Objective

Network monitoring (Annex A.10.10) generally refers to the activity that monitors the network for problems due to overloaded, underperforming, slow or failing network components and/or crashed servers, network connections or other devices. Monitoring is important to ensure availability of networks and services.

5.8.6.2 Technology

An example of monitoring technology is the intrusion detection system (IDS), which monitors a network to detect external threats and attacks. This type of system is used to observe network traffic to detect all types of malicious traffic and computer usage that can't be detected by conventional firewall protection. There are also several software tools for monitoring.

5.8.6.3 Metrics and Measurements

Monitoring normally involves the following types of metrics:

- Network response time (i.e. the time it takes to react),

- Availability or uptime (i.e. the proportion of time the network is functioning and delivering services),

- Consistency of the network to provide services,

- Reliability of the network to be able to maintain the provision of services with regard to these other metrics.

5.8.7 Network Access

5.8.7.1 Principles and Solutions

The principles of access control presented in Section 5.6 apply also to any network access scenario. There are a number of network components that can be configured to control unauthorized access to an organization's computer network. This is particularly important to control access from external users, either remote users working for the organization or other users not employed by the organization.

The old adage security is only as good as the weakest link is especially true of guarding against malicious network attacks and the people aspect of managing and controlling network access. Like all security technology it is only as good as the care and attention that is given to the management of this technology, with configuration, updates and good maintenance controls in place and of course someone with the right level of network skills and competency. If an organization does not have the right manpower to manage these technologies then it should seek help and advice from outside. There are managed services companies that offer this type of service.

5.8.7.2 Firewalls

One such network device for controlling access is the firewall, which can be configured to enforce the organization's security policy and to permit, deny or proxy network connections. It has become standard practice that network traffic to and from an organization's computer network is channeled through a firewall. This ensures that incoming and outgoing access is monitored and controlled. In particular it is important for controlling unauthorized access from some outside users and/or systems.

A firewall can also be used to segregate internal networks, for example, some internal computer networks maybe be dealing with more sensitive information and these need to be segregated from other internal computer networks dealing with non-sensitive information. It is vital that firewalls are properly configured and managed and maintained to gain the most benefit from this type of technology.

There are three basic types of firewall:

- Network layer firewalls which work at the network layer and function as IP-packet filters, not allowing packets to pass through the firewall unless they match the defined rules, at the (relatively) low level of the TCP/IP protocol stack,

- Application layer firewalls which work at the application layer and normally function to intercept packets going between applications,

- Application firewalls which are located at a level lower than the application layer and are sometimes known as operating system firewalls.

Firewalls require proper management and configuration and this demands considerable knowledge and understanding of network protocols and IT security, which the firewall administrator needs to have. Even the slightest of configuration mistakes can render a firewall compromised leaving the technology next to useless.

5.8.7.3 Firewall Best Practice

This includes configuring the firewall and its filters according to the following best practice:

- Apply strict control over communications that are known to be the cause of security compromises such as DNS, FTP, NNTP, SMTP, Telnet and various others,

- Block network packets that are known to facilitate denial of service (DoS) attacks such as ICMP Echo, TTP Echo, UDP and several others,

- Block or restrict communications to certain IP addresses and ports such as the FTP ports 20 and 21 and the Telnet port 23,

- Deny incoming or outgoing traffic where the source address is known to be "spoofed",

- Filter the network traffic using pre-defined rules to enforce the "principle of least access" and "separation of duties" principle (see Section 5.6),

- Follow the standard firewall rule "What is not expressly permitted is forbidden" as it is easier to give access than take it away. The rule the other way round should not be in force "What is not expressly forbidden is permitted",

- Be up to date with the organization's latest policy requirements and commensurate with the vendor's upgrades/patches and the latest information on Internet threats and vulnerabilities.

There are other network access technologies that may also be considered such as an Internet gateway using router technology, wireless gateways, network access servers, remote access protocol technologies and various others.

5.8.7.4 VPNs

Another way of restricting access to networks that need good security is the use of virtual private networks (VPNs). Typically this method connects two computer networks across a public network in such a way that this connection provides a private network thus assuring a certain degree of security to the end users regarding eavesdropping of confidential data, unauthorized data modification and unauthorized access. The VPN uses the standard public network protocols (an insecure transport channel) to support the private network protocols (a secure transport channel).

The VPN is a relatively inexpensive solution to achieving secure communications between two computer networks of different organizations, or across the organization itself with the ability to connect remote users, such as staff working off-site, to its computer network.

5.8.7.5 VPN Best Practice

The security of a VPN can be provided in several ways including:

- Use of cryptographic tunneling protocols such as the de facto standards IPSec and SSL/TLS, but there are many others available. These provide a measure of confidentiality (for blocking snooping and thus Packet sniffing), sender authentication (blocking identity spoofing) and message integrity (blocking message alteration),

- Use of PC firewalls for remote access to the organization's network or servers,

- Use of client firewalls for access to the organization's network or servers.

Of course, using a VPN is not the complete solution since there needs to be security measures at the user location and at the network management level, which is what ISO/IEC 27001 provides for in its requirements and controls.

5.8.7.6 IDS

The intrusion detection system (IDS), as the name infers, detects the presence of intruders in the network possibly wanting to gain unauthorized access into a computer system. These systems are designed to detect different types of malicious network traffic and computer system access and utilisation. These are events that are normally not detectable by a conventional firewall-based system such as:

- Network-driven attacks to exploit vulnerable services,

- Data-driven attacks on applications,

- Host-based attacks regarding system privileges escalation,

- Unauthorized access to sensitive and/or critical files.

Consequently there are different types of IDS depending on the protection objectives: network intrusion detection (NIDS), protocol intrusion detection (PIDS), application intrusion detection (AIDS), host based intrusion detection (HIDS) and of course there is a hybrid intrusion detection system of these types. The basic model of an IDS process is shown in Figure 5.28

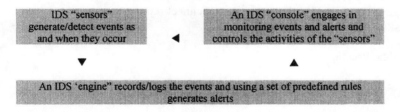

Figure 5.28 Example IDS process model

5.8.7.7 IPS

Another device is the intrusion prevention system (IPS), which is also able to exercise a degree of control over access to computer systems to protect them from exploitation. IPS, like the IDS technology, is another form of access control method performing a role similar to a firewall functioning at the application layer.

5.8.8 Wireless Security

5.8.8.1 Mobile Connectivity

With wireless connectivity there is a lack of protection, especially access to a wireless the user has no authority to use. This is a growing issue, especially when it comes to broadband (ADSL) connections and services, as well as the many access points that could be available. There are various wireless components that radiate their existence to anyone in the vicinity with a wireless capability on their laptop, mobile phone, PDA or other mobile device. Wireless base stations, modems, firewalls and routers are all capable of radiating the existence of a wireless network in the immediate vicinity.

5.8.8.2 Standards

Wi-Fi is the name associated with a set of WLAN (wireless LAN) technology based on the standard IEEE 802.11. The Wi-Fi concept originated by the Wi-Fi Alliance and the logos Wi-Fi and Wi-Fi Certified are their registered trademark.

5.8.8.3 Wi-Fi Jargon

There is a set of wireless jargon that has been deployed to indicate the location and presence of a wireless access point such as:

- "War chalking", marking on walls of a building (or on a pavement) to highlight the presence of an access point in the building/office,

- "War driving", searching for Wi-Fi access points whilst driving in a car or other vehicle and posting the results on a Web site,

- "War walking", searching for Wi-Fi access points whilst walking along streets and roads and posting the results on a Web site.

Of course there are signs put up on walls, such as in railway stations or airport departure lounges, by service providers advertising there is a Wi-Fi access point (wireless hotspot) provided by their company, normally these are protected and access is only possible if the user pays for it.

5.8.8.4 Wireless Best Practice

Wireless access points (WAP) by default are all open, unprotected access points to a wireless network hence they are insecure in this mode of operation. There are several measures to deter unauthorized users from getting wireless access and providing a degree of confidentiality including:

- If the service set identifier (SSID) has not been disabled then turn it off this is a basic/weak form of protection which needs to be supplemented with other security controls such as the use of encryption and authentication,

- Use of the IEEE 802.11 Wi-Fi security standards WPA (Wi-Fi Protected Access) and WPA2 (IEEE 802.11i). An earlier standard WEP (Wired Equivalent Privacy) is no longer being recommended since it was found to be flawed. Of course, Wi-Fi technology is advancing rapidly and therefore implementers should be alerted to the fact that any further security vulnerabilities might influence the currently recommended best practice. Industry will always need to be working on the next generation of security technology and Wi-Fi is no exception.

Many computers, especially laptops, have a wireless capability built in avoiding the need for a wireless receiving device (e.g., USB device or a PCMI device) needing to be connected to the laptop. If the user has this permanently switched on then it is continuously broadcasting the fact of its wireless accessibility which any other computer with a wireless capability could detect. This might be a security concern and one which users and organizations need to pay particular attention.

5.8.9 DNS Security

The DNS (Domain Name System) is a critical Internet tool and facility since it can store many important pieces of information and associates this with the domain name and then maps this to IP addresses. In addition it provides a list of those mail exchange servers, which accept emails. Like many other Internet standards originally, they were not designed with security in mind and DNS falls into this category.

Some of the problems relate to spoofing issues, which the DNSSEC standard (RFC 2535) is designed to counter, including:

- Lack of origin authentication of DNS data,

- Lack of data integrity,

- Lack of protection to control denial of existence.

The DNS facility can be used to deal with public domain Internet functionality and information or it might be used for an organization's Intranet system. In both cases there are security problems relating to the information the DNS is handling. An organization's DNS can and does have information, addresses and identifiers about the systems connected to its Intranet, which could be useful to outsiders that want to launch a network attack on the organization.

Therefore this information is quite sensitive and critical for the protection of internal computing resources and so this needs to be protected in such a way as to avoid unauthorized access to this information. There are several ways of achieving this such as the use of proxy servers and a public facing DNS servers and an internal DNS server arrangement.

5.8.10 Network Service Providers

The provisioning of network services should be done through a provider that is capable of delivery services to suit the needs and security requirements of the organization. Service level agreements (SLAs) and contracts with service providers (as described in Section 5.7.2) should state:

- Responsibilities for networks and services both for the contractor and the organization,

- Capacity requirements,

- Availability, continuity and accessibility requirements to a particular set of services,

- Requirements and methods for ensuring the non-disclosure of confidential information,

- Requirements on restriction on methods of service connection,

- Process of dealing with security incidents and service interruptions.

- Change management process.

Service contracts and SLAs should be reviewed on a regular basis and updates should be made as and when necessary and appropriate.

5.9 USE OF CRYPTOGRAPHIC TECHNOLOGY

5.9.1 Business Use of Cryptography

Cryptographic tools such as encryption and digital signatures can provide a secure way of protecting information such as for the purposes of:

- Confidentiality of sensitive information,

- Integrity and authenticity of information,

- Authentication and identification applications (such as A.11.4.2 and A.11.4.3) including Identity Management Systems,

- Anonymity and pseudonymity applications,

- Non-repudiation applications such as for a digital proof of the sender and/or receivers of messages,

- Digital Rights Management (DRM) and Digital Copyrighting to protect the intellectual property rights (see A.15.1.2) of an organization regarding the products they have in software, electronic books, DVDs and CDs containing music, pictures or movies.

There are many technologies and products available to provide both encryption and digital/electronic signature capability. These products vary in their strength, performance and ease of use and application. Together with any specific technology that might be used there is also a need to consider the management of those parameters such as secret-keys and public-keys. The cryptographic security can and does present many challenges for business implementers of this type of technology.

5.9.2 Policy in the Use of Cryptography

ISO/IEC 27001 is not concerned with what specific type of encryption and/or digital/electronic signature techniques, methods or technology is used to provide confidentiality or integrity support. What ISO/IEC 27001 is mainly concerned with is the need for establishing a policy on the use of cryptographic techniques (see A.12.3.1) and aspects of key management (see A.12.3.2).

There are plenty of good reference books going into the technical details of these techniques as well as many good ISO standards that provide specifications of cryptographic systems and their application such as for authentication purposes.

A policy is necessary to inform staff:

- What is allowed and not allowed regarding the use of cryptographic technology both for internal and off-site use (acceptable use),

- Authorization process for approving user utilisation,

- User responsibilities and approved methods for the utilisation.

- Which types of information, which applications (e.g., sending confidential files over an email system) and which ICT (e.g., on laptops used for off-site visits and meetings) need to be protected using cryptographic technology,

- The arrangements for key management,

- Who is responsible for management of the use of cryptographic technology in the organization,

- Legal aspects and restrictions (see Section 5.9.3).

5.9.3 Legal Aspects

In addition to the policy side there is also the legal aspect, which ISO/IEC 27001 is concerned with (see A.15.1.6). For many years there have been export regulations regarding the export of products containing cryptographic technology. This includes its use both in software and hardware products.

In recent years in many countries these restrictions have been relaxed although certain limitations and export licenses still exist in some of these countries such as the United States. Those participating in the so-called Wassenaar Arrangement also have similar restrictions. Advice on this aspect should be obtained from someone knowledgeable about laws and cryptography.

5.10 AUTHENTICATION AND IDENTIFICATION SYSTEMS

5.10.1 Do We Know Who You Are?

Knowing whom someone is and being able to check and verify his/her identity is fundamental to avoiding several security problems. The authenticity of certain attributes linked, especially those that are unique, to a user needs to be checked to collaborate the user is who he says he is and whether the user is masquerading as the real user. These attributes are something to determine:

- What the user knows (such as a login name, a password, a PIN,

- What the user has (such as a computer readable token, a Smartcard, or a card key),

- Who the user is (such as some form of data related to the user e.g., biometric fingerprint, retinal pattern, iris pattern, hand configuration),

- What the user does (such as voice recognition of a user, or the user's signature).

Protection of these attributes against fraudulent use is of the essence. There are several methods and technologies of achieving the identification and authentication of a user and some of these methods will be listed below.

5.10.2 Authentication: The All Important Preprocess

The organization needs both a method of identifying and authenticating users sometimes referred to as I&A. In many applications authentication is an important preprocess combined with other security measures such as:

- Authorization, which verifies that someone has the authority to do something including making payments, withdrawing funds, signing contracts, having access to something,

- Access control, which checks that someone has the rights and privileges to access something.

Sometimes the "authorization" process is used in the context of authentication and authorization combined.

5.10.3 Why Do We Need These Measures?

These methods are needed to support the implementation of several of the controls in ISO/IEC 27001 Annex A, for example:

- To allow users to logon and have access to information, information systems, applications and business processes (e.g., A.10.7.1 and A.11.4 to A.11.7),

- To give users access to networks and service (e.g., A.11.4),

- To give users physical access to buildings, office and ICT equipment such as PCs and laptops, mobile phones, PDAs and BlackBerries, storage device access such as USB sticks and external hard drives access (e.g., A.9, A.10.9, A.11.6 and A.11.7).

5.10.4 How Can We Achieve Protection?

There are many ways to achieve authentication. The simplest is considered to be that based on what a user knows (a password or a PIN) commonly referred to as "one-factor" authentication. If two of the factors/attributes mentioned in Section 5.10.1 are combined such as what a user knows and has (e.g., a PIN and a bank card) then this is commonly referred to as "two-factor" authentication. It goes without saying that "one-factor" is the weakest form of authentication whereas those methods based on "two or more factors" are much stronger.

A word of caution in the use of the terms weak and strong authentication can often mislead. If what a user knows, has, is or does is not protected then even a "two or more factor" strong authentication could be compromised. If a user's PIN is known (e.g., obtained by shoulder-surfing at an ATM or in a store or shop) and the user's card is stolen then this "two-factor" authentication has been weakened and broken.

There have been cases where complete files of PINs have been stolen from an organization's server. The message is that whatever the user knows, has and so on, needs to be protected against visible, physical or electronic theft. Identify theft is a growing problem which users are experiencing everyday and the cost of this threat to users and organizations is rising fast. Identity management is a fast growing and developing area of standards and technology.

Cryptographic methods are often used to implement the strong authentication solutions (see Section 5.9). Other types of technology include:

- *One-time password devices* involve the generation of a dynamic password (e.g., every 60 seconds) associated with a user PIN. the passwords are "random" making it hardly likely for any repetition of passwords at least to the extent that the security of passwords could be compromised. The user has a small pocketsize hand-held device that generates the password based on the user's PIN, and the computer system uses the same password generator to check the user's PIN plus password combination,

- *Digital certificates/IDs* are used for authentication purposes, for example, in Web on-line applications or VPN clients where the security is normally provided by a security protocol such as SSL or IPSec, the authenticity of the user and certificate are checked by a system (usually a Certification Authority or CA), although this provides a good level of security it does depend on the integrity of the certificate being maintained,

- *Smart cards, USB tokens and other tokens* are technologies which rely on the utilisation of various techniques such as dynamic passwords or digital certificates,

- *Single-sign-on technology* provides a unified approach to achieving identification and authentication where more than one application is involved so rather than the user being authenticated for each application he/she wants access to is authenticated once,

- *Biometric technology* covers many different types of characteristics associated with the user such as fingerprint, retina features, facial geometry, voice and several other user biometric features.

Figure 5.29 provides an overview of the above techniques. In addition to what is detailed below consideration also needs to be given to the level of resource needed for managing the utilisation of these technologies.

Technology	Security Level	User Impact	ICT System Impact
Passwords/ PINS	Low	Low	Low-medium
One-time Passwords	High (H/W)	Medium (H/W)	Medium (H/W)
Digital Certificates	Medium	Low	Medium-high
Smart Cards/Tokens	Medium-high	Medium	High
Biometrics	Medium-high	High	High

Figure 5.29 Overview of technology

Chapter 6

ISMS Utilisation and Keeping Up To Date

6.1 ISMS APPLICATIONS

"A journey of a thousand miles began with a single step (千里之行，始于足下)." from the Tao Te Ching

6.1.1 Scenarios

The following sections present a number of scenarios based on real-world models of some of the applications of ISMS. For obvious reasons the names of organizations have been removed. These scenarios will be referred to later in this chapter to illustrate specific security features of these applications.

6.1.2 SME Design Services

A small company with 11 full-time staff provides household designs for domestic users. This includes customised fitted kitchens and bathrooms, studies and living and dining rooms. The company consists of consultants and designers, salespeople, showroom staff, the owner and a secretary.

The company has been in business for 7 years and are well recognised as a supplier of quality designs. The company has just one showroom/office located on the ground floor of a five storey building in a busy high street of a town in the UK. The company is already implementing an ISMS. It now wants to expand its IT solutions to network its PCs, give remote access via consultants' laptops when it is on customer sites, add Web site services to its customers and wants to expand its business to open another office in the Netherlands to provide the same sort of services.

The company has carried out a SWOT (strengths, weaknesses, opportunities and threats) analysis to assess the feasibility of the objectives and potential success of expansion. Based on this analysis it decides to go ahead. Its business implementation plan includes an extension of the scope of its ISMS to include its Web site presence, remote access and its office in the Netherlands.

Through a gap analysis it identifies what its existing information security system includes:

- An information security policy,

- Procedures on backups, viruses and handling personnel and customer information,

- Password control on all office PCs and consultant laptops,

- Physical access controls to its offices, rooms and filing cabinets.

A target ISMS scope is defined to cover all existing operational needs as well as future plans for expansion. A risk assessment is performed on existing assets and the acquisition of new assets and ICT resources, the results of which are evaluated and developed into a risk treatment and ISMS implementation plan.

As its future business plan rolls out over the coming six months so does the implementation of its ISMS and within the next six months the company has plans to be fully operational. Its Internet side of the business starts to grow as they are getting more customer enquiries and orders, as does the number of staff employed by the company.

6.1.3 Legal Services

A small legal firm with 17 full-time staff provides legal advice for both commercial businesses as well as citizens. The firm has three offices in the UK: London, Edinburgh and Belfast. It has been established for over 25 years and has many high-profile businesses on its books. Over the last 3 to 4 years it has relied more and more on the use of ICT and the Internet. It is now becoming quite clear that it needs to do something about its information security.

The firm doesn't really have any management system for information security. It does have some of the basic controls in place but none of these are integrated together or utilised in a way to provide any effective protection of its own and its clients' information assets.

The decision to go down the route of using ISO/IEC 27001 was made after the firm was made aware of other firms in the legal services business going down the same route. Its main ICT resources and Internet capability consist of:

- A number of office PCs networked together to a central server (one in each office),

- Internet access through this server,

- Laptops, BlackBerries and mobiles (all Wi-Fi enabled) used by legal professionals.

Its information assets include:

- Client confidential case files, reports, letters, statements and other documents,

- The firm's internal confidential and restricted information, documents and files,

- Library of legal books, works of reference and generally other publicly available information.

The task it embarked on (with the help of external consultants) was a risk assessment relating to its information assets and they utilised its ICT resources commensurate with the nature of its business. This revealed a number of exposures including:

- The unprotected use of the Internet to communicate between the firm's offices as well as to its clients,

- Direct connection between the internal server and the Internet (no firewall in place),

- The use of the laptops and other mobile devices in the Wi-Fi enabled mode, especially in public places and for remote access into the firm's servers,

- No information security policy or procedures,

- Lack of awareness of the risks,

- Limited/weak access control over the confidential information assets.

This led the legal firm to fix all these problems and to establish and implement an ISMS, to the requirements of ISO/IEC 27001. It followed this with an audit carried out by an independent certification body and achieved a clean bill of health.

6.1.4 Electronic Accounting Systems

The management of a large retail company decides to install a fully integrated electronic accounting system but before the decision is made they checked the requirements for achieving an effective level of information security. The current accounting system does use PCs, but these are not networked together to provide a streamlined start to finish process for handling sales, purchases, orders, invoices, payments, delivery and dispatch notes. Its future plans require the installation of an ICT system networked throughout the company and external customers and suppliers, with appropriate software application packages, which enable staff to process and share information on-line within the company and also to electronically send orders, payments and other documents to suppliers and customers.

Although the company has information security measures in place it decides to carry out a complete overhaul of its information security taking account of existing controls. It recruits someone as its security officer and together with IT departments such as sales, purchasing, finance, operations and IT it develops an ISMS design based on ISO/IEC 27001.

The company gets management approval and commitment to implement this ISMS design across all the five locations. As the project is quite sizable and it wants to achieve this electronic accounting system development as soon as possible to take advantage of the business benefits of such a system and provide added value to its customers they decide to supplement the internal project team with external consultants.

The project is not without its setbacks, as commercial pressures indicate a greater need to have the system fully operational as soon as possible. In addition, the gap analysis and risk assessment were not as easy to accomplish due to the multisite nature of the project, the current lack of coordination, consistency and integration of the current system and some local resistance from staff regarding issues to do with change and questions on security. It is then agreed that the senior management must get more closely involved to show full support and to commit to more resources. After several months of delay in making progress the company rolls out a fully operational electronic accounting system with information security in place. Due to this experience management is persuaded to recruit a second full time employee to support the security officer to maintain the ISMS. The company, over the next six to nine months, prepares itself for third party certification, which it achieves.

6.1.5 Government Payment System

A government department in Southeast Asia operates as an off-line and on-line payment system refunding citizens for their Social Security claims. As with many governments around the world, the attraction of its converting business processes to utilize e-commerce technology exists and this trend is growing. This is irrespective of whether it will be dealing with supplier chains, citizen information on government departments, payment claims from social security to state health schemes, e-tax, e-driver licences, e-voting, e-procurement or many other applications that involve government to government, government to business or government to citizen transactions and sharing of information. Another government department whose responsibility it is to advise on information security matters recommends the ISO/IEC 27001 ISMS route.

This particular government department always had information security measures due to the sensitive nature of the claims it was handling, especially as it was involved general personal data as well as more specific details such as health-related information. Its future plans covered moving over to a more electronic way of submitting claims to social services Internet café type facilities in government centres and offices around the country, all networked to the department dealing with social services. The ISMS had to deal with citizen privacy technology, citizen smart cards for identification and authentication purposes, as well as accessing the system, secure exchange of citizen information and secure information processing facilities in the government department concerned. Of course around this is the management framework for making this function effective.

The scale of this project is large and complex and so it is decided to roll this out in phases focusing on one particular town of a medium-sized population to trial out the ISMS design to improve the design where necessary and then to proceed with other towns to gradually cover the whole country. This first trial was successful although the ISMS did need various adjustments. For the subsequent phases work is still in progress.

6.1.6 Outsourcing Call Centre Operations

A major international European-based company outsources its call centre operations to a company in Asia. This type of business change in operations has become very common and popular over the years and one that is not expected to change but to grow. Its call centre operations cover customers all over Europe and the daily number of enquiries continues to grow due to its business successes. However, for reasons of streamlining the business and cost cutting it decides to outsource its call centre.

Dealing with the risks of outsourcing needs a lot of attention. It is of utmost importance that an information security risk assessment is carried out before undertaking such an operational change, especially to overseas countries. This is not say that the risks cannot be managed to safeguard the company assets but without doing such an activity and putting in place the appropriate measures to manage the risks then the company will very likely lose all the benefits it expects to gain from an outsourcing deployment of its facilities if the impacts of no information security take their full effect.

Chapter 4 provided an example of the risks associated with third party services (Chapter 4, Section 4.2.1). In this particular business scenario above the geographical location and the risks of the location are important considerations to take account of, such as:

- What hazards apply to this particular area of the world? Is it in an earthquake zone or an area prone to volcanic activity, tornadoes,

typhoons, tsunamis or other natural phenomenons? Many areas in Asia
have these types of problem,

- Is the location in an area of political and social stability? Is it
  economically stable?

- Are the communication systems able to cope with the volume of customer
  traffic?

- Can the outsourced company supply an adequate number of competent
  staff to fulfill the contract requirements (e.g., communication skills,
  knowledge, experience and language skills)?

- Can the outsourced company supply enough facilities and resources to
  fulfill the contract requirements (e.g., sufficient capacity to meet demands,
  effective information security, backup, disaster recovery and business
  continuity arrangements, response times, performance and service levels)?

- Can the location and its facilities be easily secured from a physical
  perspective from local threats?

Of course, all the information security risks also apply to other organizations,
equally to the outsourcing company. ISO/IEC 27001 is very often used by
outsourcing companies to demonstrate to its customers that it is "fit for purpose"
and in several cases such companies have been certified to this standard. It could
be the case that the customer itself requires the outsourced company to be
certified; there are also real examples of this and the outsourced companies did
get certified.

6.1.7 ICT Services

An ICT services group of a company designs and produces various quality
products for organizations that use trophies, shields, glass awards and other items
that are given to customers for its business loyalty. It also produces a number of
corporate publicity items for conferences, exhibitions and other events. The
company relies heavily on the use of ICT for its design work, its automated
production line, handling on-line orders and for customer deliveries. Its business
is derived both from on-line and telephone customers. The company has
developed a worldwide network of customers through its on-line process, in fact
40% of its business is from overseas customers and this marketing is growing.

Management tasked the ICT services group to review its current information
security management position and status. The group has always had various ICT
security controls in place; its task is now to review this and to progress towards
developing an ISMS for its ICT services with the possibility of then becoming

certified against ISO/IEC 27001. The ICT services group achieves an ISMS implementation, which has now gone into operation. Over the coming six months the ICT services group are presented with a number of minor problems, which they took action over to resolve. Its next plan of action is to prepare for the ISO/IEC 27001 certification of its ISMS.

6.1.8 On-line Services

A small-medium sized company provides various on-line services in Germany for several publishing houses. It has built up a very viable and profitable business in the provisioning of these services. It has established a reputation in the market for the quality and speed of response to its customers' demands. As the number of its customers' orders increased then so did the company resources expand both in staff numbers and its ICT facilities.

Even from the start the company always took the topic of information security seriously and implemented a "light-weight version" of ISMS based on ISO/IEC 27001. With the increase in company size and its ICT resources it decided to take its ISMS a stage further and to implement more information security measures, as well as tighten up the deployment and utilisation of these measures. One specific area it improved in was its incident handling process as well as the introduction of more stringent policies and procedures in certain areas, such as its "acceptable use policy" regarding company ICT resources (see Section 6.3.13).

6.1.9 Manufacturing Systems

A successful medium-sized manufacturing business is certified to ISO 9001 Quality management system (QMS) requirements standard. It has now decided that it should consider applying ISO/IEC 27001 across its business to complement its ISO 9001 capability. It would eventually like to integrate the two systems together to create an efficient and effective management framework to gain the cost-benefits of having an integrated certification audit.

Its current information security practice seemed to have been sufficient in past years but there is growing awareness of the threats and risks it faces from observing market trends in their particular industry sector. An additional drive towards gaining more awareness was the fact that one of its competitors suffered a damaging attack on one of its ICT-based automated production lines. It employed a consultant to do a gap analysis and risk assessment of its current systems. The results of this were quite startling for the company as it turned out its current information security provisions were only 35% compliant with ISO/IEC 27001 and in fact 20% of these had been picked up by the recent ISO 9001 surveillance audit as things that had an impact on its QMS implementation. Even more startling was the large areas of noncompliance, 55% of which turned out to be high-risk areas based on the results of the consultant's risk report. The main areas of risk were:

- Insufficient access control for operating systems, internal networked services and applications,

- Lack of procedures in a number of key areas, such as for information handling and backups,

- No real information security incident handing process,

- The gateway to the Internet was wide open to external threats allowing relatively easy access to its internal network,

- Lack of information security awareness and training across the whole company,

- Lack of information security considerations in its contracts and SLAs with third party service providers,

- No vulnerability management controls,

- Many open doors to the threat of social engineering, both on-line and off-line,

- A very flimsy attempt at business continuity.

After several management decision making meetings it decided to go ahead with developing an ISMS for the whole company. It contracted the work to a small company specializing in ISMS standards, which had a track record in different parts of the world in helping clients to establish an ISO/IEC 27001 compliant system. After an intensive contracting period it got there in the end. The company even went a stage further and got certified to ISO/IEC 27001, out timing its competitor. The next challenge was to work with its Certification Body towards planning an integrated ISO 9001 and ISO/IEC 27001 audit.

6.1.10 Identity and Access Management System

IAM (identity and access management) has become a fast-growing area of enterprise-wide security. Theft of user identities, credit card details, private and personal data, company confidential information and other information assets has accelerated with the growing utilisation of the Internet, e-commerce, mobile and wireless communications and various other technological advancements. The combination of identity, authentication and access control measures to protect such information assets has become a powerful tool against the above-mentioned types of theft.

The application of ISO/IEC 27001 as a management framework for IAM deployment across an enterprise is considered by some organizations to be an international solution that works and has brought them immediate benefits. Some have used ISO/IEC 27001 as an all-embracing management framework to meet all its information security management requirements, not just for IAM. This is what ISO/IEC 27001 was designed for. The best practice management measures in ISO/IEC 27001 Annex A supporting IAM include:

- Asset management (Annex A.7) such as,

    - Acceptable use of assets,
    - Information classification,
    - Information handling,

- Operational and communication measures (Annex A.10) such as,

    - Operating procedures,
    - Third party services,
    - Backup procedures,
    - Control of malicious software code,
    - Information handling,
    - Exchange of information,
    - E-commerce and e-office protection,
    - Monitoring usage,

- Access control management (Annex A.11) such as,

    - User privileges, access rights and responsibilities,
    - Operating system access,
    - Network service access,
    - User authentication,
    - Applications and information access,
    - Mobile computing access,

- Development, acquisition and maintenance of systems (Annex A.12) such as,

    - Security requirements for IAM,
    - Message authenticity and integrity,
    - Use of cryptographic techniques,

- Incident handling measures (Annex A.13),

- Legal measures (Annex A.15) such as,

  - Data privacy and protection laws,
  - Computer misuse.

6.1.11 Supply Chain Management

Supply chains are the life-blood of most organizations. They need to work efficiently and effectively with their customers. They need to survive in fast moving and dynamic customer markets, where market competition, customer satisfaction, timeliness and profitability are the name of the game. The supply chain can be viewed as a networked system of organizations, human resources, operations and communications, information and ICT resources, all working together in delivering a product or service to the end customer.

Typical examples of this are on-line purchasing of books, food supply chains, car parts, components and subassemblies to support car manufacturers, energies supplies, supply chains supporting the construction industry, supply chains supporting the travel industry, such as airline travel, or chains supporting the production and supply of medicines for the healthcare industry. All of these supply chains need to run both efficiently and effectively to fulfill customer and consumer needs and demands.

Supply chains link together an organization's value chain of activities, such as the logistics of both its inbound and outbound traffic, its operations in producing things or delivering services, its marketing and sales support and its maintenance support.

Outsourcing companies (sometimes referred to as third party logistics provider or 3PL) are available to support an organization's supply chain, such as in the provisioning of integrated warehousing and transportation services.

Again, like with other case studies given in this chapter, ISO/IEC 27001 can be applied as a management framework for supply chain management. Some organizations that supply logistic support services have been certified against ISO/IEC 27001 for this very purpose, especially those that also provide international logistic support.

6.1.12 Utility Metering and Data Collection Services

In the energy supply industries, such as in the supply of electricity or gas, the supplier needs to collect information about the consumption of energy per household or per business to be able to send customers monthly or quarterly bills and consumption statements. In several countries there are many competing suppliers in this field, so several of them subcontract the work on an outsourcing basis. Therefore, independent companies have been established to handle thousands of suppliers at any one time. So typically you might have an outsourcing company handling the data for over 10,000 suppliers, as well as handling over 350,000 energy consumers.

An important aspect of this work is to keep consumer details confidential but also that of the competing suppliers, as well as keeping the supplier details separated from each other to avoid disclosure of tariff rates and other competing facts. The metering of consumption can be done remotely or manually using hand-held recording devices.

This seems a clear example of the ISMS route being a useful way of protecting all this data. In fact, a UK company not only used the ISMS approach but became certified by a third party certification body.

6.2 EFFECTIVE INFORMATION SECURITY

"Cause is the effect concealed, effect is the cause revealed." which is also expressed as "Cause is the effect unmanifested, effect is the cause manifested." A translated interpretation from the Upanishads.

6.2.1 Management of Risks

Proper management and treatment of the risks can cause lead to achieving effectiveness of information security, whereas information security incidents are the manifestation of a threat, or threats, exploiting one or more vulnerabilities. The management of the risks to avoid this manifestation from becoming a problem should be a key objective.

Achieving effective information security is one of the main goals of ISO/IEC 27001. Achieving and maintaining effectiveness can be done at different levels. To be effective is "to do the right things" to affect the level of performance or accomplishment to be achieved. In ISMS terms we need to accomplish the effective management of the business information security risks. As was understood from Chapter 4, having the knowledge of the causality of the threats and vulnerabilities and understanding the incidents related to the ISMS enables us to make the right decisions on how to manage the risks and impacts to meet the business objectives of the organization.

6.2.2 Measuring

There are a number of things that can be done to measure the effectiveness of the ISMS in response to these security causalities, such as:

- Appropriate monitoring and measurements being taken,

- Having a business-wide incident handling process in place,

- Having procedures in place that are suitably utilised and working properly,

- Training and awareness of staff that works in the organization,

- Having suitable and regular management reviews and audits and the gathering of appropriate information via staff feedback, scorecards and/or brainstorming exercises.

The sections that follow in this chapter take the reader through these issues and present a process to measure effectiveness and monitor and manage changes and improvements.

6.3 ISMS MEASUREMENT SYSTEM

"Man is the measure of all things." Protagoras (c.490 - c.420 BCE)

6.3.1 Introduction

Metrics are important in information security management to measure the effectiveness of the various processes that are used to deliver information security to protect the organization's information assets and that of its customers and suppliers. Taking measurements enables the organization to:

- Accomplish a valued assessment as to how well it is doing and how well the risk controls it is utilizing are performing,

- Gather information on the risks it faces for informed decision making,

- Make improvements,

- Set benchmarks,

- Demonstrate to the CEO, directors, senior management and the board the value of information security.

Taking measurements is at the root of achieving, maintaining and improving ISMS effectiveness. To comply with the requirements in ISO/IEC 27001, the organization needs to define:

- A set of metrics to measure against,

- What is to be measured and what are useful units of measurement,

- What procedures and methods should be used and how should these measurements be utilised,

- How often the measurements should be taken,

- How to deploy measurement methods to measure the effectiveness of the ISMS,

- What are information security thresholds and how are the thresholds estimated and calculated,

- Key performance indicators and how to undertake reviews of the effectiveness of the ISMS measurement system.

Whatever system of metrics and measurements an organization puts in place, the metrics and measurements should be objective, reliable, accurate, repeatable, verifiable and relevant and quantifiable against the business targets.

6.3.2 Some Examples

The following are some examples to illustrate different things that can be measured:

- Measuring the ISMS risk assessment and treatment processes,

- Measuring the performance of the information security incident handling process,

- Measuring the results of regular ISMS audits,

- Measuring the costs and benefits against information security being in place and not being in place, costs of recovery, costs against impact analysis, other costs and information security dependencies,

- Measuring the operational performance of staff and their knowledge and utilisation of security procedures,

- Measuring the usage and demand for information processing resources to help with capacity planning.

6.3.3 Reporting of Measurements

The results of measurements need to be communicated to its intended audience in a way that is meaningful and useful. Some may only have a use to and be meaningful for security managers, security administrators and managers of networks and ICT services. Other measurements may be targeted at senior management and need to reflect its areas of business interest. Being overtechnical is one problem that might occur, whereas oversimplified or overcomplicated results and messages are not the best way forward. A balance is needed to the amount of technical detail included, too much or too little can result in not giving or masking the important messages. At the end of the day these measurements will be used in decision making, so how they are represented and presented could make a huge difference to whether or not well-informed decision making can be achieved.

6.3.4 Review and Improvements

It is important that whatever metrics and measurement system is in place there is a need to review how good the system is at delivering meaningful, useful and timely results. The ISMS PDCA cycle requires such reviews to take place regularly. There is always room for improvements, no one can get these measurement processes fully correct from the word go and it is unlikely that such a goal can never be attained. What makes measurements a moving target is that changes, both internally and externally to an organization, are a reality, a fact of life and this will always mean that new challenges and problems will arise. So review of the measurement system is an opportunity to make improvements.

However, not only are changes affecting the organization a reason for a review, but there are other issues that could be addressed in the review, such as:

- What are the resource costs for operating this ISMS measurement system?

- How much money has it saved the organization so far in terms of countering security problems and harmful business impacts?

- Have the measurements provided a better insight and understanding of the effectiveness of the organization's information security?

- Is the organization getting value for its money?

- Are some metrics and measurements better than others at delivering value-added results?

A final thought is that measurements can be taken at different times during the ISMS PDCA life cycle. Measurements are taken during the risk assessment phase about the risks and impacts the organization faces, during the treatment of risk and the selection of risk controls phases and also during the implementation and utilisation phases. These different aspects should be an interlinked chain of measurements to provide a coherent and meaningful end result.

6.3.5 Measurements in Practice

There are a number of key points that should be kept in mind and the organization should guard against them if it is to achieve an effective measurement system such as the:

- Quantity, quality and timeliness,

  - Measuring the wrong things,
  - Measuring too many things,
  - Measuring at the wrong time frame (i.e. insufficiently often or not frequently enough),
  - Collecting too many measurements that are not used,
  - Gathering imprecise measurements or irrelevant measurements,
  - Measuring too few things,

- Use and interpretation of measurements,

  - Wrong use,
  - Inappropriate use,
  - Wrong interpretation of measurement results,
  - Right use (e.g., to gain a better understanding of the state of information security, to motivate or encourage staff, to assess the competence of individual members of staff).

6.3.6 Compliance with Policy Procedures and Legislation

At the core of the ISMS is the information security policy, then the procedures and control measures for implementing this policy and to achieve compliance against the legislation, regulation and contractual obligations also need to be complied with.

The compliance aspect presents a number of possible metrics and measurements such as the:

- Number of recorded incidents, involving noncompliance issues,

  - Problems with data protection/privacy of an individual's personal information,
  - Computer misuse, hacking, downloads of undesirable information and media,
  - Abuse of copyright laws and licensing agreements,
  - Noncompliance with the company's information security policy and procedures,

- Number of staff that lack training and awareness of information security policy and procedures,

- Number of systems, processes and applications that are not compliant with the company's information security standards, such as ISO/IEC 27001 if this has been adopted by the company,

- Number of failures of delivery services against an agreed contract or SLA.

6.3.7 System Accounts Management

It is often presented in many surveys and reports that a high percentage of the risk of exposure appear through internal activities. Of course, internal staff has more access rights and privileges to systems, processes, applications and information. The insider therefore has a better chance of causing a security breach than an outsider. Hence, if there are weaknesses in the management of user accounts, the subsequent utilisation of these accounts might result in the organization having a problem. If there are further problems with the user identification and authentication system and the access controls that dictate what the user can do with information then the problem might be building up to a disaster.

The ISMS should be properly implemented and utilised to ensure the system accounts are correctly managed, user accounts are carefully monitored and that a regular review is carried out to update accounts as and when necessary, for example, when an employee leaves the organization or when the job role changes.

The management of user accounts presents a number of possible metrics and measurements, such as the:

- Number of system accounts,
  - Normal,
  - Special privileges,
  - Administrator privileges

- Number of log-in accounts,

  - Never logged in,
  - Logged in not within the last month,
  - Infrequently logged in,

- Number of unused accounts of ex-employees still in the system,

- Number of failed or unsuccessful login attempts,

- Number of recorded incidents related to user account problems.

6.3.8 Effectiveness of User Training and Awareness

Users, staff, management and even contractors (sufficient to honour its contractual obligations) should have an awareness and understanding of the organization's information security policies and procedures. In the case of contractors, what they are allowed to access should be sufficient to honour its contractual obligations. For internal awareness and training staff this can range in depth, depending on the job role and how much involvement they have in information security. It should not be forgotten that all staff has some involvement. In-house courses and training, on and off the job, provide some of the ways in which training and awareness can be given. In addition, staff might be sent on external courses, this is especially the case in the more specialist areas, such as firewalls, intrusion detection systems, network security and other technical topics.

The metrics and measurements that can be considered include:

- Number of employees attending awareness training and how much training do they get,

- Types of training given, depth of scope and content, relevance,

- Exams, test and course assessments results, scores and marks, to evaluate the success of the training,

- Has staff had sufficient training and do they understand enough to enable them to put into practice and to utilize the policies and procedures correctly and properly in its job function (e.g., regarding backups, reporting incidents, processing information)? Checks should be made on the operational deployment and utilisation of staff training through regular reviews and audits, operational observations, feedback, questionnaires, interviews, scorecards and on-line self-tests,

- Regularity of refresher training given and how many staff are given such training,

- Cost of training.

6.3.9 Case Study of Personnel Group Tracking Trends

The Personnel Group, from the same organization as the ICT services group referred to in the scenario in Section 6.1.6, has been tracking the trends of some of its awareness and training programmes. The trends for the year 2006 are illustrated in Figure 6.1.

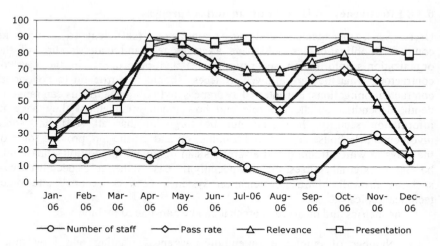

Figure 6.1 Awareness and training trends for the year 2006

The group considered: the number of staff that went through training, the overall percentage pass rate for each month, an overall percentage of relevance of the training content to their particular jobs according to the feedback provided by each member of staff, and finally it looked at the knowledge and presentation skills of the tutors as perceived by each member of staff when they went through training.

On analysing this information, the Personnel Group identified that the dip in results during the January/March period may be due to the skills of the tutor since in late March they employed a new tutor and also this tutor was absent during the August period during which the results dipped again. The only other time the results dipped was during December, which it was not really able to comment on.

Other aspects not related to the tutor were analysed, such as seasonal variances in attendance, such as in August and December, course content and different teaching methods. One possibility it is now considering is one on the job interactive training, coupled with using some on-line teaching packages, which users can utilize at their workplace.

6.3.10 Case Study ICT Services Group Tracking Trends

The ICT services group referred to in the scenario in Section 6.1.6 has been tracking the trends of some of its most serious incidents. The trends for the year 2006 are illustrated in Figure 6.2.

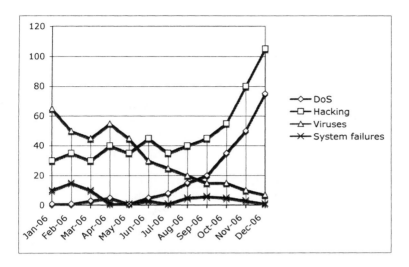

Figure 6.2 Serious incident trends

As can be seen from this chart the ICT group has been successful at curbing the number of virus incidents due to a concerted effort across the company to stamp down on this particular problem. The number of system failures has also been reduced. The increase in the number of incidents of failures, supposedly due to the roll-out of a new batch of PCs and applications software for the sales and marketing department and time needed to resolve any teething problems with its utilisation is a trend that needs to be monitored and kept in check.

The worrying trends shown on this chart are those related to the number of unauthorized access attempts together with the rise in the number of denial of service attacks. Taking measurements to indicate these trends has enabled the ICT services group to have a better understanding of the success of its ISMS implementation and which areas to focus on for future improvements.

6.3.11 Incident Handling Process

In section 6.4 we will go into more detail about what is involved in establishing and deploying an information security incident handling scheme. There are a number of metrics and measurements than can be associated with this scheme, such as:

- Frequency of incidents,
    - Over a period of time (e.g., months/years),
    - In particular areas,

- Incident penetration,

- Localised incident,
- Widely spread incident across the organization,
- Incidents involving and impacting external parties,

- Types of incident,
  - Number and types of major, business critical or minor incidents identified,
  - Number of vulnerabilities identified and their type,

- Resolution of incidents,
  - Number of incidents resolved versus number still outstanding,
  - Number of vulnerabilities remedied and fixed,

- Cost of incidents,
  - Cost of resource in identifying, assessing and evaluating incidents,
  - Cost of recovery,
  - Cost of replacement,
  - Cost in terms of business impact.

6.3.12 Case Study of ICT Services Group Assessing the Incident Patterns and Trends

In the case study in Section 6.3.9 we saw an example of a measure of the rate or frequency of the occurrence of certain types of information security incidents that have cumulated over a period of time to assess if certain trends and patterns emerge that could point to a risk of exposure and a serious incident occurring. For example, questions such as the following could be asked: When did they occur, during a specific time such as evenings or weekends? Did they follow certain work patterns, such as out of normal hours? This could indicate the user might be involved in some insider trading or other private business. Were they seasonal? Were they on the decline or increasing? and many other questions.

Going a stage further, a measure applied to the prevalence of such incidents in different parts of the organization and with regard to different business processes and applications being utilised (e.g., a virus attack that is widely spread across the organization's computer network and that has taken a long time to eradicate has a high incidence of risk).

The ICT services group produces further charts such as in Figure 6.3 to assess what other patterns or trends emerge. In this case, the number of incidents during normal working hours goes to a minimum during vacation times, such as summer, Easter and Christmas time when staff are away. What is of most concern is the trend in incidents that have occurred during the evenings and at weekends and of course during this time, as indicated in Section 6.3.9, there was a rapid increase in the number of hacking and denial of service attacks. This increase may be purely incidental, but further analysis is required to check if there are any links between these two incidents which might indicate an internal threat and possibly an insider job.

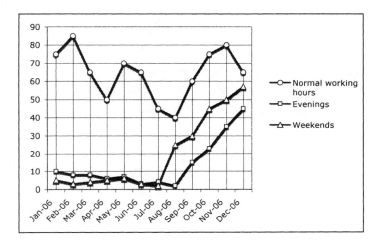

Figure 6.3 Number of incidents recorded

A further stage of analysis would consider measurements regarding the causality between the security threats an organization faces, the known vulnerabilities of the organization, its risk of exposure and resulting types of incidents that have occurred and subsequent business impact. By considering the cause-effect-cause-effect chain of analysis, it has a better understanding of the problems and possible direction for their resolution.

6.3.13 Case Study of ICT Services Group Incident Response and Recovery

Taking the case study example, we can look at another aspect: measuring the speed of response and recovery. The incident handling process involves a range of activities from the reporting of an incident, assessing the information about the incident, through to taking action to resolve the problem. Timeliness of response is key to be able to resolve the problem and to implement solutions to recover and get the business operations back to normal.

Figure 6.4 indicates what the results of the incident handling process reveals as regards the types of incidents that have occurred as per each group in the organization and the time to recover.

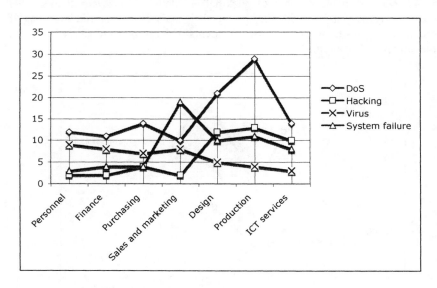

Figure 6.4 Results of the incident handling process

How much these measurements tell us and how this information is utilised need care and attention. This information could be further amplified with what types of application were subject to these incidents, levels of damage and business impact. In the chart above, the peak number of failures in the sales and marketing group could be due to the fact that they had a new system and applications software installed.

The number of denial of service attacks in this case did affect everyone, however the design and production groups were especially affected as they are more reliant on the ICT to deliver results and thus it seems likely that the recovery time would be longer to get the design and production lines fully operational again. This type of analysis can also provide a benchmark measure, but again care must be taken on how to interpret the results and to compare as best as possible like with like and not compare with dissimilar and widely differing attributes.

What this example did not illustrate is the measurements that could be taken regarding response times. For example, How long did it take to discover and report the incident? How much time and effort did it take to gather enough information to be able to understand and assess the problem? How much time and resources did it take to find a solution, to test and implement it? These questions are very general and the answers can and do vary considerably depending on the type of incident, how far it has penetrated across the organization, what type of business processes and applications did it affect and many other varying circumstances.

Virus attacks are normally relatively easy to detect, Trojan horses not so. A rapid decrease in system performance and responsiveness could indicate a denial of service attack or system failures. Identifying hacking attacks and theft or damage to information is not necessarily straightforward. If a hacker causes some immediate effect on the system, this is different from a situation where the full extent of the effect is only detectable days or weeks later.

6.3.14 Case Study of ICT Services Group Incident Costs

A final example, but of course not the last type of measurement, that can be associated with incidents concerns that of costs. The cost of recovery from a major incident affecting the business can often be difficult to calculate and the full extent of the cost may not be known for days, weeks or even months depending on the type of incident.

A virus attack can destroy many of the organization's critical business files; however, if the organization has kept regular backups of such files then it should not be a major resource cost to recover these files from its backup system. Detecting and eradicating the virus from all the systems should also not pose a big problem as long as the anti-virus software has been kept up to date and contains the relevant virus signature to deal with the virus.

Another normally straightforward cost calculation is that related to the cost of replacement of equipment in the case where the incident has resulted in damaged or stolen equipment the information content of a stolen laptop is another level of complexity as was discussed in Chapter 5 (see Sections 5.4.3.6, 5.6.1 and 5.6.5.5) on theft of assets.

A more complicated set of examples relate to denial of service attacks or damage to the organization's image and reputation. An organization's image, which may have taken years to establish, can easily get damaged or tarnished in a short period of time by a whole range of events. This might be a result of competitors, bitter disputes with current staff or ex-employees, political activists, various groups disputing the organization's business activities, such as waste-disposal and green issues, animal rights and other public issues, as well as denial of service attacks which slow down the operations resulting in lack of services to the organization's customers, or being unable to produce and/or deliver products. Another example is the case of the on-line shop or on-line travel agency whose Web system goes "off the air," for say, three, four or more days. This can damage its image as a reputable and reliable supplier of on-line shopping, resulting in a loss of customers and revenue. This may only have a short-term impact or it might have longer-term effects.

Calculating the cost of a damaged reputation is quite difficult without knowing the long-term implications. The same can go for denial of service attacks, depending on the severity of the attack and whether the organization can recover fast enough and absorb any impact without harming its market presence, customer confidence, or without losing the ability to continue to deliver services and products with a minimum of delay to have little or no real impact on its customers. Recovery costs might also include retaining customer loyalty, for example by introducing immediate special offers to its long-standing customers, such as reduced travel or hotels through its on-line booking service for a limited period of time. Of course, how these offers might be marketed is a different issue to avoid its loyal customers getting the wrong impression. Some companies have spent a lot of money in building up their brand and the value in this brand and brand equity. Protecting the brand and the brand equity is a serious issue, without proper management a major information security incident could have dire consequences.

Another issue is the effects of negative publicity of an incident being reported to the press or the media. Of course, where an incident has involved some criminal activity and/or the incident has involved or had an impact on another organization then dealing with the press or media needs to be handled with great care and attention. There is a cost in resources to deal with the press or media. Also, legal action might be taken against the organization resulting in more costs for it to bear.

Costs can be categorised as one-off, short-term or even long-term. Also, the overall cost might not be known in the short-term. Metrics and measurements can be reasonably well calculated and some more estimated.

6.3.15 Defending Against Viruses and Other Malicious Code

Defending against malicious code attacks such as viruses, worms, Trojan horses and the like is a continuous process, which the organization needs to keep track of and take regular action. Although this is one of the many incidents covered by Section 6.3.9, malicious software does present some specific challenges, which will be addressed by this chapter.

Viruses are well known to most organizations and citizens as the media have always provided some form of news and presentations about the latest dreadful attack that might happen tomorrow or next week.

Apart from staff being aware of the dangers of viruses, some of the things that they need to look for and the things they should not to do, there are many other things an organization can arm itself with, such as to have virus checking software in place, doing regular scans of computer systems and verifying that the virus checking software is regularly kept up to date.

Associated with this there are several metrics and measurements that can be utilised in the fight against viruses. These include:

• How many systems are regularly scanned for viruses?

• Is virus scanning carried out automatically or done manually by the user?

- How many systems do and do not have virus checking software?

- How many systems should have virus checking software but don't?

- How many systems have not updated their virus definitions?

- How many systems have suffered virus attacks?

- What length of time did virus problems take to solve?

- What was the cost of the cleanup operation after a virus appeared?

- What have been sources and the nature of the attacks, such as were they internal or external, malicious or accidental?

These are some of the questions, which could deliver measurement information on a weekly basis to determine how effective the organization's process is at defending against virus attacks.

6.3.16 Case Study of a Consultancy Agency

A consultancy agency offers a wide range of independent advice to customers on various financial matters: taxes, loans, investments, insurance and several other related financial services.

Most of its financial consultants spend most of their time on the road using laptops on clients' sites, in their home-based office and on trains, airport lounges and other public places. They remotely connect to the office servers when on the road, as well as sending emails with attachments to colleagues working in the back office.

The agency's servers have their virus checking software updated every week or more often, if necessary. The PCs of the back office support are subsequently updated every week with any new virus signatures. However, the staff in the back office does not do regular virus scanning.

The agency is experiencing a high virus infection rate. Looking at the measurements of infected computers for February they indicate that the laptops may be the cause and that the infected computers in the office are due to the remote connections and emails being sent by the travelling consultants. Figure 6.5 gives the results for February. It appears from further investigation that most of the viruses were spread from infected laptops to PCs via email attachments.

Virus measurements can also provide a lot of information regarding the organization's other vulnerabilities, not just a lack of regular virus signature updates or virus scanning. As indicated by this case study, the information security of remote working arrangements is an issue for the consultancy agency. Other examples might be to address the weaknesses in its backup system, incident handling process or the effectiveness of their firewall setup.

   With regard to this case the agency will need to tighten up on the
information security for remote working and the use of laptops and the Internet.
Proper and correct use procedures, suitable training and awareness, doing regular
and automated virus scanning and virus signature updates all need to be
mandatory to all staff.

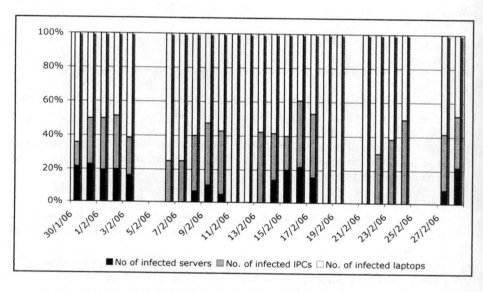

Figure 6.5 Incident trends for February 2006

6.3.17 Effectiveness of Backups

The metrics and measurements taken in regard to backups can be anything
ranging from the:

- Frequency and types of backups taken,

- Efficiency and performance of the backup process,

- Recovery times to restore damaged or corrupted files,

- Restoring a complete system of information and software after a disaster
  and/or major system failure,

- The cost of recovery and the storage of backups such as off-site storage.

6.3.18 Vulnerability Management

The management of vulnerabilities presents a number of possible metrics and measurements. For example, patch management can be quite a challenge. A typical scenario is that a vulnerability in a piece of software is discovered, the details of the vulnerability are published on the Internet, the software vendor develops a patch to fix the problem, the user downloads the patch, tests it out on a nonoperational system, then the patch gets installed on operational systems and finally deployed in operational use. The series of events can take some time for various reasons, such as the testing does not go well and clashes and incompatibilities with other pieces of software occur, or simply the time that is taken to install the patch on many computers.

Another problem is, whilst this scenario is being enacted, a malicious attacker might be working to exploit the vulnerability and hence there is a race against time a window of opportunity for the attacker (that is the time a threat is released + the time vendors release patches + the time taken to test and install the patch). A term that is sometimes associated with this problem is "zero-day attack" which can occur because this time window exists and the time for the organization to react gets shorter and shorter. So the types of measurement that could be considered include:

- Time between announcement of the vulnerability and the availability of an appropriate patch,

- Time taken to respond to the announcement of new patches and the downloading of the patches,

- Time to test and install the patches,

- Number of systems that failed, crashed or have problems after the patches had been installed,

- Number of recorded software vulnerabilities,

- Number of computers scanned/not scanned for patches,

- Number the patches installed or not installed,

- Costs of patch management,

- Resources for patch management.

6.3.19 Internet Services and Access

Another source of risks is in the utilisation of the Internet. Policing and managing the Internet is not a realistic solution due to its ubiquitous, virtual and dynamic nature. However, managing how the organization uses the Internet in a secure way is a relatively easier problem to solve, despite the fact that many organizations are still struggling to meet the challenges with information security as a top priority to resolve or fully recognising it as a problem. Monitoring the usage of the Internet with information gathered from various tools such as firewalls, IDS, computer system audit trail logs and records, incident handling records, Web cookies and via other means can provide a number of measurements including:

- Number of failed access attempts,

- Number of attempts at accessing blocked or forbidden sites,

- Number of file downloads,

- Amount of spam traffic,

- Amount of virus and other malicious code traffic,

- Statistics of time spent "surfing" the Internet and the types of sites visited,

- Statistics of denied external access attempts,

- Number of noncompliance incidents relating to the information security policy on Internet access, acceptable use of the Internet, or unacceptable email usage.

6.3.20 Case Study of On-line Services Company

The On-line Services Company referred to in Section 6.1.7 has recently introduced a strict Internet usage policy to improve staff productivity, customer services and to direct staff to spend less time surfing the Internet during busy times in the office. This seemed to work for a short period of time and then some staff became disgruntled and at odds with management. The company experienced an increase in the number of unauthorised access attempts during the first two weekends in March. There is also an increase in the number of blocked viruses.

On inspecting the Internet usage measurements it noticed that a pattern between blocking external access attempts and internal access attempts. More detailed analysis of other monitoring records kept by the organization showed that those attempting internal access were those same people that expressed their strong objection to the recently introduced policy and three of these worked during the weekend of the 3rd and 4th of March.

They interviewed the staff and then started disciplinary procedures. During the process the names of friends finally emerged that were involved in the external attempts. It also emerged that some of the unexplained loss and damage of company files could be traced back to the activities that took place over the weekend of the 3rd and 4th of March.

The relevant authorities were called in to help in the case and to make charges where appropriate. This group of collaborators, staff and friends, were responsible for gaining unauthorised access, destroying files and planting viruses in the company's system. The enquiry concluded with internal staff and external individuals being charged by the police for criminal activities.

6.3.21 Firewall, IDS and Other Network Tools

There are various pieces of network software that function by observing and controlling network traffic. In the case of the firewall it will monitor incoming and outgoing traffic and permit or deny traffic to have access according to a pre-defined set of rules.

It also can look at and filter traffic based on a predefined set of key words, look for the presences of virus or spam and it can block traffic of a predefined type, block traffic from specific addresses or ports. These types of network software offer many measurement opportunities, for example, data from the firewall could be used to record and provide measurements on:

- Number of blocked ports and addresses,

- Volume of traffic coming from blocked ports or addresses,

- Number of authorised or unauthorised connections,

- Number of failed or dropped connections,

- Number of different types of attack and the patterns of these attacks.

6.3.22 Spam and Ad-ware Controls

The amount of spam and ad-ware getting through organizations computer systems continues to grow. Not only does it use system resources, such as bandwidth and storage, but it also distracts staff and wastes operation work time. The organization needs to spend time blocking the majority of spam while at the same time allowing business emails with legitimate content to get through. This can add up to significant losses to the organization. There are a number of measurements that could be considered in this area including:

- Number of incoming emails passing through the computer network and the number of these that are tagged as junk mail or rejected as having spam content,

- Number of outgoing emails being junk mail or containing unacceptable or spam content,

- Consumption of resources on junk email or spam bandwidth or storage,

- Number of Web page spam and ad-ware being identified,

- The rate of real versus false identified spam passing through the computer network.

There are various controls that are being considered and developed to help curb this ongoing problem. For example, spam controls and the idea of "spam mass" devised by Zoltán Gyöngyi and Hector Garcia-Molina of Stanford University, in association with Pavel Berkhin and Jan Pedersen of Yahoo, as a "measure of the impact of link spamming on a pages ranking" this has led to the development of Web search techniques that separates useful Web pages from spam to avoid the threat of malicious Web spam subverting search engines.

6.4   INCIDENT HANDLING

"Don't curse the darkness, light a candle." Chinese Proverb

6.4.1 Basics

Incidents can cause an organization's systems to be severely damaged, the work significantly interrupted and the incidents can involve legal action (both civil and criminal), or in the worst case they might even lead to the organization becoming bankrupt as a result of the severity of the impact of the incidents.

It is no good expressing anger and annoyance about the problem *("Don't curse the darkness ... ")* don't ignore the inconvenient truth that it has happened and take immediate action to find out what the problem is and get something done about the problem *("... light a candle")*. Doing something well thought out and planned in the necessary time frame to resolve any problems caused by the incident and to reduce any impact to a minimum saves money, time, reputation and image and the future well-being of the organization.

The longer an organization avoids taking appropriate action, the worse the problem might become and the greater the resulting cost. Timeliness is critical to protect the organization.

These problems could be system failures or malfunctions, virus or other malicious code attacks, compromise of the access control system, information theft, ID theft, fraud or physical destruction. The severity of the incident could be minor as the overall impact is relatively low, or it could be major and the impact is very high. Daily, weekly incidents occur at varied frequencies; some are minor and some are major. It is generally expected that the majority of incidents is minor, but this is not to say they should be ignored. Over time the minor incidents could grow into major ones.

6.4.2 Cyber Space Attacks Hit a Pharmaceutical Supply Company

A medium-sized pharmaceutical supply company is experiencing a number of external hacking attacks to its computer networks. None of these were successful but management was worried by this concentrated spate of attacks. This was then followed by its firewall detecting and blocking a rapid increase in the number of viruses and Trojan horses trying to penetrate its computer system. At the same time the email system was being bombarded with a continuous stream thousands and thousands of unwanted emails, enough to overload its system. This chain of events further worried management by this rapid build-up of events, as it seemed that the company was being targeted. Fortunately for the company it had an incident handling management process in place, which they had tested out and made major improvements to only three weeks ago.

It turned out after consulting with one of their customers that the customer was the real target, its suppliers were indirectly targeted to interrupt their supply, which followed an incident involving its supply management system being compromised. After several weeks of investigation involving the customer and three of its suppliers, several men were charged with criminal offences, including some from the company itself. The impact on all companies involved was costly and resource intensive, especially for the pharmaceutical company. The media coverage also had an impact on the company and its suppliers. Finally, over a period of time, the situation got back to near normal and the company started building back the confidence and loyalty of its consumer market. All those involved learnt many lessons in incident handling that should help them in avoiding future incidents such as this.

6.4.3 Case Study "Down Tools on the Production Line"

A medium-sized company producing a range of electronic components is hit by a spate of system problems. Its design and production line are highly dependent on the use of ICT for CAD/CAM applications for the design work and its automated assembly and testing facilities. The processes seemed to become erratic, unreliable and produced faulty results, which slowed down productivity and on two occasions the complete system had to be restarted. An incident management team was assembled to resolve the problem as soon as possible. In collecting all relevant information about these incidents it discovered the problem seemed to be related to a few new customized application software packages that had been deployed two months ago. The supplier of this software was immediately contacted and asked to solve this problem. Over the next 24 hours software engineers found a number of bugs in the software products and produced several patches to resolve the issue. The customer tested these and found everything to be functioning as intended. The company got back into to it normal operational working and productivity after three days of downtime. Since then several improvements have been made to its information security and software management controls.

6.4.4 Case Study "Insider Job"

A small-sized company involved in financial investments for a number of clients has been very successful in the marketplace for delivering products across a whole spectrum of investment options and services: stocks and shares, insurance, banking accounts, dealing in currencies and other investment options. An incident occurred not so long ago involving a senior partner and an outsider, which resulted in criminal action being taken against the company and hence against the individuals involved. Both individuals were accused of illegal insider trading.

6.4.5 Case Study on Incident Reporting

A large company introduces an on-line incident reporting facility to support its existing reporting procedure to take advantage of ICT to streamline the incident handling process with the hope that it would improve the efficiency and effectiveness of the process. One of the electronic forms they introduced allows staff to detail the type of incident that has occurred (as illustrated in Table 6.1).

Incident Reporting Form				
Name		Date	Contact	Tel. No
Department/Location		Time	Details	Mob. No.
Incident		*Description of the problem, location, estimated severity and impact, actual/attempted, internal/external*		*Date & Time*
Computer Systems and Networks and Communications				
Unauthorised access to: computers, networks, services, information, processes, software				
Unauthorised modification to: information, software, system configurations, processes				
Unavailability of resources, systems and services				
Hacking incidents				
Page 1 of 3				

Table 6.1 Incident report form

Incident Reporting Form					
Name		Date	Contact	Tel. No	
Department/Location		Time	Details	Mob. No.	
Incident		*Description of the problem, location, estimated severity and impact, actual/attempted, internal/external*			*Date & Time*
Compromises relating to, information handling and processing					
Malicious software code: virus, worm, Trojan horse					
Spyware or adware					
Spam					
Phishing attack					
Information theft					
Software theft					
Software failures					
Configuration faults					
Other attacks and incidents					
Staff, Contractors and External Parties					
Operator errors					
User processing errors and mistakes					
Social engineering and/or staff coercion					
Staff abuse or physical assault					
Unacceptable and/or suspicious behaviour					
Fraudulent activities					
Misuse/abuse/unacceptable use of resources					
Breaches of system privileges and access rights					
Theft of property and equipment					
Theft of information, identities					
Unmanned equipment, sensitive papers left out overnight					
Staff shortages					
Staff training					
Other incidents related to human factors					
System Failures, Crashes and Malfunctions					
Hardware failures					
Software failures					
Communications failures					
Other incidents related to system failures					
Page 2 of 3					

Table 6.1 Incident report form (continued)

Incident Reporting Form					
Name		Date	Contact	Tel. No	
Department/Location		Time	Details	Mob. No.	
Incident		*Description of the problem, location, estimated severity and impact, actual/attempted, internal/external*			*Date & Time*
Legal and Regulatory Compliance					
Noncompliance with data privacy/protection laws					
Noncompliance with laws related to unauthorised access, computer misuse, hacking					
Breach of copyright laws, software license policy and laws of piracy					
Downloading illegal software, undesirable material such as pornographic material					
Fraud					
Breaching contractual agreements					
Falsification of evidence					
Compromise of information for noncompliance company policy and procedures					
Physical and Environmental					
Physical break into building, office, rooms, filing cabinets and safes					
Damage to equipment					
Radiation, emanations and emissions					
Sabotage					
Fire, water leakage, flood					
Electricity, gas supply					
Other environmental hazards					
Page 3 of 3					

Table 6.1 Incident report form (continued)

6.4.6 Timeliness of Response

As described in Chapter 4, an incident can be thought of as the coming together of a threat and vulnerability. When a hacker is able to exploit the weaknesses in an organization's access system the result is an incident of unauthorized access. The impact can vary depending on what the hacker is able to do and how fast the organization is at stopping the hacker. Time is of the essence in dealing with incidents, especially major ones.

The hacker may start by getting access to files and downloading the information, then the intruder might be installing malicious code in the system and finally use the organization's network vulnerabilities to connect to the network of one of its major customers. This whole chain of events, if allowed to happen, could result in various financial and legal impacts as well as in the loss of the organization's image and reputation. If this chain of potential disaster is interrupted and averted early enough in its cycle then the damage can be limited and so timeliness of response is very important.

6.4.7 Incident Handling Team

The information security incident management process involves those activities to identify, analyze and correct problems. This process should involve a team and as the issues involved can be multidisciplinary a range of skills need to be involved such as:

- Management,

- Information security,

- ICT and non-ICT,

- Physical security,

- Human resources,

- Legal,

- Those handling external relations and the press and sometime external parties, emergency services, policy and maybe even trade unions.

The team needs to be able to analyze the situation, determine the scale and severity of the incident and to initiate appropriate action to correct the problem and prevent it from reoccurring and to liaise and communicate with all the relevant internal and external parties. The incident handling team should have a leader whose task it is to coordinate the process and to facilitate and involve those of the team that need to be deployed in the process.

6.4.8 Past, Present and Future

The situation an organization faces is taking action today based on what happened in the past and its current experiences of the present yesterday's causes become the results of today (the effects) and tomorrows results are caused by today's events. The causes and effects are both events; the cause of the security compromise yesterday has an effect on the organization today, the effect of not resolving this problem today causes a continuing or set of new problems tomorrow and so on.

We should learn from the mistakes of the past that cause our security problems to help us do the right things today and to protect our future. Figure 6.6 illustrates this situation.

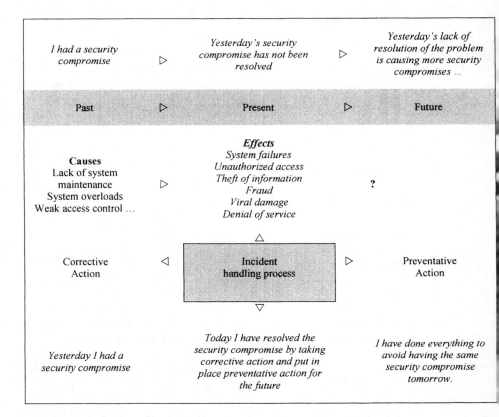

Figure 6.6 Past, present and future events and incidents

6.5 PROCESSES

6.5.1 Planning

Being prepared is a vital position to be in. A fairly commonsense thing to say is "taking the right action to being prepared," but this is not often done in practice. In many cases producing a set of procedures for incident handling and having them tested and tuned to respond only takes place after a few major incidents have happened. Some organizations partially address the problem, for example, they may have an anti-virus system in place but nothing else to protect against other incidents.

So it is important to have a set of procedures in place defining a typical set of incidents, the process for identifying and evaluating these incidents, defining how to respond, explaining what the resolution and recovery process is and what the next process might be. The procedures should also identify who is responsible for what part of the process and the means of communications during an incident occurring. It is important that this is not just a paper exercise but these processes are tested in advance of any potential incident occurring.

6.5.2 Identification and Evaluation

The process needs to identify and record:

- What is the incident (is it minor or major)?

- Where in the system is it occurring (internally, externally or both)?

- What further information can be gathered about the incident, what might be the cause and how did it occur?

- What resources are being affected (internal and/or external)?

All this information needs to be analysed and evaluated by the team to assess the extent and scale of the incident, the severity of the incident and to ask questions such as:

- Is it contained in one area or is it spreading?

- How fast is it spreading?

- Is it isolated to just internal systems, has it come in from the outside or is it spreading to the outside?

These and many other questions need to be asked to be able to start the response and recovery process, knowing what should be done and what action needs to be taken. Also, both internal and external stakeholders need to be notified.

6.5.3 Response

In responding to the incident the team needs to resolve the incident in a timely way and to recover the system to its original operational state as soon as possible. Time is of the essence to stop the problem spreading and to ensure the organization can keep functioning properly in order to not damage or lose its business through excessive delays caused by the response process. Key points are:

- Get the information security incident management team started on dealing with recovery,

- Process the evaluated results and collect evidence about the incident,

- Take action to contain the incident,

- Manage the communications and information flow within the organization and between internal and external parties,

- Take steps to eliminate the causes of the incident.

6.5.4 System Recovery

Recovering from the incident gets the system that was affected back to an operational state so that business can continue. Again, time is of the essence to avoid any unnecessary losses to the organization whilst it is not fully operational and to avoid any further delays in getting its business back on track.
    Key points for system recovery are:

- Reestablish any affected computer systems and other ICT equipment, the organization's computer networking capability and connections,

- Reconfigure computer systems and networking,

- Restore any lost, damaged or corrupted information that occurred during the incident,

- Fully document the incident case and the changes that needed to be made to the system, policies, procedures and processes,

- Reestablish and restore a fully operational state and communicate this to staff, management, customers, suppliers and any other appropriate stakeholders,

- Take final steps to close the incident case file.

6.5.5 Post-Incident Review and Follow Up

This part of the process is important firstly to do a review of the incident situation and secondly to take preventative actions to make the necessary improvements to protect the organization from further incidents of this type from reoccurring.

Review activities:

- Carry out a post-incident review,

- Carry out a forensic analysis of the incident (see Section 6.4.4.),

- Review the effectiveness of the incident handling process and the information security incident handling controls,

- Undertake a business impact analysis of the incident.

Improvements and updates:

- Make recommendations for improvements,

- Take steps to improve the process and controls,

- Update policies, procedures, processes and training, where appropriate,

- Where necessary make changes to contracts and SLAs,

- Look at the trends by analysing several past incidents this is a part of the learning process,

- Finally, produce an incident analysis report.

6.6 FORENSIC INVESTIGATION AND EVIDENCE

"It has been said that man is a rational animal. All my life I have been searching for evidence which could support this." Bertrand Russell

6.6.1 Basic Terms

Investigations that involve the use of forensic techniques are normally utilised in a lot of different disciplines to gather and evaluate information related to an incident that has occurred, such as crime scene investigations, an ICT system which is suspect, fails or is compromised; major engineering disasters due to materials, product or structure failures, aircraft crashes or the causes of death.

The "forensic" disciplines cover many different topics and is generally associated with the term "forensic science"; the term derives from the Latin word *"forensis"* meaning "in open court, for public scrutiny" from the Latin word "forum" and more accurately the term "forensics" is another term for "legal", or "presented before the court." Hence, not only does "forensic science" provide a scientific method of examining evidence relating to an incident, but it is necessary for the legal system and law courts (see ISO/IEC 27001 Annex

A.13.2.3 "Collection of evidence" and A.15.1 Compliance with legal requirements).

6.6.2 ISO/IEC 27001

ICT system compromises tend to focus the investigations on computer forensic analysis. However, the scope of ISO/IEC 27001 is information security of which ICT security is only a subset. ISO/IEC 27001 covers many broader areas not involving ICT aspects such as people, corporate governance, processes, information and non-ICT information systems, business continuity and legislation. Therefore, ISO/IEC 27001 related forensic investigation needs a more detailed examination of the whole information security management system.

Information forensics is a closer forensic science match to ISO/IEC 27001 as it embraces both information system forensics and computer forensics. It considers forensic analysis on business and system processes; human factors and their implicating influences: work patterns and any mitigating circumstances: other implicating factors, methods and standards used for handling and processing information and the use of ICT.

6.6.3 Cause and Effect

The causes of the incident are: the threats, the vulnerabilities they are exploiting and any other implicating factors and conditions that allow the incident to manifest. The effect is the incident itself and the damage it causes. Information on the effect and the object(s) of the effect itself might provide evidence of the cause of the effect. Forensics provides a means of gathering and recovery of evidence from the scene of the incident, helps to analyse this evidence and to reconstruct the events that led up to the incident happening.

Today's enterprise business information systems are often very complex. In particular those based on ICT, both new systems and legacy systems, often are susceptible to a number of security compromises related to a combination of human factors and the technology: fraud, misuse, abuse, mistakes, errors, failures, sabotage and many other information security risks.

6.6.4 Forensic Tasks

The forensic process involves several different tasks, such as:

- Searching, gathering and recovery of evidence associated with the scene of the incident and about the incident itself, for example, from corporate accountants and financial records, business processes, paper documents and files, personnel records, personal and key witness statements, criminal records: physical items including communication devices, recording devices, computer hardware and storage media, software items, electronic documents and files, IP and MAC addresses, network records of banking transactions, telecommunication and postal records, mobile phone identifiers, CCTV recordings and footage, system audit trails and records: residual information from physical characteristics, damaged or corrupted information data; traces from specific objects or items such as fingerprints, facial recognition and voice analysis using biometric techniques,

- Preserve and protect the information and evidence collected to ensure a minimum of damage is introduced in the evidence collection, storage and handling processes,

- Authentication, evaluation and forensic analysis of information gathered Does the evidence give sufficient information about the events that happened? Does evidence translate into a reconstruction of the information security incident that has occurred?

- Present a report on the evaluation and analysis of the evidence.

6.6.5 Computer Forensics

Computer forensics involves the utilisation of people with specific skills, knowledge and experience, specialized tools and techniques for the recovery and analysis of electronic/digital evidence, as well as the other tasks mentioned in Section 6.4.4. One of the prime objects of evidence computer forensics need to deal with is that of storage devices, as well as system and network audit trails and logs, electronic records of transactions, electronic records of user activities, applications still remaining open or recently used applications, recently worked on documents and files, email information (headers, footers, content and attachments), objects in the computer system's vicinity such as mobile phones, MP3 players, iPods and many other items that may contain evidence or provide links to sources of evidence.

Having the computer system in the same operational environment it was in at the time of the incident is an ideal opportunity to collect evidence, but this is not always the case. The forensic analysis should not be performed on the suspected computer system itself to avoid destruction of evidence. Therefore, it is important to make sound copies of all evidence to carry out the forensic tasks.

If an organization does not have forensic expertise in-house then it is very wise to use a recognised outside company with good references and credentials. Non-specialists should not carry out such forensics work, as those without the necessary skills and knowledge could easily make things worse by destroying, inadvertently corrupting or modifying evidence, or devaluing the evidence.

At the end-of-day the evidence is vital as it could exonerate, or mitigate those in the organization and the organization itself from legal action, litigation, financial liabilities and damages and/or from criminal sentences. It is also important to have the necessary evidence in place in order to exonerate, or mitigate customers, shareholders and suppliers and not to present them with unjustified liabilities and legal actions.

6.6.6 Rules and Standards on Evidence

The collection of evidence, as mentioned in ISO/IEC 27001 (Annex A.13.2.3 "Collection of evidence"), is only of use if it complies with the admissibility rules and standards of the jurisdiction in which the evidence is to be used. This is likely to include a definition of what is considered as "relevant evidence" and the limits of relevancy, types of evidence such as expert witness statements, written and recorded, rules on hearsay evidence, excluded evidence, liability and confidentiality issues, as well as many other aspects.

6.7 BACK IT UP

"Chances rule men and not men chances." Herodotus

6.7.1 General Issues

The purpose of this type of policy is to define the requirements for backing up the organization's information assets. The slogan "Back it up before you lose it" is a very expressive way of illustrating this basic requirement. Hence, performing regular information system backups is vital to ensure an organization's information is adequately protected and preserved from damage or loss. The policy should state the business importance of doing backups and consider what needs to be done to face the consequential risks of failing to implement an effective backup process that could severely impact business operations. These risks should include the risk of exposure to legal proceedings, not being able to respond to customer orders and supplier payments, deliveries cancelled or production lines being halted or running inefficiently. On the other side of the coin, having a good backup system enables the organization to operate normally in case of problems, to continue trading and supplying customers with services and/or products even if the original information has been damaged or lost.

6.7.2 Roles and Responsibilities

The owner of an information asset is accountable for its safe and secure handling. Of course, the deployment of risk controls to provide such protection may be delegated to others for practical purposes, but the owner still remains accountable. It should be made clear that it is essential that all information that is processed by all departments, operational groups and staff, whether they are owners or custodians of information assets, should be the subject of regular backups.

Much of the information an organization has and its processes are indispensable for it to do business. Also, the organization might be responsible for handling information owned by other organizations and customers. The consequences of loss of information, or its destruction or damage, can have severe commercial and financial consequences, as well as dire legal implications so *"back it up before you lose it"*.

6.7.3 The Technology Is Available Use IT!

Backups can be implemented in many different ways and today's technology makes the process simple. Many pieces of software providing network and PC security offer backup facilities. For example, such a piece of software might offer virus protection, a personal firewall for a PC, spam protection and backup facilities.

6.7.4 Managed Backup Services

One option that an organization could consider is the use of managed backup services. There are, of course, advantages and disadvantages with this approach:

- Advantages include the organization uses less of its resources for implementing and managing backups, less time in keeping up with the advances in technology and the maintenance of ICT for backups; it can reduce the organization's risk of data loss due to lack of focus under operational pressures, human errors and/or accidents; it reduces the day-to-day responsibilities of backups and it provides a way of achieving the automatic availability of off-site added protection.

- The main disadvantage is that the organization is entrusting its information assets and the management of the risk to a third party and not to internal staff or another part of its own organization, whilst at the end of the day the organization is still accountable for these information assets, which could involve information owned by its customers or suppliers and certainly it could (is likely to) contain personal data.

If managed backup services are the option that an organization selects then careful consideration needs to be given to the managed service contract and SLA to ensure the organization is adequately and suitably protected.

6.7.5 Backup Processes

Best practice for backingup data includes:

- Assign one member of staff with the main responsibility for the central backup, with a second or third person to cover for absence (such as sickness, vacation or other personal reasons),

- Use a different tape or disk to back up each day of the week and have a schedule for rotating them,

- Keep backups secure, preferably off-site from the main business premises,

- Staff should receive some training in doing backups to safeguard their essential information on their PCs that is not backed up centrally as well as, if necessary and appropriate, knowledge on how to use the central backup system as per the backup procedures,

- Backups should be encrypted and/or password protected to ensure their confidentiality and integrity,

- Archive a sample of copies of the backup every 2 to 3 months,

- Finally always consider and plan for the worst-case scenario.

6.8 ISMS PREPAREDNESS AND BUSINESS CONTINUITY

'Defer not till tomorrow to be wise, tomorrow's sun to thee may never rise.'
William Congreve

6.8.1 Business Value

There should be little doubt as to the importance and value of business continuity and the essential role that ICT and ISMS readiness contributes to the ability to keep the business running. The business impact of not having appropriate contingency and protection processes in place can all too well be seen by the various real cases that have hit the world headlines from man-made situations to natural hazards, or a combination of both, for example, where a natural hazard triggers a disaster relating to some man-made situation.

Several examples can be given, such as the New York telecoms system being out for hours crippling businesses that have communications on the phone and through the Internet for the best of the working day, bombings in various parts of Europe and the United States, the SARS and avian flu epidemics (see Section 6.6.5.2), the tsunami event of 2004, the Taiwan earthquake incident of 2006 (see Section 6.6.5.1), failure of corporate governance, 175,000 credit card numbers being stolen on-line, the UK reports that in 2005 and 2006 the number of fraud cases in English courts continued to grow to staggering heights (such as those related to ID theft, card scams, bank insider frauds and money laundering) and many, many more cases.

All these examples raise awareness, attention and concerns of organizations and the citizens and consumers alike. This situation does trigger some organizations to rethink "Could it happen to us?" and how good their processes and systems are at coping with these issues. However, there are still many companies that have not insured themselves with an effective business continuity process and some do not have such a process at all.

Sometimes the reason why business continuity is not in place might be that it presents too many challenges, the organization may see it as too expensive or they are just too complacent to do anything. These are particularly some of the reasons why small-sized companies do not go for business continuity as the cost, know-how and resources are out of their reach.

This should not be the case since there are many routes available for getting simple advice on what can be done. At the end of the day the company needs to weigh up the costs of the resulting impact of not doing anything against the cost of doing something and the reduction in the business impact. However, it should be clear that there is business value in business continuity: no matter how perfect the solution is, take the first important step of doing something and the rest will fall in place with the right guidance. One of the important things to do first is to get management commitment and this can be helped by doing an initial business impact analysis demonstrating the potential losses to management.

6.8.2 Business Impact

One of the important questions to ask is, "What are the critical things that are essential to the organization to enable it to continue to operate?" Once we know this we can then test these essential things out by looking at some examples that might be appropriate to the organization running its business. These can then be used to calculate the business impacts the organization might be challenged with in the face of adversity in the event of disastrous incidents occurring.

If the organization is not prepared and has not planned for the advent of a disaster, disruption to its operations, major system failures, or external influences from the markets it's involved in then it leaves itself wide open to being exposed to high impacts which could ruin the business. For example, such impacts could be:

- Supply chain failures and disruptions,

- Denial of service attack shutting down or grossly restricting operations dependent on ICT systems, services and a networking capability,

- Critical loss of supporting infrastructure (e.g., electricity, gas or water supplies) and services (e.g., telecommunication services, ISP services, outsourcing facilities),

- Major losses of tangible assets such as through fraud, theft, embezzlement,

- Strikes, political activists, labour relations,

- Environmental hazards and disasters,

- Bombs and explosions,

- Critical depression in market conditions (e.g., share prices, interest rates, world/country economies),

- Legal, regulatory or contractual penalties and liabilities.

These examples cover financial, operational, customer/supplier, staff-related and legal issues.

6.8.3 Processes

Business continuity processes are the way to ensure that the right resources are available to keep the business running and operating. This includes ICT resources, but many other aspects are also included that make up the full business continuity domain.

The process of doing an impact analysis is similar to other processes such as the ISMS risk assessment process as it involves gathering, analysing and evaluating this information to assess the impacts with regard to loss of confidentiality, integrity and availability. The results of this can then go towards a review and decision-making process to determine the organization's requirements and what should be done to guard against such business impacts occurring.

Information can be gathered through different means such as:

- Scorecards,

- Workshops and meetings,

- Incident handling reports,

- Risk assessment reports,

- Financial and marketing analysis,

- Audit findings.

There are other processes that the ISMS should be dealing with that are also important to business continuity, such as backups (see Section 6.5), incident handling (see Sections 6.4 and 5.4), system acceptance (see Section 5.7) and capacity planning (see Sections 5.7 and 5.8.5).

6.8.4 Getting Ready and Being Prepared

Business continuity plans provide a basis for being prepared for the disaster and business interruptions. The ISMS, like ICT, is only a subset of the broader scope of business continuity. The first step in developing an ISMS preparedness plan is to do a gap analysis to: understand the organization's current state of readiness, define where it needs to get to and be, to fill the gaps and what actions it needs to take to get there. This includes:

- Get management buy-in and commitment,

- Identify the critical business components,

- Do an impact analysis,

- Produce a business continuity plan,

- Implement and test the plan,

- Review effectiveness of the plan on a regular basis and update the plan when necessary.

The following are some of the best practice messages related to business continuity:

- Whatever assumptions are made in the planning phase, get them checked out, if the assumption were grossly inaccurate then this exercise could be a waste of time and resources,

- Do not leave it until the disaster strikes,

- Always ensure you have an effective backup process in place,

- Do not forget the important role that people play in the overall process,

- Do not ignore the warning signs and alerts provided by the incident handling process and be quick to take action against pending incidents,

- Ensure you have adequate disaster recovery provisions in place, which are working to enable the organization to survive and continue to fully function and operate after the events,

- Consider the use of third party services, where appropriate, for backup services and/or recovery services,

- Do not forget the legal and contractual aspects.

6.8.5 Legal and Contractual Aspects

When disaster hits an organization, liabilities and claims relating to third parties are likely to be an issue. An organization needs to be alert to these issues and to plan and react appropriately to limit its liabilities by assessing these risks and their impacts. The liabilities might arise for several reasons, including the failure to honour contractual obligations regarding supply of goods or services, failure or noncompliance when delivering systems, negligence on the part of the organization, damage to property associated with the supply of services, loss or damage to data, safety issues, accidental mishaps and many other situations.

The organization needs to be alert to how its business continuity plans and response can cope when disasters strike with respect to the legal and contractual obligations either under contract or in tort. This is a subject not to be forgotten when developing business continuity plans; it should be part of its business impact analysis.

6.8.6 Case Studies

6.8.6.1 Telecom and Internet Chaos

In December 2006 a 7.1 magnitude earthquake on Taiwan's coast disrupted telecom and Internet services across Southeast Asia. The disruption frustrated organizations that had to desperately grapple with the situation; this included those dealing in stock market trading, those doing on-line transactions and other customers and suppliers to business as well as the private citizens. This incident highlighted the problem of the world's dependence on ICT for business and private use.

The problem was that the earthquake severely damaged submarine telecommunication cables, which carry traffic in the Southeast Asian region and beyond. The damaged cables sent a disruptive shockwave to China, South Korea, Singapore, Japan, Hong Kong, Malaysia and as far as Australia.

Telecommunication companies tried to re-route their traffic through other networks or to use other cables, but the reduced the capacity could not fulfill the rapid demand for services resulting in very slow network and Internet access and services. Some sought cooperation from their counterparts in North America and Europe to use satellite links.

The problem was reduced by the afternoon as the re-routing of the telecoms traffic started to take effect. By then, of course, the disruption had become quite widespread, which included jammed phone lines, Internet access slowed down, connections to the United States were disrupted and it was reported in several newspapers that trading was affected as the Bloomberg systems were affected.

Although the business and financial impact was high, it could have been much higher if the incident had not happened on a quiet trading day after Christmas.

Lessons learnt included:

- The heavy reliance of ICT and networking for modern day business,

- The heavy reliance on submarine cables to carry telecoms traffic,

- Not to put "all your eggs in one basket" drop the basket and all the eggs could be broken.

6.8.6.2 SARS Epidemic

In 2002 to 2003, when the SARS (severe acute respiratory syndrome) epidemic was at its height, some companies in many parts of the world were quick to respond. They did so by reviewing their business continuity plans, reassessing their business impacts and then revising their plans to take account this new hazard. Most other hazards involved the provisioning of duplicate ICT resources, backup premises and being able to mobilise their workforce needed to relocate to continue operations.

With the SARS incident it was more the case of not knowing where it would hit, so it was not so much a question of where to relocate ICT facilities but how to distribute key staff skills and resources to enable remote working, working at other offices or at home.

For example, rather than keep all the ICT support staff in one location it is better to partition the ICT team to avoid the situation where all ICT staff is under the threat if all are only in one location. Replicating the key staff in different locations reduces the threat that all ICT staff is affected. Some staff could be located in the ICT centre, other staff located at home having remote access to the centre and some staff relocated in other offices, again with remote access. The same partitioning also applied to other key staff that could facilitate the continuation of business operations. It was reported that fortunately none of these organizations had to use their revised business plans for this particular epidemic. The main lessons to be learnt:

- Always keep alert of new threats to the organization and never underestimate your protective capability,

- Always review and update your business impact analysis,

- Always test and review your business continuity plans on a regular basis
  and revise where necessary.

6.8.6.3 On-line Business Capability Outage

After many months of labour disputes between senior management and several
staff over pay and privileges at one of its office locations, the company makes a
hasty decision to subcontract some of the key roles to other staff from some of its
foreign offices. The organization did this to ensure the continuity and availability
of its on-line business services, which it provides to a global network of
customers. This does not help the situation as the staff becomes more disgruntled
and malcontented and they even gain support from other staff. The situation
severely gets worse when the backup resources arrive from one of the foreign
offices.

In the turmoil that emerged a few of the frustrated and disgruntled staff
planted several booby-traps for the foreign workers which took effect when they
started to take over the work of the displaced staff. This included several Trojan
horses when the foreign workers started to use their newly allocated system
accounts.

Within hours the systems started to significantly slow down customer access
to the organization's Internet services. In addition, the email system crashed and
several critical information resources became inaccessible.

The result was that the organization's on-line business came to a grinding
halt. This situation lasted for 72 hours before the organization was able to get to
grips with the problem and it took another 24 hours before it was able to resume
a 50% operational system and another 12 hours to become fully operational.

The business impact to the organization was severe, both financially and to
its image and reputation. The lessons it learnt included:

- The need to regularly review the business continuity plans,

- To review information security management system and controls,

- To review its use of staff resources, especially the subcontracting
  services between offices,

- To improve management and staff working relationships.

6.9 SYSTEMS ACQUISITION, DEVELOPMENT AND MAINTENANCE

6.9.1 Systems

From time to time new business requirements or business changes will be addressed by the organization and this can lead to the need for improving existing systems, acquiring new systems and/or developing new systems. Whatever the decision is, information security should be a key part of the discussion process and the provisioning information security should feature from the word go in improvements, new developments and new acquisitions.

It has often been the case in the past that information security was an afterthought, a "bolt-on" or "knee jerk" reaction maybe following a major incident, it may have been through lack of knowledge of information security risks or even lack of funds available at project initiation. If information security is added as an afterthought not only might it end up being more expensive to implement but it also leaves the organization open to many risks and impacts.

So for system improvements and upgrades, new system developments, or new system acquisitions, information security requirements should be an essential element of the project specification. All the ISMS processes of risk assessment, risk treatment and selection of controls should be an integral part of the project plan and its implementation.

6.9.2 Current Systems and Legacy Systems

There is no universally agreed strategy as to whether an organization should replace its ICT or stick with what it already has. Some think that their existing legacy systems have worked so far, so what is the point of changing? Their systems are tried and tested, durable, reliable and they produce the results they need; so what is the point in spending more money for the sake of replacing its technology with no added value or advantage, to buy a new systems without any guarantee that it will perform reliably.

Of course, there are other organizations that do not agree with this strategy and have a completely different view. What is clear is that both strategies have a place in business and industry needs to work together to achieve an appropriate level of interworking between the two. There are issues, such as backwards compatibility, limited removing for improving or expanding legacy systems, system interoperability between old and new if a hybrid strategy is taken, aspects related to replacing safety systems, aspects related to information security and aspects related to high availability requirements either with replacing the old or with developing or acquiring new systems. In addition, the cost of maintaining legacy systems, cost of retraining staff in the use of new systems and the disruption of operations when the new systems are being installed and deployed need to be addressed.

Whatever the strategy the organization decides on, an old, new, or an old/new hybrid system, information security should be at the heart of the decision process. Achieving, utilizing and maintaining effective information security management are critical must do activities.

6.9.3 Acquisition

In the acquisitioning of new systems, whether they are subcomponents/subsystems (such as new software applications, new hardware or new services) or complete ICT systems, the following should be considered:

- Has a capacity plan exercise been carried out to determine the current and future needs and demands of the organization?

- Does the evaluation of the options for new systems/subsystems take account of the organization's information security requirements?

- Will these new systems/subsystems integrate with existing systems or legacy systems to avoid potential conflicts, interworking and interoperability problems and security compromises?

- Licencing arrangements and terms and conditions, Are they appropriate to the organization's intended use of the system?

- What are the maintenance costs including the costs to maintain effective information security management?

- What vendor support is provided for effective information security management?

6.9.4 Development

In developing new systems or new sub-components/sub-systems (such as new software applications, new hardware or new services, or complete ICT systems), the following should be considered:

- Do the design and specification options take account of the organization's information security requirements?

- Will these new systems/sub-systems integrate with existing systems or legacy systems to avoid potential conflicts, interworking and interoperability problems and security compromises?

- Should the development be done in-house or subcontracted?

- If the development is to be subcontracted, What are licensing arrangements and terms and conditions? - Are they appropriate to the organization's intended use of the system?

6.9.5 Installation, Testing, Integration and Deployment

The installation of new systems and possibly the integration with other systems need to be carried out in a way that does not cause the operational environment to be compromised. If there is a 24/7 high availability for the operational facilities then care and attention needs to be taken of how the installation might be done to minimise any disruption to the business.

Another aspect, which can have a profound effect on the success or failure of deploying new systems, is the testing of these systems, especially if they are being integrated with existing or legacy systems. These tests should be carried out before accepting the systems for utilisation into the operation (ISO/IEC 27001 Annex A.10.3.2).

There are many different types of testing, such as individual component or module testing, integration testing, or full system testing, as well as functional testing, performance testing, implementation, or installation testing. All have the right place in the procurement/development process. Areas such as hardware tests, software testing and specific security testing are all separate special fields of testing.

For system developments that are not in-house but are carried out by an outside company, appropriate measures need to be in place to ensure that the installation, integration and deployment activities in the operational environment do not cause any security compromises to existing facilities.

Many of the problems that occur in developed systems focus on software problems, especially brand new software applications. Some vendors provide pre-releases of software for users to test out on their own systems in order to gain feedback regarding its functionality, its performance and any faults discovered during use. Downloading and using such versions in an organization need to be strictly controlled and certainly this should not be allowed on operational facilities (for example, see ISO/IEC 27001 Annex A.12.4.1).

A further control specified in ISO/IEC 27001 Annex A.10.1.4 covers the separation of development, testing and operational facilities. Such separation is important to avoid any risk of system security breaches in the operational environment. Developed systems should not be created on operational systems and untested developed systems should not be tested on operational systems before being pre-tested and the system acceptance process has been gone through. Testing should be carried in a test environment or preproduction environment, which is especially important regarding software development and all this should be separate from the operational facilities.

6.9.6 Asset Inventory

The organization's asset inventory needs to be updated with all the information related to new systems that have been acquired or developed. This also includes revising entries where the new systems are replacing old systems. In such a case, a proper closure process needs to be involved to ensure there is a record of assets that are no longer on the organization's books and how and where they were disposed of. Of course, all the necessary information security procedures need to be carried out to ensure the secure disposal of such assets Chapter 5 (see Section 5.4.3.).

6.9.7 Training and Operational Procedures

It should be clear that any new systems require staff to be adequately trained in the use of the systems. Specific procedures need to be created, approved and distributed to all users regarding the operational use of these systems. Existing procedures need to be updated to reflect the changes that have been made because of the new system. It should be ensured that the training activities have been completed before the new systems are used in the operational environment.

6.10 SOFTWARE MANAGEMENT

"A mind without instruction can no more bear fruit than can a field, however fertile, without cultivation." Cicero

6.10.1 Software Assets

Alongside the secure handling of information comes the secure management of software: operating systems software, applications software, software for networks and communications service provisioning.

Software is another one of those important assets that should appear on the asset inventory. In addition, the organization should keep a record of all the software licenses and agreements it has for its software. The organization should have control over what software is installed on its systems, PCs and laptops. The downloading and/or otherwise installing of illegal software must be strictly prohibited to avoid both legal and information security problems. The downloading and/or otherwise installing freeware and/or shareware should be prohibited unless prior authorization has been given and there is a good business case for doing so. Any such action should be backed up with a risk assessment to ensure control over any associated risks. A critical factor to be taken into account is the help, support and maintenance that are provided for such software, which very often are none.

The organization's ICT runs on software and this software needs to be applicable, reliable and secure for the organization and their applications, processes and the handling of information.

6.10.2 Software Upgrades and New Versions

Software upgrades and new versions appear from time to time. Sometimes this is to repair vulnerabilities in the current version and other times it could be to introduce more or improved functionality. Whatever the case may be, it is important to manage the process in an appropriate way to ensure the effectiveness and security of the system are not compromised:

- Has the necessary authorization been given for the upgrades or new versions to be acquired and installed on the system (ISO/IEC 27001 A.6.1.4)?

- Have the upgrades and new versions been subject to change control procedures (ISO/IEC 27001 A.10.1.2)?

- Have the upgrades and new versions been subject to a system acceptance process (ISO/IEC 27001 A.10.3.2)?

- Are controls in place to protect against software vulnerabilities (ISO/IEC 27001 A.10.4.1, A.10.4.2 and A.12.6.1)?

- Are agreements in place regarding any exchange of software with external parties (ISO/IEC 27001 A.10.8.2)?

- Are there procedures being utilised regarding the installation of software in an operational environment (ISO/IEC 27001 A.12.4.1)?

- Are effective controls in place to prevent the unauthorized access to software source code (ISO/IEC 27001 A.12.4.3)?

- Are procedures in place for the implementation of software changes (ISO/IEC 27001 A.12.5.1)?

- Has a technical review been carried out regarding the system and its application after changes to operating systems have been made (ISO/IEC 27001 A.12.5.2)?

- Are there any restrictions or limiting conditions on changes to software (ISO/IEC 27001 A.12.5.3)?

- Is a process in place and being deployed to control and manage any software development being carried out by a third party (ISO/IEC 27001 A.12.5.5)?

- Are controls in place to ensure compliance with any laws, regulations or licensing agreements and controls regarding software use and deployment across the organization (ISO/IEC 27001 A.15.1.2)?

6.10.3 Software Vulnerabilities and Patch Management

Software vulnerabilities can range from programming bugs, errors, flaws or mistakes in the software code, failure of the software to function or perform as intended by its design or specification, developer's backdoors through to the intentional introduction of malware (viruses, Trojan horses and worms) and malicious executable code in general.

Software vulnerabilities can exhibit a wide range of problems and effects, with varying levels of business inconvenience, risk and impact. Some of these vulnerabilities exhibit subtle effects in the software's functionality, which may not be detected for a long time. On the other hand the vulnerabilities may show immediate effects, such as causing the ICT systems to crash or fail to function. This can lead to the unavailability of business processes dependent on these ICT systems for information processing, to denial of network resources and services, or other incidents that cause the normal flow of business to be severely interrupted with a loss of productivity, service delivery and performance.

Software vulnerabilities can result from malicious activities with the intent of causing harm or damage; they can also result from accidental actions, such as a careless or incompetent programmer, faulty programming tools, or lack of understanding of the requirements of the specification.

Software vulnerabilities create all sorts of information security problems, such as the leakage of information, unauthorised access leading to theft of information, theft of user details and identifiers, unauthorized execution of commands, installation of executable malicious code, unauthorized modification of information, unreliable and inaccurate results in information processing due to a lack of information integrity controls, or unavailability of information.

Vulnerability disclosure is a hotly debated subject. Once a vulnerability is known and then disclosed work can start on finding a fix of the problem, such as a software patch or upgrade, but on the other hand work can also start on how to exploit the vulnerability. One school of thought supports a full public disclosure of the vulnerability to enable all users to be fully aware of the risks they are running. Another school of thought supports the idea of a restricted disclosure to allow enough time to be able to fix the problem before the vulnerability has been exploited.

These two schools of thought have appeared in other areas in information security, such as the disclosure of encryption algorithms. Publicly disclosing the algorithm details can give time for analysis into how strong the algorithm is at withstanding an attack thus enabling users to judge whether the strength is good enough for the specific application they have in mind. But at the same time this disclosure can put users at risk if the encryption code is broken. On the other hand, the restricted disclosure or *"security by obscurity"* approach enables it to be more difficult to break the encryption code, but can also put users at risk since they may not be able to establish the strength limitations for specific applications.

Of course what has happened over recent years is the so-called "zero-day" attack. So called "zero-day protection" is the attempt to guard against "zero-day exploits and attacks." Many techniques have been used to limit the effectiveness of vulnerabilities. For example all operating systems are working to improve their security over time, stopping "zero-day exploits" before they cause any harm. We now have is a group of software engineers who work to release nonvendor patches for zero-day exploits the zero-day emergency response team, or "zert".

Various best practice measures can help to reduce the likelihood of a vulnerability being exploited, for example:

- Be constantly alert and be vigilant to the threats and vulnerabilities,

- Pay careful attention during software maintenance, software upgrades and patches phases,

- Use firewall and access control mechanisms in the deployment and utilisation phases,

- Use auditing practices throughout the software development life-cycle, as well as during the deployment phase.

6.10.4 Malicious Code

Malicious code is one case of those pieces of software that are designed specifically to do damage and harm and to put organizations infected with such code at risk. As is well known by many cases, viruses once in the system attach themselves to applications software and can then replicate and spread themselves very fast like a fire in a forest that has not seen rain for weeks or months. In their path through the system the viruses cause destruction and damage just like the fire and even when they have been discovered they may not be immediately eradicated, just like a fire that has taken hold of the forest. So for a period of time the virus is out of control. The virus might be deleting files, damaging software programs and applications; it might even be aimed at reformatting the hard disk. The more benign types of viruses can also cause the organization problems since continual replication of the virus can eat up memory, trigger erratic behaviour and maybe make the system crash; all this can result in degradation of performance and possibly a denial of service.

The worm is a self-replicating piece of software code which does not attach itself to an application, but nevertheless causes widespread damage across networks, such as the Internet. Since it is self-replicating it is like the benign virus that eats up network bandwidth, consumes computer system memory, slows down systems and in the worst case causes a widespread denial of service attack. Worms such as the "Morris Worm" of 1988 caused global disruption and chaos in many systems connected to the Internet once the worm had invaded these systems. Several of the worms that are released into the Internet only replicate and spread themselves, however, some worms have been produced to carry "*pay-loads*", such as to delete files, send files via email to other systems, install "*back-doors*" in systems and even encrypt files. The "*back-door*" problem can result in an opportunity for the attacker to create a "*zombie-computer*" within the infected system, which, when similar "*zombie-computers*" are networked together, form a "*botnet*". This "*botnet*" subsequently can be used by those responsible for sending spam, which in turn can create several security incidents as has been discussed previously.

The Trojan horse is a piece of software code that contains and/or installs a piece of malicious code into a system. This piece of malicious code is often called a "*payload*" or simply a "*Trojan*". These Trojan horses might appear as useful and harmless pieces of software, but beneath the surface lurks the malicious code which, when the seemingly useful piece of software is executed, triggers off a sequence of damaging events. A Trojan horse can cause a whole lot of unauthorised activities to occur on the victims systems without their knowledge or consent, such as:

- Downloading and uploading files from the Internet,

- Sending out emails using the victims email address book, including the distribution of spam,

- Phishing in the victims files to gain access to credit and banking details,

- Causing the system to restart,

- Attaching the system to a "botnet",

- Deletion and corruption of files.

Trojan horses can infect systems in several ways, such as an email attachment, or by the user downloading a file from a rogue site on the Internet.

There are a number of products on the market commonly called anti-virus software, which attempt to detect, prevent and eradicate viruses and malware from computer systems. They generally scan the systems files and folders located on hard drives and other memory devices, but also some of them try to identify any suspicious behaviour in software, which indicates the presence of a virus.

The anti-virus software relies on a dictionary of known viruses to compare against when scanning the system.

The effectiveness of this method relies on the dictionary to be up-to-date and the majority of, if not all, product vendors have an on-line facility for getting live updates of virus signatures to enable users to update their anti-virus dictionary. Of course, this live update needs to be done on a regular basis, at least once a week. It is a good idea to set your system to do an automatic update that is initiated whenever a new virus signature has been added to the dictionary. Most also have signatures for known worms and Trojan horse viruses.

However, on the other side of the coin, malware code writers always try to stay one step ahead of the vendors by using various techniques to disguise the virus so that the virus does not match to those virus signatures in the dictionary. Some of these use so-called *"polymorphic"* or *"metamorphic"* virus writing methods.

Anti-virus software can also monitor suspicious behaviour, such as a piece of software attempting to write to an executable piece of software code. In this case the antivirus software will alert the user to a potential problem and ask them what to do.

Of course payloads, such as those attached to a Trojan horse, are more difficult to protect against. Most of these are delivered by email and there are some email best practice measures that could help:

- Be alert to emails that are received from someone that the user does not know, are suspicious, or have unknown attachments,

- Set the email preferences to not automatically open attachments,

- Update the antivirus software automatically,

- Update the operating system with the latest patches.

ISO/IEC 27002 Clause10.4 offers best practice advice on the implementation of protection against the threats of malicious code.

6.10.5 Software Backups

Making a backup copy of software is always a good measure, assuming this is allowed under the vendor's licensing agreements. All the normal best practice for the storage and protection of backups as covered in Section 6.5 also applies to software.

6.10.6 Software Development

Software development may be carried out in-house and/or by external third parties. The outsourcing of software development is covered in several parts of ISO/IEC 27001, such as:

- Controls in place to protect against software vulnerabilities (ISO/IEC 27001 A.10.4.1, A.10.4.2 and A.12.6.1),

- Agreements in place regarding any exchange of software with external parties (ISO/IEC 27001 A.10.8.2),

- A process in place and being deployed to control and manage any software development being carried out by a third party (ISO/IEC 27001 A.12.5.5).

6.10.7 Software Maintenance and Testing

Software development maybe carried out in-house and/or by external third parties and the advice related to that is contained in the following clauses:

- Change management process (ISO/IEC 27001 A.10.1.2),

- Separation of development and testing facilities (ISO/IEC 27001 A.10.1.4),

- Contracts and SLAs with external parties (ISO/IEC 27001 A.6.2 and A.10.2),

- System acceptance controls (ISO/IEC 27001 A.10.8.2),

- Agreements in place regarding any exchange of software with external parties (ISO/IEC 27001 A.10.8.2),

- Software system/applications test data (ISO/IEC 27001 A.12.4.2),

- Access to software source code (ISO/IEC 27001 A.12.4.3),

- Procedures concerning change control (ISO/IEC 27001 A.12.5.1),

- IPR (intellectual property rights) agreements in place regarding any exchange of software with external parties (ISO/IEC 27001 A.15.2.1).

6.11 MONITORING, REVIEWING AND IMPROVING THE ISMS

"Knowing ones self and knowing others will lead to 100% success, knowing ones self but not knowing others will lead to 50% success and not knowing ones self and not knowing others will lead to 0% success" SunZi on the Art of War.

6.11.1 Review

6.11.1.1 Review Purpose

Reviewing the ISMS on a regular basis may seem like a complex, over the top, resources intensive activity, but like ISMS monitoring, in essence it should be a simple and straightforward exercise. Basically, there needs to be a way of reviewing how good the ISMS is at managing the organization's information security risks. This does not or should not imply the need for endless meetings and committees. Everything is scalable and business reviews in whatever form exist in most organizations. There is no need to set up new arrangements just for information security and it especially should not be seen as an independent subject divorced from any other important business activity or process. Existing committees might suffice to do this job with appropriate agenda items to cover the review of information security. This may not always be the case and there are exceptions which can be dealt with on a case-by-case basis, for example where a major incident has taken place or a major reassessment needs to take place, in which case a separate meeting and/or an ad hoc group needs to be established for this purpose.

6.11.1.2 Types of Review

At this point it is worth pointing out that there are different types of review specified in ISO/IEC 27001. Management reviews that bring together senior management, staff and managers from specific areas of the business, such as someone dealing with personnel, finance, legal issues, ICT services and, where necessary and appropriate, specialists. Who should attend, when they should attend and how many need to attend will depend on the nature of the review and the topics under discussion. For example, a review covering personnel security or legal aspects needs the right competent staff with knowledge in these areas to be present.

Another type of review might be at a more detailed level requiring more technical discussion, for example, to assess and review the results of the last six months output from the incident handling process, or the results of a recent risk assessment. It might be necessary to discuss future improvements in the access control system. Again, these reviews need to be dealt with on a case-by-case basis without the need to set up a permanent structure. Of course, if the organization wishes to have a more permanent structure in place then it is entirely its decision.

Another type of review is an internal ISMS audit, which is covered in ISO/IEC 27001 Clause 6. The important thing is that reviews do take place on a regular basis with specific goals and objectives to ensure that the effectiveness of the ISMS is maintained.

6.11.2 Meeting Business Demands

It should be clear by now that any activity involving the ISMS needs to be done in cognisance of and familiarity with business demands and assurance that these activities are able to meet these demands. This should be the true essence of the existence of ISMS. Any reviews relating to the ISMS need to always bear this in mind.

One way of making sure that activities are in sync to be cognisant of such demands is to make information security a topic on the agenda of management meetings at all levels, a part of management decision making, part of the overall business culture and way of thinking and an integrated part of all other relevant business activities and processes.

This is to ensure that those dealing with the ISMS do not lose sight and focus on the business goals and requirements, that senior management is fully aware of the ISMS activities and developments and that continued support and commitment are assured.

6.11.3 Review of Measurements, Effectiveness, Audit Results and Other ISMS Process Results

Any review should take into account the recent results of the ISMS measurements that have been taken and what these tell us about the effectiveness and performance of the ISMS.

6.11.4 Brainstorming

There are many ways of achieving appropriate feedback from managers, users and staff, customers and from suppliers or business partners. Meetings to bring staff and managers together for "brainstorming" sessions can be a very valuable exercise. This enables immediate, interactive feedback and discussion of perceived threats, risks, current gaps and performance of the current status of the ISMS and allows for an opportunity to think about and discuss improvements.

6.11.5 Scorecards, Gap Analysis, Questionnaires, Benchmarks and Indexing

There are many ways of getting staff involved in the process and at the same time gather important feedback on information security management being deployed in practice. This topic has already been discussed in Chapter 4. The importance of all these methods is that they can provide invaluable input for both the monitoring and review processes.

As we have already discussed, gap analysis exercises are useful to check where the organization is at any point in time regarding its information security management status. Thereby a gap analysis is giving a measure of how far it is from getting to where it should be and at every process stage of the PDCA cycle different forms of gap analysis can be carried out. This may be considered as a sort of "tick-in-the-box/check-list" type of audit, which is highly dependent on the types and the number of questions and the types of answers being given. Nevertheless, it does have value but does not replace the better form of audit based on the collection and analysis obtained from objective evidence.

Scorecards, questionnaires and other similar methods have value to the monitoring and reviewing processes. These methods should be there to support and be used in collaboration with the other processes being used to gather, analyse and evaluate the information and evidence of the real workings of an organization's information security management and its effectiveness.

Benchmarking and indexing enable a company to do a comparison and health check between its information security management status and effectiveness and other companies in a similar line of business and/or in the same industry sector. They can also be used internally between the different departments or business groups. Indexing is a way of measuring how close each group, department or individual is to conforming to the information security controls, policies and procedures implemented by the organization and how close or far away it is in achieving business targets and performance levels. Figure 6.7 is an example of where a scorecard method was used to benchmark different groups as regards the number of incidents each group experienced during March 2006, all of which had an implication on the information security effectiveness within that group.

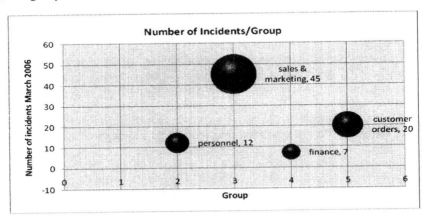

Figure 6.7 Scorecard benchmarking

6.11.6 Monitoring

Monitoring the ISMS is one of the major areas of activity in the "Check" part of the PDCA process model "Monitor and Review the ISMS." There are several aspects of the ISMS an organization should be monitoring as defined by the ISO/IEC 27001 requirements, such as:

- Monitoring effectiveness and performance,

- Monitoring change,

- Monitoring the risks and business impacts, ISMS processes and the incident handling process,

- Monitoring peoples awareness, competence and utilisation of the ISMS,

- Monitoring the ICT, network monitoring, monitoring Internet usage and Web site monitoring,

- Monitoring third party services and SLAs,

- Monitoring compliance to the organization's policies and procedures, contractual obligations, laws and regulations.

6.11.7 Monitoring Effectiveness and Performance

This chapter and Chapter 5 have addressed the topic of ISMS metrics and measurements. Monitoring these measurements is very important as it provides some essential feedback regarding the effectiveness of many aspects of the ISMS: people, processes, policies, procedures, services, internal auditing and utilisation of ICT to name but a few.

The ISO/IEC 27001 requires a continuous cycle of PDCA processes to be in place not only to achieve effective information security, but also to take effectiveness measurements and the maintenance and improvement of the ISMS effectiveness.

Impermanence or change is a natural characteristic of all things, including everything a business has and does and the infrastructure and environment that support the business. Change requires regular attention, consideration and appropriate action to ensure the effectiveness of the ISMS is maintained and improved where necessary. Therefore, organizations need to regularly monitor and check the effectiveness of the ISMS using the following guiding questions as examples:

- Is the organization monitoring the ISMS effectiveness in the face of new threats, vulnerabilities, risks and impacts to be taken care of by the ISMS?

- Is the organization monitoring the ISMS effectiveness in the face of new business requirements (e.g., expansion of its business, using different technologies, embarking on new products, downsizing or upsizing the business or outsourcing part of its business)?

- Is the organization monitoring the effectiveness of its information security in relation to its business processes?

- Is the organization monitoring the effectiveness of its staff in how they perform in their job functions and roles in relation to information security?

- Is the organization monitoring the effectiveness of its incident handling process?

There are many other questions relating to the monitoring of information security and the effectiveness of its ISMS to enable the organization to check what changes and improvements need to be made to the ISMS to maintain its effectiveness. Reviewing the ISMS measurements enable the organization to check its ISMS effectiveness and to get an indication of its performance.

Is the organization "fit for purpose" to deliver services to its customers, to produce quality products, to manage its business risks and impacts, to manage its supplier chain, to do on-line transactions whilst preserving the confidentiality, integrity and availability of its information assets and those information assets that it might be handling and processing? Taking measurements, checking and reviewing these measurements and the ISMS effectiveness are key to meeting the requirements of ISO/IEC 27001.

6.11.8 Change

6.11.8.1 Certainty of Change

"Nothing is as constant as change" is an old adage that is very apt. It is often said that change is the quality of impermanence and everything on this earth is impermanent, in a state of constant flux. The Greek philosopher Heraclitus saw change as ever-present, ever-flowing and all encompassing.

Changes may happen slowly or rapidly, decrease/increase, go forward/reverse, or progress in the same/different direction, everything at one point in time will change, whether it will be something that is physically strong of weak, tangible or non-tangible. Change can be sequential, non-sequential or consequential. Organizations need to view change as a natural process and they should monitor and review the patterns of change, the speed and direction "its velocity" and any other aspects that will affect and impact the organization.

As SunZi's words (Section 6.8) reflect that the organization should be knowing itself and its business and knowing the environment and markets it is doing business in, which can lead to a better chance of achieving 100% success and of course continuation of this success. This requires the organization to know, understand and adapt in a suitable way to both the internal and external changes. The organization knowing its information security strengths and weaknesses (vulnerabilities) and also the threats that might exploit these vulnerabilities gives it a better chance of managing its information security risks. Regular monitoring and reviewing any changes to these strengths, weaknesses and threats enable it to be in a better position to continue to improve and maintain an effective information security capability.

An organization knowing its on-line business capability and its information security strengths and weaknesses and its competitors' capability, strengths and weaknesses in this field, enables it to manage and improve its information security risk controls capability. Again, regular monitoring and reviewing any changes to these conditions to achieve continual improvement and maintenance of an effective information security capability will make the most of business opportunities.

6.11.8.2 Resistance to Change

An organization could resist the changes or could react to them by adopting any changes that happen both of which in the first instance are unwise paths to take as further analysis should be undertaken to check whether this "knee jerk" is the best action to take. There may be individuals or certain business groups and not the whole organization itself that resist the change. Taking the "path of least resistance" is a good strategy for many difficult situations in all walks of life. Using an area of the business the organization knows to be open and receptive and which offers the least resistance to a proposed change is a good starting point to introduce and test out the change; this type of action is more likely to succeed. Once this area gains confidence through the deployment of the change and other parts of the organization see this success then the organization can start to roll out the change across the rest of the organization.

It should also be borne in mind that some things may not or should not need to be changed to ensure consistency and business continuity.   Adoption of changes should be in flow with the business and not a "big bang" approach but a "path of least resistance". For example, a complete overhaul and upgrading of the organization's ICT strategy for both ICT acquisition and deployment needs a good knowledge of the internal and external factors which might have an impact on this strategy. This could include issues such as knowing what external changes have driven this new strategy, what the changes will mean to the organization's staff as well as to its customers and suppliers, or what impact these changes will have on its market positioning.

6.11.8.3 Types of Change

There are changes driven by the market, for which the organization needs to decide how to react to and there are changes driven by the organization where it can be pro-active in driving and leading the market with new customer services and/or products. In both cases, business risks need to be considered, for example, the risks of adoption of new techniques by the organization driven by the market, or taking risks to drive the market with the organization's own development of new technologies. Other examples include:

- Legislation and regulations that drive the organization to react to avoid the risk of noncompliance,

- New, or changes to existing, contractual obligations, SLAs or contracts that drive the organization to react to avoid the risk of noncompliance or breach of contract,

- Changes in the supplier chain driving the organization or by being driven by the organization,

- Changes in the risk profile due to internal or external events and activities.

6.11.8.4 Change Management

Changes to the ISMS need to be approved and authorised and should be documented. ISO/IEC 27001 Annex A has several controls in this area of management including:

- A.10.1.2 Change management,

- A.10.2.3 Managing changes to third party services,

- A.10.3.2 System acceptance,

- A.12.4.1 Control of operational software,

- A.12.5.1 Change control procedures,

- A.12.5.3 Restrictions on changes to software packages.

6.11.8.5 Methods of Tracking Change

The overall monitoring process is about getting information about changes, system usage, being attentive to the rise or fall in threat and risk levels, tracking incidents and looking for trends and patterns. Several processes can be used to provide information about changes; an obvious one is the incident handling process, which provides information about changes to threats, vulnerabilities and risks and the organization's ability to respond to these. Reassessing the risks and impacts and doing gap analysis also provide similar information.

Scorecards, staff feedback and similar types of human methods can and do provide some valuable information. Technology in the form of firewalls, IDS devices, audit trail applications, monitoring tool for networks, services, Web browsing and Web-based applications can also add considerable value in this information gathering process. All these techniques help to build up a better picture of the changes, the trends and patterns allowing future planning and allow for well-informed management-decision making. The organization should not ignore the valuable information, which might be available from customer and supplier feedback.

6.11.9 Monitoring and Review Processes

ISO/IEC 27001 specifies a number of processes such as:

- Risk assessment, risk treatment and selection of controls (see Sections 4.2.1, 4.2.2, 4.2.3 and Chapter 7),

- Information handling and processing (see Section 4.3 and Annex A.7.2.2, A.10.7.3, A.10.9.2, A.11.6, A.12.2, 12.4, A.13.2.3 and A.15.1.2 to A.15.1.4),

- Incident handling (see Section 4.2.2 and Chapter 7 and Annex A.13),

- Backups (see Annexes A.10.5 and 10.7),

- Effectiveness (see Sections 4.2.2, 4.2.3, 5.2.2 and Chapter 7),

- Audits and reviews (see Sections 4.2.3 and Chapters 6 and 7),

- Access control (see Annexes A.9 and A.11).

All of these processes need some form of regular check-up, examination and assessment to check whether they are working effectively. For example, risk assessment should be an ongoing cyclic process; it occurs in the "Plan Phase" when designing the ISMS and again during the "Check Phase" when the ISMS is being monitoring and reviewed. In a similar way, the selection, implementation and utilisation of controls are a series of processes during the Plan and Check Phases and during the Do and Act Phases. The cyclic nature of the PDCA model requires regular use of these processes and others, to ensure that the ISMS attains effectiveness and maintains and improves the effectiveness.

Monitoring these processes is another one of the activities, which can have a profound effect on the success or failure of ISMS being effective against the very changing profile of business risks and impacts. Getting the monitoring right is a beneficial consequence to the achievement of effectiveness. Getting it right is not always easy. The organization will need to check that what it monitors and how it monitors against the real business values and requirements and monitoring should not just be done because ISO/IEC 27001 says so, as this might be a waste of the organization's resources. Taking, monitoring and evaluating the ISMS measurements should be a ceaseless and unremitting activity.

An implemented control might be working effectively in itself but unfortunately if the processes that lead to the selection of this control result in the wrong control being selected, then the whole exercise is a waste of time and money. There are many ISMS elements that need to work in an ordered and collaborative way to achieve effective information security, whether it is the processes driving the ISMS design, implementation and maintenance or the controls that are being implemented and utilised.

The best security technology in the world does not provide effective security if it is not configured, managed and maintained in a proper way commensurate with the business applications and environment in which it is utilised. The selection of the right technology for the job needs to be done based on a proper risk assessment and treatment process.

What drives the risk assessment process? Knowing the business, its objectives and requirements and the legal, regulatory and contractual requirements; these are the things that need to be understood, as they are vital inputs to the risk assessment process in addition to the threats, vulnerabilities, risks and impacts the organization faces. These and other ISMS processes seem very obvious but are not always achieved in practice.

There needs to be a series of interconnected and integrated monitoring and review activities, which brings together the various ISMS activities to achieve an effective end result. This is the intrinsic nature of the ISMS philosophy. Monitoring the ISMS processes is just as important as monitoring the controls. Monitoring has a major place in the process and the organization needs to schedule the right level of resource to see that it is done.

It should be noted again that everything that is in ISO/IEC 27001 can be scaled up or down depending on the complexity of the ISMS and the business, especially so when it comes to SME deployment. Monitoring should not be perceived as an onerous barrier. Take the first important step to get started the rest will develop.

6.11.10 Monitoring and Review of People's Awareness, Competency and Utilisation of the ISMS

6.11.10.1 Competence

Staff competence is generally considered to be the knowledge, skills and behaviour that the organization requires of an individual to properly perform a specific job function or role. For instance, a specific management role might require skills in influence and negotiation. A network manager's role should include technical knowledge, staff management and analytical skills. Someone working in the personnel group handling all the staff records needs to have a working knowledge of the legislation that applies to the handling of personnel data, information security to protect personal data; he/she will need knowledge of handing personnel affairs, skills at handling many personnel issues and good communication skills to name but a few of the abilities he/she needs to possess.

An individual may not be considered competent for a different job function or a change in this role but he/she does not lose the skills, abilities, qualities and knowledge that he/she possesses.

It is often said that a part of human nature and psychology tends to make people self-examine themselves and either under- or over-estimate their competence: those that are grossly incompetent at tasks tend to grossly overestimate, while those that are very competent people tend to underestimate themselves. Good management should always motivate rather than de-motivate their staff as they are one of the most important assets of the organization. Even in organizations that are fully automated there is still the need for staff. Providing a good management leadership and right motivation, giving the right amount of responsibility and incentives and enabling good communication channels between management and staff are pathways to success.

6.11.10.2 Security Culture

Staff are a significant driver in their own productivity, therefore, it follows that if they are disgruntled, dissatisfied, operating under poor working conditions, or are not being stretched to their levels of skill and competency their productivity will not be as good as it could be. Whichever area of business life, this seems to be generally true, including information security. Developing a healthy security culture within the organization should be one of the main aims of the organization. This topic of "security culture" is very important as a management control for information security; it is being addressed by various institutions and organizations, including the OECD in their paper "Guidelines for the Security of Information Systems and Networks – Towards a Culture of Security, July 2002."

Some organizations have had "security culture" for many years, others are only starting to realize the importance and benefits it offers to the protection of their information security. It is often said that ICT is not the problem of information security it's the people using the ICT, which matches up to many of the security surveys which report that people are the cause of many security breaches and incidents.

6.11.10.3 Monitoring

Monitoring people in relation to their responsibilities and roles regarding information security is extremely important. However, this should not be done in a "big brother" way, over-surveillance of staff, covertly or any way that is going make staff feel ill at ease, de-motivated, overly restricted, limited, or contained in a "workplace prison" which can lead to mistakes, accidents or unintentional errors being made, which might impact the effectiveness of the information security.

Many organizations have "acceptable use policy (AUP)" to regulate the use of ICT and Internet services, such as email. To ensure compliance the organization needs to operate some form of monitoring, for example monitoring and recording employees' emails.

Regulations such as RIPA (The UK Regulatory Investigatory Powers Act) provide some provisions for the legal intercept and monitoring of communications that enter and leave their networks.

However, in other countries this is not always the case as no such laws exist or it is deemed as an offence to do such types of monitoring as has well been demonstrated by the number of court cases that have appeared over the years, such as in the dismissal of employees for using the organization's email system inappropriately for private use.

6.11.10.4 Awareness, Training and Career Development

Developing and improving staff knowledge and skills require an appropriate level of training and awareness. Formal classroom training, on-the-job training and on-line training and learning are some of the ways the organization can help its staff in attaining the right levels of knowledge and skills for the job. As people are of such importance to an organization to meet its objectives and performance levels, it is equally important to look after staff training, awareness and career development. Not only does this ensure that the organization has the right competent people to do the job but it also motivates staff as their career development is being looked after and avoids unnecessary loss of skilled staff that do not receive such attention. Section 6.3.8 covers example measurements concerning staff awareness and training.

Monitoring staff regarding their on-going competence to perform specific job functions enables the organization to further improve their knowledge, skills and abilities to continue to perform such a job. Of course, it might want to transfer the individual to another job function requiring a different set of competencies and monitoring the individual's ability, knowledge and career development enables the organization to provide that member of staff with retraining. The personnel group plays a key role in managing the process of matching job competency requirements to the skills and knowledge of existing staff or the recruitment of new staff.

6.11.11 Monitoring ICT, Networks and Service Usage

This, like other areas, has major implications on the effectiveness of the organization's information security management. Monitoring and reviewing the acceptable use of organizational resources, given the high level of incidents that are caused by the insider threat, whether intentional or accidental, should take place in any circumstances as this is a must in an effective ISMS (see ISO/IEC 27001 Annex A.7.1.3). Monitoring and review measures should be in place at different levels:

- Human resources level (such as ISO/IEC 27001 5.2.2 and 7, as well as Annex A.8),

- Process, policy and procedural level (such as ISO/IEC 27001 4.2.3, 6 and 7, as well as Annexes A.7.1.3, A.10.1.1 and A.10.10),

- Technical level (such as ISO/IEC 27001 4.2.3, as well as Annexes A.10.10 and A.11.4 to 11.6).

6.11.12 Monitoring and Reviewing Third Party Contracts, SLA's and Provision of Service Delivery

6.11.12.1 Service Management

ISO/IEC 27001 Annex A.10.2.1 concerns the level of service delivery, especially considering how services are implemented, operated and maintained.

In ISO/IEC 27001 Annex A.10.2.2 addresses the monitoring and reviewing of third party services. This includes reviewing the records of service performance, service levels and any problems in not achieving the requirements of the SLA, risk levels, service recovery and any incidents that may have occurred. The reasons for doing this are manifold, but one important reason is to keep track of the supplier's delivery of services and to check whether it is in compliance with the contract and SLA (as discussed in ISO/IEC 27001 Annexes A.6.2.1 and A.6.2.3). Another reason is to revise the contract and/or SLA because the organization wants to make changes: reduce or expand its current services, revise the current level of service, or to add new services.

Another aspect is the auditing of the supplier's system to check for compliance against what has been agreed between the contracted parties. It is strongly recommended that the contract and/or SLA, contains provisions giving the organization a right to audit.

ISO/IEC 27001 Annex A.10.2.3 considers the change management aspects of service delivery. Changes to how the services are provided, how the services are maintained and upgraded/updated, improvements to the services, the delivery methods and facilities and contractual and SLA changes.

6.11.12.2. Monitoring and Reviewing Service Provider Changes

For whatever the reason changes on the supplier side will happen, the organization needs to be informed of these to understand and review whether these changes will impact it. There is always a need for ICT changes at the service provider end. Maybe its success has secured it more business with existing clients or new clients to meet the increase in demand for ICT facilities and services.

It might be the case that the provider wants to make changes to stay ahead of its competitors and to be number one in its field of outsourcing, replacing outdated systems, or by introducing changes to improve, streamline and/or make its operations more cost-effective.

Whatever the reason, ICT changes might involve all or some of the hardware, software, operational environments, management tools, networking arrangements, connections and services to change.

Conveying these changes to the supplier's clients through regular channels of communication and reporting helps both sides to reassess the risks and plan for any changes that might directly affect the client. This type of reporting should be in the existing contract and a contract review process needs to be initiated to discuss, negotiate and agree to changes to the contract.

6.11.12.3 Termination of Contract

One clear reason for terminating a contract is the failure of the service provider to meet the requirements of the organization, such as being unable to meet the level of service required or being unable or not willing to expand its services or increase its service levels to meet the demands of the organization.

Other reasons might be that the service provider is taken over or merged with other organizations, has moved its location to a different geographic area which presents a greater security risk, or simply that the service goes out of business.

Whatever the scenario, there are several challenges to be considered. If a termination does go ahead how is the organization going to protect its assets between finishing one contract and starting another?

Does it have the skills in-house to protect and manage them in-house? The organization needs to take account of the fact that in any transition between suppliers all parties need to be involved to ensure a relatively problem-free change over taking place, especially no glitch in the continuation of its operations.

The business continuity process needs to address these issues regarding changes in providers, the transition period and the protection of an organization's assets.

6.11.13 Monitoring and Reviewing Legal and Contractual Compliance

ISO/IEC 27001 Annex A.15 considers some of the general requirements and provisions regarding legal and regulatory compliance, as well as contractual and and the organization's policy compliance. It is vital that an organization keeps track of its compliance with those laws and regulations that apply to it.

The more multinational the organization is the more pieces of legislation and regulation it needs to deal with, as well as considering the legislation for trading across the Internet between jurisdictions. The impact on an organization for failing to comply has been addressed in other parts of this book, such as in Section 6.8.6.3.

6.12 IMPROVEMENTS

"Knowledge rests not upon truth alone, but upon error also." Karl Gustav Jung

6.12.1 Bringing It All Together and Closure

Improving the ISMS to maintain an appropriate level of effective protection is the last phase of the PDCA process cycle but the work does not stop there. The PDCA process is a continuing life cycle of implementation, deployment, monitoring, review, maintenance and improvement of activities to continue achieving effective information security management. So what does the Act phase constitute in terms of things to do? The following are some of the activities that should take place:

- Take corrective and preventive actions to improve the ISMS based on the decisions made at the Check phase (see ISO/IEC 27001 Sections 4.2.4, 8.1, 8.2 and 8.3), such as

    - Implement new measures
    - Upgrade and improve the performance of existing measures

- Implement and test these ISMS improvements and then deploy them in the organization (see ISO/IEC 27001 Sections 4.2.2 and 4.3),

- Provide new training, or upgrading of existing training for staff, especially for those that will be directly involved with utilizing these improvements (see ISO/IEC 27001 Sections 4.2.2 and 5.2.2 and Annex A.8.2.2),

- Review the provision of resources needed to deploy and utilize the implemented improvement (see ISO/IEC 27001 Sections 5.1 and 5.2),

- Review the competencies of those staff that are directly involved (see ISO/IEC 27001 Annex A.8.1.1, A.8.2.1 and A.8.3.1),

- Update or produce new policies, procedures, processes, monitoring and measurement methods to reflect these improvements (see ISO/IEC 27001 Sections 4.2.2 and 4.3 and controls from Annex A relating to procedures, such as A.7.2.2, A.10.1.1, A.10.7.1, A.10.8.1, A.10.8.5, A.10.10.2 and A.13.2.1),

- Communicate to all staff that must know the details (i.e. to the level that is appropriate and relevant to them) about these improvements, new measures, new policies and procedures, including outside third parties, customers and other external parties that need to know about the changes, as well as updating relevant contracts and SLAs, if necessary (see ISO/IEC 27001 Section 4.2.4 and Annex A.10.2.3),

- Document and record all the changes that have been made using some form of change management process (see ISO/IEC 27001 Section 4.3).

The Check Phase identified information to formulate what needs to be done to improve. The Act Phase does the work to improve, in a very similar way to the Do Phase. In fact, not wanting to be over simplistic, the Plan (e.g., do a risk assessment) and Check (e.g., reassess the risks) Phases have several things in common, as do the Do (e.g., implement controls) and Act (e.g., implement new or improved existing controls) Phases, they are close to being duals of each other.

The success of the PDCA model reviewing the effectiveness in a "measured" way and responding/reacting in a "measured" way provides a good path to follow. Reviewing in a "measured" way but reacting in an "unmeasured" way, is likely not to get us to a point the review suggests we should be at. Reviewing and reacting in an "unmeasured" way, is likely to get us nowhere, using the same thinking process as SunZi on the Art of War quote (see Section 6.8).

To have complete closure of this Phase all the actions given at the start of 6.12.1 need to be dealt with. This may not take place overnight as some of the changes may take some time to implement, such as training, management of resources and updating of procedures and policies. There needs to be time for the actions to be completed in the improvement plan, as well as it needs to be identified who is responsible for the actions, who is responsible for the improvement project and who is responsible for a review process to check progress against the plan. All the normal things that organizations would do on other projects.

6.12.2 Resolving Conflicts or Blockages

Like most things in business, plans do not always go right the first time. There may be things in the plan which when implemented cause conflicts with existing systems, or the conflict might be with the staff. The fault might lie in the information gathering stage, the analysis stage or bad decision making, all of which can have a knock-on effect.

An extreme example might be implementing a plan to install several new networked systems that have been selected through a decision making process, but an appropriate analysis of the capacity requirements has not been done and the assessment that had been done grossly underestimated the demands of the organization's staff and those of its customers.

There have been real examples over the years, such as a major organization serving thousands of customers underestimated the demands and at switch-on, the system gradually came to a halt within half a day due to a high demand. Sometimes it is not easy to get an accurate enough measure of the demands and like most systems the demands peak and increase as time goes by, but a well-thought out analysis on capacity demands can help the organization to avoid these problems.

By way of another example, consider the case of the lack of consultation and awareness with staff and the changes that might cause staff to resist and react unfavourably to the changes. During the Monitoring and Review Phase, staff should be involved in some way or other in the process and before deciding and approving the changes management should be sensitive to this problem and communicate with the staff. This is not special to information security management but applies to every aspect of business, which can have a direct impact on their roles and responsibilities in their day-to-day work.

Communication and awareness are key to avoiding some of the problems keeping staff informed of changes is always the best strategy and discussing with them any problems which might hamper the implementation and utilisation of such changes. Of course, there will be aspects of the business and its business decision-making that are marked "In-Strictest-Confidence" and needs to be kept that way until the time and conditions are right for making major announcements.

So how an organization introduces changes and improvements needs to be handled with care and attention and with an appropriate level of staff awareness and consultation for any proposed changes.

One thing that should be done is to engender a security culture in the organization; this will help to pave the way for a better understanding of the risks and how everyone in the organization plays a part in managing the risk. It brings together staff and management to talk in a common language, to collaborate together towards a common set of risk management goals, to develop an information security community that everyone can work with and will benefit and enable the organization to do its business securely and to reap the gains of future success and profitable well-being of the organization and that of its staff.

6.12.3 The Next Phase

There is no end to this process. As soon as we have closed the loop on implementing the agreed improvements, the risk profile of the organization might have changed not just today but maybe weeks or a month or more ago. Everything we have already discussed is in a state of flux and ever changing so nothing is permanent. No sooner have we implemented a solution for last week's risks than a new one appears today.

What should we do, panic? Should we not feel complacent or feel that this is a never-ending struggle? The only thing we can be certain of is that change is constant and so is impermanence. Benjamin Franklin once said "The only two things we can be certain of is taxes and death" but even these two things are subject to the conditions and changes that are associated with these things and these conditions are subject to change. Yes, we all die, but when and how depends on the conditions.

Regarding taxes, someone can choose not to earn so much or to live and work in a country where tax rates are lower, which are conditions related to how much is paid and of course when a person retires he/she normally does not pay any income tax, but of course he/she still pays taxes on investments and on some goods he/she buys in shops. So this quote should be taken in the spirit it is said.

So what happens next? One thing that needs to be done is to regularly assess the information security risks and the business impacts the organization faces. There will also be a changing risk profile for the business, which needs to be tracked and observed.

Are there things that we can be sure about of the risks of tomorrow and the future? The answer, of course, is no, but if we have been tracking the trends and patterns using the organization's own incident handling process, the results from feedbacks and reviews and the tracking of official, authentic Web sites that post information about the current vulnerabilities and future trends, then this will give a good estimate of at least some of the risks the organization will be facing. Of course, annual or biannual surveys about information security breaches do also provide some information.

The following are some incidents that will probably occur with the business community in the foreseeable future as the trends indicate that the rate of growth of these threats is not slow or solutions to avoid or counter them are not available:

- Denial of service (DoS) and DDoS attacks,

- Identity theft and information theft,

- Environmental hazards such as earthquakes, volcano eruptions, floods and global warming,

- Continuing development of malicious code,

- Spam,

- Computer glitches, system failures and crashes,

- Insider threats,

- Terrorist threats.

What about future predictions? Here are some guesses:

- Panepidemic problems,

- Political problems,

- Catastrophic natural disasters, such as the predictions of a super volcano, super-tsunami, large-scale earthquakes, one event triggering another,

- National and global infrastructure disasters.

Removal of the GAIA (named after Gaia or Gaea, the Greek goddess of the earth or the Earth's grandmother), the thin band around the Earth (defined as encapsulating the Earth's incandescent interior and its surrounding upper atmosphere), which regularly refreshes itself as an ecosystem cyclic regulator (Do-Act process model) is essential for the survival of earth.

It is predicted, by some experts, to be the worst and ultimate threat to all sentient beings and other living organisms and systems. This GAIA is gradually and surely being overstretched by man's continuing and excessive demands, bad decision making and indiscriminate usage. Once it can't refresh itself properly or fast enough everything is doomed and so the ISMS PDCA process model grinds to a halt.

The same principle applies in the information security world: if the organization cannot respond fast enough to disaster, then it cannot recover in a timely way, or if an organization exhausts its resources dealing with severe incidents and it cannot refresh these resources fast enough then it could be heading for a state of collapse and financial ruin.

Before we get lost in a long philosophical argument let's take stock. It all sounds doom and gloom, but it is always good to be prepared for the worst case scenario and to do a realistic risk assessment as might be possible, with all information gathered from reliable sources.

One thing is certain, threats of all sorts will always be there and they can affect the organization if the conditions are right. Another thing that is certain is that an organization that fails to deal with the vulnerabilities it has is likely to be at risk as these threats exploit these vulnerabilities. So one of the real-life actions that management and staff need to do is to continue to assess its risks and vulnerabilities and do something about them to avoid incidents occurring through threats exploitation, resulting in a dire impact to the organization.

The PDCA processes for information security management are aimed at doing just this. So the organization needs to continue this cycle of improving the effectiveness of its information security management.

On a final word before starting to progress around the PDCA cycle again is the question of cost. If the cost of continuing around the PDCA loop is thought to be a barrier, then generally this is the wrong view. All the time, resources and effort in going around once would result in a loss in the organization's investment if it is not pursued in later cycles.

What would be the alternative? Having no ISMS and suffering an information security impact which could be very costly? Having an ISMS will cost, but if designed and implemented properly it will reduce these losses.

The secret is to get the balance right between the costs to and the benefit for the organization, spending and investing to the right level on the right level of information security whilst maintaining a sense of commercial realization. Not too much, not too little, just enough.

By using the continual improvement cycle, the PDCA allows the organization to fine-tune the ISMS to get this balance right and adapt it to the ever changing requirements.

Another point to bear in mind is that after the first ISMS round the organization will have all the processes, control systems, policies and procedures in place. So the second, third and subsequent rounds should be a case of fine-tuning with revisions and improvements. So these turns around the PDCA should be easier in cost and resources and staff usage.

There will always be regular maintenance costs, but these costs are likely to be small compared with the costs of letting the ISMS fall into disrepair. Of course, there will always be the unforeseen incident or the major company change.

This could happen with or without an ISMS being in place, but hopefully if the ISMS is running effectively and is being regularly maintained then the ISMS being in place will help to reduce the business impact and to learn lessons to avoid this in the future.

So having an ISMS in place that continues to provide effective information security management is well worth the investment in terms of business benefits, as has been demonstrated by the thousands of organizations that are using the ISO/IEC 27001 standards as their business information security framework and benchmarking tool.

Chapter 7

ISMS Certification

7.1 INTRODUCTION

This chapter explores the world of third party ISMS certification. The basic ideas of who does what are covered, what the process involves, who does the audit and what qualifications are needed and finally the current international trend for ISMS certification.

7.2 CERTIFICATION SYSTEM

The players involved in the process are ISMS certifications accreditation bodies, certification bodies and the end user (the organization whose ISMS is to be certified), see Table 7.1. ISMS certification uses the same model as other management systems such as ISO 9001 for quality, ISO 14001 for environment and ISO 22000 for food safety.

The accreditation body (AB) is responsible for assessing the adequacy of the certification body (CB) to carry out ISMS certifications in accordance with international standards and criteria for accreditation. This involves the AB:

- Carrying out head office visits to check that the CB has the necessary systems and procedures in place and functioning to undertake such audits and has the right level of qualified auditors for ISMS certifications,

- Carrying ISMS on-site witnessed audits to assess the competency of the auditors working in practice on customers' sites.

Examples of accreditation bodies are UKAS in the United Kingdom, SWEDAC in Sweden, TGA in Germany and JIPDEC in Japan see http://www.european-accreditation.org for a list of the European accreditation bodies and www.iaf.nu for the international list of accreditation bodies.

A certification body (CB) carries out the audit for third party ISO 27001 certification after being assessed and accredited by an Accreditation Body to provide ISMS certification services. Currently, there are over 40 certification bodies in the world that have been accredited to provide ISMS certification services (see www.iso27001certificates.com for the current list).

Accreditation body (AB)	Assess the CB to check their capability of providing ISMS certification services

Certificate body (CB)	Carries out audits on the end user's ISMS

End user organization ISMS	Designs, implements, deploys, maintains and updates its ISMS

Table 7.1 Players involved in the process

The standard ISO 17021-1 (previously ISO Guide 62 and EN 45012) defines the general requirements and criteria for accreditation. This document is applicable to CBs that carry out certification audits on ISO 9001 quality management systems, ISO 14001 environmental management systems, ISO 27001 ISMS and other auditable standards specifying management systems.

In addition, the standard ISO 27006 (previously EA 7/03) interprets and further amplifies the requirements of ISO 17021-1 specifically in the context of ISMS audits. These standards also require the auditors that are employed by the CB to comply with the relevant guidelines for auditing contained in the standard ISO 19011, which specifies what to do to plan, undertake and manage the audit process.

7.3 CERTIFICATION AND ACCREDITATION

Once the CB has been accredited it can then carry out ISMS certifications for three years, during which its performance will be monitored by the AB by regular surveillance visits. After the three years its accreditation can be reviewed and extended to another three years following another AB assessment.

The CB issues certificates to end users based on a successful audit being carried out and again this certificate lasts for three years. Similarly in this three-year period the CB will carry out surveillance audits every 6 to 12 months. After three years the end user organization can be re-issued with a certificate following a successful re-certification audit by the CB,

7.4 STANDARDS INVOLVED

The main standards involved in the accreditation and certification process are:

7.4.1 Accreditation

The following are the current standards used by the AB to assess and accredit the CB:

- ISO 17021-1 (Requirements of bodies providing audit and certification services of management systems),

- ISO 27006 (Requirements of bodies providing audit and certification services of information security management systems),

- ISO 19011 (Guidelines for quality and/or environmental management systems auditing).

7.4.2 Certification

The following are the current standards used by the CB to audit and certify the customer's ISMS:

- ISO 27001 (ISMS requirements),

- ISO 19011 (Guidelines for quality and/or environmental management systems auditing).

Organizations of course may use all the other standards in the 27000 series for supporting guidance and advice of the implementation of ISO 27001 such as ISO 27002 regarding control advice, ISO 27005 on risk management, or ISO 27004 on ISMS measurements.

7.5 ISMS AUDITS

7.5.1 Certification Scope

The scope of the ISMS (as detailed in ISO 27001, Chapter 4) is defined by the organization that wants to achieve certification. It is the role of the CB to check that this scope is consistent with its business and that it does not exclude any part of their operation, which could affect the organization's capability and/or responsibility, to provide information security that meets the security requirements determined by risk assessment and applicable regulatory requirements.

The CB should therefore ensure that the organization's information security risk assessment properly reflects its activities and extends to the boundaries of its ISMS activities as defined in ISO 27001 (Chapter 4) and it should confirm that this is reflected in the organization's Statement of Applicability (SoA, see ISO 27001 Chapter 4). If the ISMS interfaces with services or activities that are not completely within its scope the risks associated with these interfaces should nevertheless be included in the organization's information security risk assessment.

7.5.2 Audit Process

The certification of an organization's information security management system (ISMS) against the standard ISO 27001 is a two-stage audit process as detailed in ISO 27006.

7.5.3 Audit Stage 1

During this stage the CB carries out an examination of the documentation covering the design and implementation of the ISMS. This will include at least the definition of the ISMS scope and its ISMS policy, the risk assessment report and risk treatment plan, the Statement of Applicability and other core elements of ISMS. This review enables the auditors to get an understanding and appreciation of the organization's ISMS scope, policy and design. This then will provide a focus for planning the subsequent parts of the audit. It gives an indication of the state of preparedness of the organization for the audit. Once this review is complete and an audit report is produced the CB is in a position to decide whether to proceed with the audit. Before proceeding to the next stage the CB needs to bring together an audit team with the necessary competence to address the auditing of the organization's ISMS scope.

7.5.4 Audit Stage 2

During this stage the CB's audit team visits the site(s) of the organization covered by the ISMS scope. The objective of this stage is to confirm that the organization complies with and adheres to its own policies, business objectives and procedures in accordance with all the requirements of the ISO 27001 standard.

The audit team will focus on the organization's:

- Evaluation and review of its information security related risks,

- Its selection of controls and its Statement of Applicability,

- The resulting ISMS design and implementation.

The audit team also considers what the organization has put in place for monitoring and measuring ISMS performance and effectiveness, as well as reporting and reviewing against its business objectives and targets. The assessment will include checking:

- What has been put into operation to ensure that security and management reviews take place,

- That there is an internal ISMS audit process in service,

- What management responsibility has been defined for implementation and deployment of its information security policy.

An important aspect of the audit is the presentation and examination of objective evidence to demonstrate the audit trail links between the information security policy, the results of the risk assessments, security objectives and targets, the responsibilities for information security, the system of controls and procedures and what has been put in place for performance monitoring and security reviews.

7.5.5 Nonconformities

In the case of ISO 27001 a nonconformity is the absence of, or the failure to implement and maintain, one or more required ISMS elements, or a situation, which would, on the basis of objective evidence raise significant doubt as to the capability of the ISMS to achieve the security policy and objectives of the organization.

The CB can define grades of deficiency and areas for improvement (e.g., major or minor nonconformities and observations). However, all such grades of deficiency, which equate to this definition of nonconformity should be dealt with as specified in ISO 17021-1 and ISO 27006 (previously ISO Guide 62 and EA 7/03).

7.5.6 Audit Report

The audit team is required to provide to the CB a report of its findings and recommendations as to the conformity of the organization's ISMS with all of the requirements of the ISO 27001 standard. Any nonconformity to be discharged in order to comply with all of the requirements of the ISO 27001 standard should be promptly brought to the organization's attention.

The CB shall ask the organization to comment on the report and to describe the specific corrective actions it will take, or plans it will take within a defined time, to remedy any nonconformity. The closure of such follow-up actions may need a full or partial reassessment of the ISMS, or a written declaration to be confirmed during surveillance may be considered adequate.

This report should include the identification of ISMS elements audited, the assessed scope of the ISMS being audited, comments on the conformity of the organization's ISMS with the requirements of the standard with a clear statement of any nonconformity and, where applicable, any useful comparison with the results of previous assessments of the organization.

The decision whether or not to award a certificate in regard to an organization's ISMS shall be made by the CB on the basis of the information gathered during the audit, the audit report and any other relevant information. Those who review the report and make the decision to certify shall not have been those that have participated in the ISMS audit.

The certificate awarded to the organization carries the logo of the CB as well as the logo of the accreditation body that has accredited the CB.

7.5.7 Surveillance Audits

The CB will carry out periodic surveillance audits at sufficiently close intervals to verify that the organization's certified ISMS continues to comply with the requirements of the ISO 27001 standard and the ISMS remains effective with regard to achieving the objectives of the organization's information security policy. This audit should also examine the action taken by the organization on nonconformities identified during the last audit.

If nonconformities are found during surveillance audits then these shall be effectively corrected within a time agreed by the CB. If correction of any non-conformity is not made within this agreed time then the certification shall be suspended or even withdrawn. The time given to carry out corrective action should be consistent with the severity of the nonconformity.

According to the ISMS standard ISO 27001 the organization needs to conduct internal ISMS audits at planned intervals to determine whether the ISMS system of controls, processes and procedures conforms to the requirements of the standard. At the same time the audit should take account of the relevant legislation or regulations requirements and that the ISMS has been effectively implemented, is effectively maintained and performs as expected. An audit programme shall be planned taking into consideration the status and importance of the ISMS processes and areas to be audited, as well as the results of previous audits.

7.5.8 Recertification

Recertification is normally carried out every three years and its purpose is to verify the overall continuing conformity of the organization's ISMS to the requirements of the ISO 27001 standard and that the ISMS has been properly implemented and maintained.

Recertification and surveillance audit programmes should normally include:

- Verification that the approved ISMS continues to be implemented,

- Consideration of the implications of changes to the ISMS system of controls initiated as a result of changes in the organization's operation and ensuring the overall effectiveness of the ISMS in its entirety in the light of changes in operations. This includes changes to the ISMS documented system,

- Confirmation of continued compliance with the requirements of ISO 27001 and a demonstration of the commitment to maintain the effectiveness of the ISMS and the effective interaction between all elements of the ISMS,

- Aspects of system maintenance, which are the internal ISMS audit, internal security review, management review and preventive and corrective action.

The ISMS processes based on the PDCA model as specified in the ISO 27001 standard provide a management framework for an organization to realize a programme of continual improvement. This should provide the organization with effective ISMS implementation and deployment for the common good and governance of its business and which also matches the aims of the re-certification and surveillance audit activities mentioned above.

7.5.9 Audit Trails

An important aspect of a certification audit is the collection of objective evidence. In gathering such evidence an auditor commonly looks for a sample of audit trails. For example the organization should have carried out a risk assessment, risk treatment and selection of controls exercise leading to a Statement of Applicability (SoA). The auditor should be able to back track this process looking for evidence that the organization has carried out the process correctly, for example:

- The Statement of Applicability shows a specific control set has been selected for implementation question, What was the decision making that went behind this selection?

- Tracing backwards, the auditor might then want to discuss this decision making process in relation to the risk treatment options selected,

- Tracing back further the auditor might then ask, What risks were identified in the risk report that led to the risk treatment option of reducing the risks?

- Tracing back the auditor might want to look at the risk assessment report and discuss the control set that has been selected commensurate with the assets, threats and vulnerability they relate to and the associated risks that have been identified,

- The auditor will want to check by gathering answers and evidence that there is a correspondence from the controls in the SoA back to the risk assessment that has been carried out.

Other examples include checking on the incident handling process that is in place from:

- Detection, reporting and recording the incident,

- To the analysis of the incident,

- To the corrective actions taken to resolve and recover from the incident,

- To the closure of the incident action,

- To follow-up actions and activities to ensure preventative measures are deployed to avoid reoccurrence of the incident.

Again the auditor could build up an audit trail of objective evidence that the correct procedures and deployment incident handling controls are in place to manage the risks of incidents past, present and future.

There are many examples in the implementation and deployment of the controls from ISO 27001 Annex A (i.e., the control statements from ISO 27002). These might include establishing audit trails relating to:

- Access control measures and procedures,

- Backups,

- Business continuity plans and testing,

- Email and Internet policies,

- Legal and regulatory controls,

- Third party contracts, SLAs. and service delivery,

- Physical security measures

Like the two examples given earlier the auditor should be looking to build up audit trails of objective evidence that the correct procedures and deployment of controls are in place to manage the risks of the business. The auditor will also be looking at the on-going management of these processes and controls looking for indications and evidence that the organization is monitoring and reviewing its systems to check how effective its security is and what measures are planned to improve in areas where the security is not so effective.

7.5.10 Auditor Competence and Qualifications

Confidence and reliance in the certification audit process depend on the competence of the auditors conducting the audit. ISO 17021-1 and ISO 27006 (see Chapter 7 and Annex A.2) require the CB's to have a system in place to analyse the necessary competencies in information security management it needs to have and to be able to select auditors with these competencies to ensure that the audits are carried out effectively and uniformly. The general criteria for auditor competence are given in ISO 19011 and are based on a demonstration of the ability to apply a range of knowledge and skills gained from the formal education and IT and ISMS work experience, ISMS auditor training and auditing experience.

Auditors are expected to develop, maintain and improve their competence through a programme of continual professional development and by participating regularly in ISMS audits.

IRCA (International Register of Certificates Auditors) has defined a set of criteria for auditor certification based on ISO 19011 (general auditor competence) and ISO 27006 (ISMS specific competence). This covers the minimum requirements that auditors need to satisfy in terms of formal education, work experience, auditor training and auditing experience to be certified as either an ISMS auditor or ISMS lead auditor, see www.irca.org. Also IRCA has defined the criteria for ISMS training courses based on the ISO 27000 series of standards. Training organizations can apply to IRCA to have their courses approved according to the criteria.

7.5.11 Costs and resources

The cost to the end user organization of implementing an ISMS and having the ISMS certified breaks down into components: the cost of the CBs certification work (initial audit, follow-up surveillance audits and re-certification audits) and the cost of internal work (preparing for certification, on-going surveillance audits and maintenance and operational costs).

How these costs are calculated varies and is dependent on several factors, for example, the complexity of the ISMS being implemented. In ISO 27006 Annex A.1 and A.3 there are some examples of what makes up this complexity as well as some guidance on calculating auditor time.

As regards the internal costs then this includes:

- Reviewing risks and taking measurements of ISMS effectiveness,

- Implementing and deploy ISMS controls,

- Producing documentation,

- Awareness and training,

- Resources for specific security functions (e.g., a security officer/manager, firewall administration, or physical security manager).

Of course, this might seem an expensive exercise but it should be realized that some of these items should be everyday expenses for a lot of companies since documentation, training and awareness are required in other areas of the business. Also depending on the size and system's complexity these costs maybe not be large at all. In effect if security is integrated, as it should be, with other parts of the business then some of these costs will be absorbed and shared by other business functions and operations.

If information security is seen as an important aspect of the business and it is rare to find a company where some aspect of information security is not required, then resources will need to be part of the business budget whether or not the organization goes for certification. Of course it is a commercial balance and a trade-off between implementing just the appropriate level of security and going over the top with unnecessary expenditure. This is why it is important to carry out an information security risk assessment so that management can make the right decisions on what to spend money (see ISO 27001 Chapter 4). Hence we must not lose sight of the fact that the business needs to survive in today's dynamic and competitive markets and so the more accurate its analysis of the risks the company faces the better informed management is to make the right decisions to do the best for the company and how best to invest in information security.

7.5.12 International Certification Business

ISMS certifications are carried out in over 55 countries and involving organizations small, medium and large, from a diverse range of business sectors:

- Telecoms and network services and suppliers,

- Financial and insurance industries,

- Manufacturing,

- Retail industries,

- Utilities (electricity, gas and water),

- IT vendors, suppliers and services,

- Research and development,

- Professions (e.g., legal profession),

- Government departments and agencies,

- Academic sector.

This diversity demonstrates not only the importance of information security to every business but also the wide applicability of the ISO 27000 series of standards to meet the demands of business for a "common language" for addressing information security issues.

The motivation for going for a third party ISMS audit is also varied for example:

- To comply with legislation and regulations (e.g., data privacy and protection, governance and computer misuse and hacking),

- As part of customer and supplier chain contracts (there are more tenders and RFPs that are now including ISO 27001 compliance clauses),

- To demonstrate "fitness for purpose" (see Chapter 2),

- Insurance reasons (there are instances where insurance premiums have been lowered as organizations can demonstrate they have an effective risk management system in place),

- Market competition (demonstrating ISMS excellence in a particular sector).

The growth in ISMS certifications continues bolstered by the introduction of the international versions (ISO 27001 and ISO 27002) of the previous UK standards BS 7799 Parts 1 and 2. The current growth trend is Asia, followed by Europe, then the Americas and finally Africa and the MiddleEast. The current breakdown (at the time of this writing) is:

- Asia (including Australia and New Zealand) 71%,

- Europe 21%,

- Americas 7%,

- Africa and the Middle East 2%

Even though this percentage looks asymmetric, the growth rate in areas of the world is continually increasing and predictions from the market are that the lower percentage regions are expected to increase in the near future.

An international register is available on-line that lists all of the certifications. This register is kept up to date on a regular basis using the information provided by Certification Bodies, which is sent to the Registrars at edward.xisec@zen.co.uk and aexisap@aol.com. The Web site www.iso27001certificates.com is the official site for Register listings.

Bibliography

Peter L Bernstein, Against the Gods The Remarkable Story of Risk, John Wiley & Sons, Inc, New York 1998

BS 7799 Part 1, Code of practice for information security management, BSI, 1995 and 1998 versions

BS 7799 Part 2, Information security management system requirements, BSI, 1998 and 2002 versions

BS 7799 Part 3: ISMS Risk Management

BSI BIP 71 Guidelines on requirements and preparation for ISMS (Information security management system) certification based on ISO/IEC 27001:2005

BSI BIP 72 Are you ready for ISMS Audits? - An assessment workbook for ISO/IEC 27001:2005

BSI BIP 73 Implementation and auditing of ISMS controls - Guidance for organizations preparing for certification

BSI BIP 74 Guidelines on Measuring the Effectiveness of ISMS (Information security management system) Implementations

Code of practice for information security management, DTI, 1992

Mark Haynes Daniell, World of Risk – Next Generation Strategy for a Volatile Era, John Wiley & Sons, Inc, New York 2000

Gerd Gigerenzer, Reckoning with Risk', Allen Lane, New York, The Penguin Press, Penguin Books Ltd, 2002

Information security – Protecting Your Business Assets, DTI Publication, URN 04/626; 07/06 www.dti.gov.uk

Information security - Business Assurance Guidelines, DTI Publication, URN 04/625; 07/06 www.dti.gov.uk

ISO/IEC 27001 Information security management system requirements, ISO, 2005

ISO/IEC 27002 (previously ISO/IEC 17799) Code of practice for information security management

ISO/IEC 27003 ISMS Implementation Guide

ISO/IEC 27004 Information security management measurements

ISO/IEC 27005 ISMS Risk management

ISO/IEC 27006 Accreditation Requirements for Certification Bodies

ISO/IEC TR 15947 IT intrusion detection framework

ISO/IEC 18028-1IT Network security - Part 1: Network security management

ISO/IEC 18028-2 IT Network security - Part 2: Network security architecture

ISO/IEC 18028-3 IT Network security - Part 3: Securing communications between networks using security gateways

ISO/IEC 18028-4 IT Network security - Part 4: Securing remote access

ISO/IEC 18028-5 IT Network security - Part 5: Securing communications across networks using virtual private networks

ISO/IEC 18043, Information technology - Security techniques - Selection, deployment and operations of intrusion detection systems

ISO/IEC TR 18044 Information security incident management

ISO/IEC 24762, Guidelines for information and communications technology disaster recovery services

ISO 9001:2000, Quality management systems - Requirements

ISO 14001:2004, Environmental management systems – Requirements with guidance for use

ISO 19011:2002, Guideliens for quality and/or environmental management systems auditing

ISO 17021:2006, Conformity Assessment – Requirements for bodies providing audit and certification of management systems

ITU-T X.843|ISO/IEC 15945 Specification of TTP services to support the application of digital signatures

NIST SP 800-30, Risk Management Guide for Information Technology Systems, NIST, USA

OECD Guidelines for the Security of Information Systems and Networks – Towards a Culture of Security, OECD, Paris, July 2002

About the Author

Edward Humphreys is CEO of XiSEC, a UK business providing information security management consultancy services around the world. He has been an expert in the field of ICT and information security for more than 31 years. During this time he has worked for major international companies (in Europe, North America and Asia), as well as organizations and institutions such as the European Commission, Council of Europe and the OECD. He is also a research professor of ISMS Studies attached to Korea University and other establishments.

He has played a major role in developing and shaping the BS 7799 standards and international ISMS certification. He is the chair of the ISO/IEC Working Group responsible for the ISO 27000 family of ISMS (information security management system) standards, which includes ISO/IEC 27001 (replacement for BS 7799 Part 2), ISO/IEC 27002 (ISO/IEC 17799), ISO/IEC 27003, ISO/IEC 27004 and ISO/IEC 27005. He is internationally recognised as the father of the ISO standards and for the key role he has played in the development of the ISMS 27000 standards in particular for his editorship of BS 7799 Part 1: 1999 (which became ISO/IEC 17799:2000, of which he was editor), the editorship of the 1999 and 2002 editions of BS 7799 Part 2 (now the ISMS standard ISO/IEC 27001), the originator of the European accreditation criteria published in EA 7/03 (now ISO/IEC 27006), as well his far reaching involvement in the deployment of the global ISMS certification around the world. He has also been involved in the development of the IRCA ISMS auditor and auditor examination criteria. He is the founder and director of the ISMS International User Group. He is also an external assessor with the UK accreditation body UKAS.

In 2002 he was honoured with the Secure Computing Lifetime Achievement Award and in 2005 he was honoured with the international KPMG ISMS Lifetime Achievement Award. These international awards acknowledge his noteworthy achievements in shaping and promoting the development and standardisation of information security management best practice and ISO/IEC family of ISMS standards. He is a FBCS CITP (a Chartered Fellow of the BCS) and he also has an honorary CISM award from the ISACA.

INDEX